The Chicago Neighborhood Guidebook

The Chicago Neighborhood Guidebook

Edited by Martha Bayne

First Edition 2019
ISBN: 978-1-948742-49-8

Belt Publishing
3143 W. 33rd Street, Cleveland, Ohio 44109
www.beltpublishing.com

Book design by Meredith Pangrace
Cover by David Wilson

Contents

Contents

Contents

NORTHWEST SIDE

INTRODUCTION

Welcome to the *Chicago Neighborhood Guidebook*, a book that is, on its face, blithely uninterested in telling you where to go and what to do, eat, or buy in the third-largest city in the country. It's a book that trusts you, dear reader, to figure it out for yourself—and in that DIY, roll-up-your-sleeves, trial-and-error spirit, it is, I would argue, a book as fundamentally born of Chicago as an overdressed hot dog. It is a book about the places people live and the ways in which they live there, and a book above all else about the neighborhood changes those people have witnessed, suffered, and effected.

This book comes at a time of change for the city. I'm writing this a few days after Chicago's history-making 2019 elections, which saw Lori Lightfoot—a gay, black woman—ascend to the mayor's office on a pledge to once and for all dismantle Chicago's famed political machine, and an unprecedented slate of progressive and Socialist candidates sweep into a City Council hobbled by scandal. Just what the Lightfoot administration will do, and just how different it will be, remains, of course, to be seen.

Under outgoing mayor Rahm Emanuel, some of the city's neighborhoods—mainly on the North Side—have been radically transformed; their shiny new townhomes and transit-oriented developments are his lasting legacy, as are the rising property values and waves of displacement that they have triggered. On the South and West Sides, change is slow, elusive, and harder won. In neighborhoods struggling under the decades-old weight of racist housing codes and the economic sucker punch of deindustrialization, residents work to effect positive change far from the lights of the Loop. They struggle to desegregate white enclaves, come together to fight gun violence, and promote alternative neighborhood narratives grounded in shared experience.

A friend joked that I should call this book *Chicago's Other Neighborhoods: The Ones You've Never Heard Of,* and to some degree she's right—though of course that depends on who the "you" is in that statement. When I started work on this project, I had big plans of seeing all seventy-seven of Chicago's official community areas represented herein. But rather than trying to find stories to fill a predetermined set of seventy-seven boxes, I let the contributors be my guide. What they came up with—and what's left out—tells its own interesting story. You'll find no entry here, for example, for Lincoln Park, one of Chicago's wealthiest, and whitest, neighborhoods. I'm sad about that, because despite its white-bread reputation, Lincoln Park has a fascinating history. (Check out Daniel Kay Hertz's *The Battle of Lincoln Park* for more on *that*.) The omission is fitting, however, as this book is an attempt to balance the scales. There are two entries, for instance, for Austin, on the far West Side, and another two for West Ridge, all the way up north. In between there's Audrey Petty's elegiac sketch of South Shore, in all its painful beauty, and Scott Smith's breakdown of Beverly, as it attempts to repair decades of racial inequity. You'll find tales of living in the Loop and on Edgewater's most Halloween-happy block, as well as idiosyncratically personal takes on the Chicago River and Bridgeport, the South Loop, and the Near North Side.

This book speaks to the lived experience of everyday life in contemporary, confusing Chicago. Its contributors range from established writers to young people just finding their own voices. They speak of their neighborhoods with frustration, anger, love, and equal parts loss and hope. Reading their work has expanded my own understanding of the place I've called home for twenty-four years. I've lived here longer than anywhere else and, while I get restless sometimes, and spent a lot of 2018 out of town for one reason or another, I still always come home to Chicago. Each time I do, I see the city anew, and the work collected here is a big part of why that magic trick still works.

I'd like to thank all the contributors for committing their time and talent to this project, and Anne Trubek, Dan Crissman, David Wilson, Michael Jauchen, and the rest of the crew at Belt as well. Many thanks also to Nell Taylor, of Chicago's Read/Write Library, for her helpful input, which included brainstorming with me the spiraling path the book takes across the city, from Austin down to the South Side, then up through the Loop to the north and back again. Thank you to Ryan Schnurr and Zoe Zolbrod for their encouragement and editorial insight. And thank you, again, to Chicago.

— **Martha Bayne**

WEST SIDE

Austin: Austin and Division

SHAINA WARFIELD

We were rarely allowed far past our front porch, and the property had few amenities that could persuade us to stay of our own free will. Most of the approved activities were inside games. My usual distraction from perpetual cabin fever was this wooden puzzle that formed a map of the United States. The pieces, loose impressions of the states they represented, were painted in primary colors, the outer edges lined in thick black. To make things a bit more exciting, and to demonstrate my developed understanding of colors to my observing parents, I took to separating out the pieces by color before placing them where they belonged. Wyoming was the yellow surrounded by red, Mississippi was the red next to the green, Illinois was the green near the blue. I placed Illinois last because my parents had told me that this green wooden place was important, it was my home. I tried to make it mean something to me, to find something there that I could recognize, but the puzzle piece seemed inaccurate. I looked outside, and I saw brown; the dirt meeting the concrete, the dogs on the roof of the neighbor's garage, all the faces.

Summertime on Chicago's West Side was uniquely limited. We could ride our tricycles, creaking and wheezing under their overgrown riders, but were only allowed to go as far as the neighbor's fence on either side. We'd watch our older sister on her two-wheeler, outfitted with lopsided training wheels, from back behind the boundary. Being eight years old meant she could now go as far as the fire hydrant. At that rate, she could've hoped to see the main street sometime in her early thirties. For now, she stopped and turned around about a fence and a half from the corner. That fence and a half grew as the sun sank into late afternoon, the shadow looped around in a sort of tunnel. It covered her in phantom iron bars up to about an inch behind the hydrant. Then the tunnel would swallow her back down to where she came from, returning her to us looking as thrilled as a career world traveler, having seen it all before. We'd watch her trace her path over and over until we could almost see the line segment imprinted in the concrete, an invisible waiting arrow, missing its directional point.

Sometimes, when we got desperate, one of us would stay back to keep an eye on the house while the other two snuck soundlessly around the corner to watch the old men sitting out in lawn chairs, day drinking at the door of the bar. The drunkest of them would stand, holding himself up by the security bars on the windows. The way they drank themselves silly made it hard to believe that they thought they were anywhere on earth at all, telling stories in loud voices that could reach God, heat waves fanning out around their bodies, with their arms wide, flailing softly. That crowd wouldn't move until the streetlights came on at nightfall. We would've watched them smoke and spit and cuss until then, but we could only spare a minute. We had to reappear back at the end of our gate before the blinds opened to reveal our mother watching from the front room.

Back inside our own gate, a chain-link fence that sagged in the middle where the riffraff leaned all night, drinking out of wrinkled brown paper bags, the three of us would try to make our own fun. Our games were mildly destructive, a reaction spawned from rebellion, or maybe a childish logic that reasoned that the destruction of the container must set its contents free. We'd dig dirt holes around back, whole deep patches, scratching the twig branches into the dry bald spots on a lawn of weeds, but after we found that hot shiny rock, the one Dad snatched away and called a shell, the activity lost its charm. We'd peel loose paint chips off the side of the house, the exterior, a map of cracked powdery blue mess. We'd hear neighborhood kids pass, whispering that our old house was ugly. To us, it seemed no uglier than the stretch of land it sat on, an old, cracked, dirty mess itself. In the heat of the afternoon, we'd listen to the tired melody coming from the speakers on the ice cream truck about a block down and pretend we didn't even know what ice cream was, just to shut off the urge to run up the porch and ask our mother if we could go out and follow behind it. We'd see the fence behind us reflected in her eyes, and we'd have our answer.

We would play Rock Teacher on our front steps. Our "teacher" was a position reserved for the eldest sister, with all her worldly wisdom. She stood down at the bottom step with a piece of gravel hidden in one of the two hands held out to her "students." Winning felt important, like a test of my ability to tune into my world, a piece of the earth I stood on, my playground. I'd watch my "classmate," discouragingly more skilled at the game than I ever was, as she graduated further and further up the steps. With every correct guess, her body slowly vanished into the shade of the porch, as if the house had rescued her up from the street just to eat her. I glared at her as she descended back down the steps, annoyed by how pleased she looked with herself, how satisfied she was, scooting around catching wood splinters in the thread of her pants from climbing so fast. With dirt-ashen fingers she reached out to accept the rock from her teacher and started another round.

Only once do I remember going around the corner to Davis Park, back in the early 2000s, before its renovation. The equipment, faded in color from the sun, stood lonely most days. The basketball court next to it, however, was packed regularly with shirtless, sweaty youths. Moving together in a quick, flowing mass, they reminded me of a black plastic bag in the wind, flying down the street. Our mother said we had to leave by noon to avoid prime time for pharmaceutical transactions. We played on the swings until then. I watched my sisters compete to see who could get the highest. I stayed low and comfortable, afraid I might fall back onto the wood chips if I went too high. They teased me, claiming they could see everything from up there, the whole alley. I didn't care, it wasn't worth it. Soon, we were back at the house, back to my puzzle, where I reasoned that the world out there wasn't all that big, or all that thrilling, not knowing that if we were ever allowed around the block at the unfortunately unpredictable wrong time, the truth of our world would have revealed itself to be a fairground of the worst kind—gun violence territory.

Running errands on Saturdays felt like a prison break, although my first remembrance of those car rides proved to be a rather confusing lesson in geography. Crossing what I now know as Austin Avenue was enlightening, and a bit disorienting, to a child that measured distance in fences and half blocks. Staring out the window from the intersection of Austin and Division, quite the coincidental place to cross, I saw on the other side that these new blocks were not like my own. Waiting at the traffic stop felt comparable to watching my sister down at the fire hydrant from back behind the fence.

Across the street, there were parks. Not vacant lots occupied by overgrown weeds and Hennessey bottles. Not the dirty, designated weed dispensary of the hood. Real parks. They passed one after another; the grass seemed to roll on forever. There were towering homes with lush, manicured lawns. There were giant grocery store chains. We walked in trailing my mother, amazed to see more than chips and pop on the shelves. We laughed when we saw a sort of demented pickle-looking thing sitting outside of its jar. We tried to read the sign: Zucchini?

The most prevalent difference, a change you could sense with your back turned, was that there were white people, a lot of them, walking their blocks in family groups, casually flanking two or three across, going somewhere forward, seemingly satisfied with wherever the block decided to take them. My childhood in Austin rarely introduced me to white people, though I knew white people existed. Teachers were usually white, and I assumed they had families that were white as well. I had a television, and the faces I saw most on screen, walking the streets confidently, roaming all night on adventures with their little friends, were very often white. But there was something about those blocks, those parks, the grass, the stores, even the zucchini, that seemed "white" too. I worried that on the drive back home, when we reentered the atmosphere, the zucchini in the bag would begin to rot at the intersection, unable to withstand the climate. "White" things don't stay here for long.

It wasn't until I thought I was too old for that wooden puzzle, and for our silly front yard games, until I had crossed that boundary into Oak Park many, many times, that I understood geography to be more than just streets and dirt and lines you can't see. People are geography too; where they live and don't live, where they gather, where they work and play and buy their food. It all begins to draw a line, a color line you can see the moment you've learned your colors.

Thirty years before my time, Austin's shifting demographics began to change the ethnic and socioeconomic makeup of the neighborhood's population to what I am familiar with today. The racial demographics in Austin in the 1960s read 99.8 percent white, 0.0 percent Negro. As of 2016, the demographics are 4.2 percent white, 84.2 percent African American. The average annual household income in Austin is $31,425. The average annual household income in Oak Park is $78,384. In Chicago collectively it's $47,834. The terms "redlining," "blockbusting," "profiteering," and "white flight" would not enter my vocabulary until the later years of elementary school, and when they did I had to grab them quickly, catch them at random before the teacher read on. The moment I saw them in print, I knew I had found the missing pieces to an outrage that I had thought was misplaced, but that never failed to ignite any time it seemed that I had only to cross the street to enter another world.

Crossing over, going back the way we came, I'd see the flashing blue boxes on top of the streetlights, the M & M Quick Foods Mart, the bus station, and so many fences; the steel iron security bars on the windows, the tall barbed wire, and my own sagging chain-link fence. I'd see familiar faces, faces like mine, and I knew I was home without ever reading a street sign.

The moments in my childhood when we had all gone back inside, when the streetlights came on and the muggy summer night settled in, when I would listen to the sudden pop pops, the police sirens, and the dark voices floating up from the alley, when I would cry a little, and pray to be white, now rang with a new clarity. What I wanted was a park, the stretch of green that puzzle piece had promised me. Riding my bike as far as my neighbor's gate, I would imagine that the cracked pavement underneath me, littered with glass shards and blackened gum, was really a glorious "White Park" a thousand fences long.

Austin: Cakewalk

RASAAN KHALIL

On the West Side, it is the one time of year
when many live like royalty.
Aristocrats of tax return monarchies scramble for children to claim
Experts in the field of finesse,
foreign cars, blare anthems
reminiscent of freedom songs and McCarthyism
while black youth play God and adjust precipitation levels
On gentrified blocks undergoing photosynthesis because
Money trees is the perfect place for shade.
Their pockets a green pasture for Ben Franklins to lie down in
Decreeing *let there be light* around the necks of them and their
homies, young
cast members
caste members
who guarantee a director's cut. the climax isn't all that climactic,
considering the factors
that would equal a product
at twelve, I made my debut
and every year since, my brother and I would cakewalk through
stores
That smelled like commercials:
expensive, illegal
with collard green frosting on our fingers.

Humboldt Park: Queen of the Tunnels

LILY BE

There's this fantasy I have that takes place in a dystopian future where I am the queen of the tunnels in Chicago. Y'all may not be aware of this, but Chicago has sixty miles of tunnels deep under the city of which, in my fantasy, I am the queen. I am the queen of these tunnels because, let's be serious, the way this country's headed with Trump as our president, people like me (poor, brown, and female) might have to make our way there to survive.

Anyway, in this fantasy, I see myself having to lead *Star Wars* rebel-like forces to defeat the evil powers that be. I see myself standing up to authorities, carrying grown-ass men on my back, and pulling babies out of fires. I see myself standing before the rebels, giving speeches of hope and encouragement to those that have lost the will to live in these conditions. Men do not rule these tunnels, especially not straight white men. If they want access to the tunnels, they have to serve women of color and take a pegging from either myself or someone in the court. Anyone of privilege (and I mean anyone), regardless of race, would have to prove, by bringing me the head of a Trump voter, that they are not moles or that they are not out to destroy our civilization. Even then they would have to be a servant to the cause. They would not get weapons or have a say in any of the plans or take up any space outside of helping the weakest of us get strong, like our elderly and children. Imagine me being Khaleesi from *Game of Thrones*, only less problematic and with way more badass Dothraki.

In 2016, my son (nineteen at the time) and I went grocery shopping, and after putting away groceries, we walkup to my room so that we could watch a movie and hang out. When I got upstairs to my room, he noticed that I was out of breath and said to me, "Mom, you can't be fat and a smoker."

I ain't going to lie; I was a bit shook.

"What the fuck you say to me?" I knew that he could see that I was upset.

"I said, you can't be fat and a smoker." This time he quickly added that he knew I was in a good place in life and that I seemed to be getting along fine, but seeing me out of breath after climbing two flights of stairs had him concerned for my health. He said that he did not see me being around long enough to see his kids and that if I *was* around, I would not be able to enjoy my time with them because of all the health problems I would have.

His explanation hit me hard. I mean, it's not like I didn't know. It's not like dudes I had crushes on hadn't called me fat or that dudes I wasn't interested in, who had hit on me and been rejected, hadn't called me "fat-ass bitch" before, but this was different. This particular fat commentary was from my son, and no self-affirming "YASSS QUEEN! You are beautiful goddess, fuck what they say" pep talk would make me forget or not care about what he said to me.

"Well, what the fuck do you want me to do?" I said. "I'm fat, and a smoker, and I am okay with it. You're the reason I'm fat in the first place! I gained like a hundred pounds after I had you! I was so thin before I got pregnant with yo' ass."

Before I could continue, he interrupted to say that he was not attacking me and that he did not want to make me upset. He sat on the edge of the bed and with a calm, stern voice said, "I would like it if you lost weight and quit smoking, but if you only did one, I'd be cool with it."

I looked at him, looked at myself in the mirror behind him, and thought about it. "Well, I guess I'm losing weight then, motherfucker."

A few weeks after he went back to college, I started going to the gym. I would go to not hear his fucking mouth. I started walking on the treadmill for thirty minutes and doing some time on the elliptical. I went every day, not putting in any real effort, until one day I started noticing the little changes. I lost a couple of pounds; my face wasn't as round, my legs were a little bit less jiggly. So I started to Google shit about dieting and changing my eating habits a little bit. Less sugar in my coffee, more nutrients. I gave up soda and started to be more conscious of the shit I put inside my body. I began lifting weights, and that's when I felt the shift. I began with five-pound weights and noticed that after a few weeks, I needed to go up to seven-pound weights and then ten-pound weights after that. My arms and legs started not only to lose their jiggles, but they began to take a different form. I had muscles, yo. I could see them. I could *name* them. My biceps, my triceps, my quads, my lats. Before I knew it, it was nine months later, and I was fucking S-T-R-O-N-G, and I saw no end to this locomotive train of remarkable health.

One day, after putting in a fantastic upper-body day at the gym, I was heading home. I always walked home from the gym with my Bluetooth headset in my ear. Well, not all the way in, because my gym was on the West Side of Chicago (the part still untouched by gentrification and a bit dangerous). I heard a voice call out, "Lady, help me!" I looked across the street and saw a young boy, maybe fifteen, with floppy black hair, wearing a black shirt, standing behind a car. Approaching him, running alongside a bike, was another boy, the same age and with no shirt, yelling, "I'mma fuck you up." I didn't hesitate. Growing up in this hood, I knew what this was, and I dialed 911. The 911 operator and I did the ol' 911 song and dance while the boys did theirs.

"What's your emergency?" the operator asked.

"I just left the gym and there are two boys that look like they are about to fight, and it might get ugly," I responded.

"What is your location?"

"I'm at the Blast Fitness just north of Division on Central Park."

"What do the boys look like, what do they have on, what are their races?"

I got annoyed. I can't with this line of questioning. Why did that fucking matter? THEY'RE CHILDREN!! Who gives a fuck what race they were? They shouldn't want to hurt each other. I responded though.

"I don't know, one could be white, and the other could be Latino. White or black."

I made sure to keep saying "white" in case that sped up their response time because, again, I was on the side of town where a 911 operator and the cops were probably aware of the racial makeup of the community and I wanted help to arrive fast.

The operator finally said, "Thank you, ma'am, we have a unit two minutes away."

But I could not bring myself to walk away. I couldn't bear the thought of leaving before the cops came and later turning on the news or reading on Facebook that I left and something terrible had happened to the boys, either because the police did not come on time or because they did and shit went the way of Trayvon Martin, Laquan McDonald, or any of the other brown boys born to mothers like me. I stayed on the phone and watched the scene of these two boys, now chasing each other around a car, unfold.

The boy without the shirt was so angry; I could see the veins popping out of his forehead as he kept yelling that he was going to fuck the floppy-haired boy up. The floppy-haired boy was so scared his voice was still squeaking for help as he glanced over at me and kept his eye on the boy chasing after him.

"The police are on the way," I said, approaching them enough that they heard me, but staying away enough that I didn't get in the way.

It had now been four minutes on the call.

The boy without the shirt picked up a bottle.

"One of the boys has picked up a bottle, where are the fucking cops?" I yelled frantically into my headset.

"They're on their way ma'am."

Five minutes.

The floppy-haired boy was starting to be unable to outrun the boy around the car; the distance between them got shorter and shorter. I kept looking down the street for the cops. Nothing.

I was now in the middle of the street, watching cars drive by and do nothing, watching the crowd of bystanders that had now formed do nothing. I walked to the sidewalk and stood in front of the floppy-haired boy and faced the boy without the shirt. I put out my arms in a T pose, fist down, flexing a little (so they saw my guns), and I started talking to the boy holding the bottle.

He was young, but his anger aged him. His face was red from yelling, and he had the bottle down by his side, shifting his feet left to right as he told me to get out the way.

"Ma'am. . ."

I'd had enough of these "ma'ams"; I'm not *that* old.

"Ma'am, move out the fucking way!" he said as he looked past me at the boy behind me.

"I'm not even in a gang; I'm over here to visit my grandmother," said the scared young boy behind me.

"I don't give a fuck, I'mma fuck yo' bitch ass up, King love, bitch. Please, ma'am, move out the fucking way."

I was learning a lot about this boy as I stood in front of him.

One, he was in a gang. Latin Kings to be exact.

Two, he was probably just lip boxing (just talking, all bark).

Three, that "ma'am" coming from this boy's mouth let me know that someone in his life at some point was there to tell him that you address any "older" woman as "ma'am." Those "ma'ams" gave me hope and they were what prompted me to talk to this boy.

"You don't have to do this, yo. He ain't worth it, this ain't worth it."

"I don't give a fuck! I'm fucking him up."

"And then what?" I replied. "You go to fucking jail, for what? Trust me, G. I know this hood. I grew up on Cortez and Kedzie, you don't know how many homies I have lost to bullshit like this. The cops are on the way, G."

"I don't give a fuck," he yelled at me, and he took out his phone.

I could only hear his side of the conversation.

Meanwhile, 911 had been on the phone listening to me for six minutes, occasionally chiming in with protocol shit that I actively ignored to be in the moment with these boys.

"I'm on Central Park by the Blast Fitness," he said to whoever was on the other end of the call.

That's what I been saying, I thought to myself as the call approached eight minutes.

He hung up and went back to telling the boy behind me that he was going to get fucked up, only now he added, "Just wait."

In less than a minute from when he hung up his phone, a car with tinted windows pulled up behind him and the window started to lower.

I thought two things almost simultaneously: "Please don't pull out a gun," and "I need to be on the phone with whoever this boy just got off the phone with because that response time was ridiculous." *Holy shit* that was fast.

Another teenager peered out and said, "Ay yo, five-o," and drove off.

The boy dropped the bottle, picked up his bike, and rode away.

Seconds later, a blue Dodge Charger pulled up in front of us and lowered its window. My heart did a little skip, thinking the kid sent more of his boys before I realized these were different boys—the boys in blue—but they were undercover cops in plain clothes.

"Which way did he go?" they asked, knowing that he could have only gone in one direction since they came from the only other direction he could have gone.

I pointed, but it didn't matter. They were late.

They drove off, and I hung up my almost ten-minute call with 911.

One of the other bystanders then said, "Hey, yo, that Charger was parked on Central Park and Grand this whole time."

I was shook because I knew it was. The entire time I was waiting for a blue and white police car to pull up, looking up and down the street, I saw that Charger, too. And if I could see Central Park and Grand, Grand and Central Park could see me. They were watching this the entire time. All eight minutes of it. They were watching me the whole time and didn't do anything *until* the boy rode off. I was seething at the thought that this would never happen in a more affluent or gentrified part of town. I knew damn well that a white woman in Lincoln Park outside a Starbucks would never have to wait almost ten minutes for help to arrive. Those cops watched a poor brown woman stand between two brown boys and they did nothing. Like they were waiting for one of us to be a chalk outline before it even mattered. At that moment, I told the other boy to go home. He was okay. He thanked me, and I walked home, disgusted and lost in thought.

I have this dystopian fantasy of being the queen of the tunnels. That dystopian future is already here for people like me. God knows that I have *already* carried many men on my back. I have stood up to plenty of authority, and given those speeches of hope and encouragement to those of us that have lost the desire to live in these conditions. Most of all, I have pulled many a baby out of the fire, starting with my own. I'm a teen mother from the West Side of Chicago. My son, a poor brown boy, born to children of immigrants, was already set up to crash and burn in the fire lit by the fucked-up powers that be that allow undercover police in blue Chargers to sit and wait for them to be nothing but ashes before they even care. I like to think that one day I will be the queen of the tunnels of Chicago and beyond, but I know that what you all have just read is an introduction to who I already am.

Garfield Park: Perspectives

GABRIEL X. MICHAEL

Garfield Park lagoon at sunset, August 2017.

My artistic motivation is to photograph under-recognized historic architecture and cultural history in Chicago's underserved and neglected neighborhoods. These photographs are meant to convey the beauty of Garfield Park's remarkable interplay of nature, infrastructure, and historic built environment, amidst brutal socio-economic conditions that have persisted for decades. Many believe that bureaucratic systems of historic preservation and formal recognition have mostly eluded or failed these neighborhoods, and my intensive, street-level work attempts to create a uniquely personal record of today's built environment in Chicago.

3116 - 3118 West Lake Street, built 1869.

Under demolition, 734 South Sacramento Boulevard, built 1894.

Morning light on the mosaic at North Francisco Avenue and West Madison Street.

4661 West Lake Street, March 2012.

Behind the 3100 block of West Jackson Boulevard

North Lawndale: An Interview with Alexie Young, MLK Fair Housing Exhibit Center

F. AMANDA TUGADE

Alexie Young is the gatekeeper to what she considers an "untapped gem" in North Lawndale, a neighborhood on Chicago's West Side. "I do believe that the MLK Exhibit Center is going to be one of the spaces that will be a catalyst to change the atmosphere," says Young, seated at a white folding table inside the dimly-lit memorial site on South Hamlin Avenue.

In January 1966, Dr. Martin Luther King Jr. and his wife, Coretta Scott, moved into an apartment in North Lawndale as a way to understand, experience, and combat the housing inequality that African Americans faced during that time. A life-sized, black-and-white print of the couple inside their apartment on 1550 S. Hamlin Avenue hangs down from a wall in the room's back corner.

Young's role at the MLK Fair Housing Exhibit Center ranges from marketing coordinator to tour guide. But her priority remains the same: to transform the nearly 1,000-square-foot space into a hub for cultural gatherings.

"Until then, it's just sitting . . . until someone decides to really step in and activate it completely," she says.

F. Amanda Tugade: Before you found the MLK Fair Housing Exhibit Center, you were an entrepreneur from North Lawndale looking for a storefront to house your wine and painting classes. What was it like for you to find?

Alexie Young: When I met [Lawndale Christian Executive Director] Richard Townsell looking for a storefront, he had mentioned to me after some time, "How about you consider renting the MLK Exhibit Center whenever you might need to do a class?" And I was like, "Wow! That's a great idea!"

And the rent was extremely affordable. It did not cut into my profit margins, which was extremely unique because a lot of entrepreneurs, they want to do pop-ups and stuff like that, and there's a lot of places that are really great places to host events, but most of the time they're not on the West Side of Chicago. They don't have the aesthetic that people are looking for.

But then also because of the historical value—I really appreciate MLK, the work that he's done, so that we can enjoy some of those freedoms that they fought for. I think that some communities get really stuck in the trauma of the past, and I often feel like there [are] more opportunities now to celebrate that we have come really far and how can we use those historical references to inform how we move forward and inform how we celebrate that forward motion.

Tugade: Your neighborhood's history is so embedded with the work that Dr. Martin Luther King Jr. did here. Do you think that history still carries in your neighborhood?

Young: There's been stories about how this community was a bustling community at some point back in the day, and after the assassination of Dr. King on April 4, 1968. North Lawndale was one of the communities in Chicago that suffered from the riots. A lot of things were burned down. Businesses were burned down.

So now, I feel like there's a sense of openness to rebuilding, even though we're decades away from the riots. My outlook is extremely positive because I'm involved with lots of community organizers, and I go to meetings and I know people in the community and we know each other by name and face and we know everyone's skill or talent. I kind of feel like we're building a pretty strong ecosystem.

I believe that we're kind of shifting towards seeing the fruits of the organizing labor. So all of the strategic plans and the development ideas that we have for ourselves that we want to see happen, those things are starting to feel a little bit more tangible, whereas before everything felt so conceptual, like we're just being dreamers in a community that doesn't look like the affluent ones.

Tugade: What's your vision for the MLK Exhibit Center?

Young: If people are thinking about hosting a podcast, interviews, or pop-up shops, things like that, I want this space to be considered for those types of events and eventually programming that will be huge. It would be really great to have the funding to install some programming here that is engaging people intergenerationally where there's events for families, documentary screenings, opportunities to hear people speak about the Civil Rights Movement, or even current development and leadership in the community.

It doesn't necessarily always have to be historical because what we're doing right now is historical, and to my son's generation, what we're doing now will be their history, right? I want the exhibit center to just be recognized as a staple on the West Side of Chicago.

Tugade: What does it mean to have a space like this?

Young: I just see this as being one of the spaces that will allow people to enjoy that on this side of town. If you're driving down Sixteenth Street, especially from Kedzie all the way to Pulaski, you can see it's pretty barren. It doesn't have a lot to offer, but I do believe that the MLK Exhibit Center is going to be one of the spaces that will be the catalyst to change the atmosphere and the perception of Sixteenth Street, especially while Ogden is being developed. If you go to Ogden, you go to the Green Tomato [Cafe] where it feels like *Cheers*. You walk in there, everyone knows everyone, and that's beautiful. Ogden wasn't always like that. Ogden was once barren, and it didn't have much to offer a few years ago. I just hope that Sixteenth Street can change in some way where it's good for the community.

Tugade: What do you think gets overlooked when people talk about the West Side?

Young: I believe that when people view the West Side there's this perception that there isn't any culture—that there aren't any real art spaces. That there's just an oversaturation of nonprofit organizations and churches and barbershops and hair salons and those viable businesses that do work in these types of communities.

You don't necessarily see the offbeat artisans that are doing co-ops, or you don't necessarily see the future of business or arts and culture or things like that. You might see murals. You might see gardens popping up, but what gets overlooked is that there is culture, and I think that we're all trying to figure out a way to demonstrate that we do have very deep rich culture.

Tugade: What's it like to not only witness but be a part of the change that's taking place in your neighborhood?

Young: I think it really just anchors me to this neighborhood. I can't think of anywhere else I would rather live. There are obviously other places that have everything you could possibly want just a couple steps away from your apartment or your home, but I believe that I'm here during a time that is really calling for the people here to care more and to really get involved to counter gentrification.

That's like the biggest thing. People are in fear of losing homes or in fear of tax rates increasing, in fear of displacement and all that comes along with gentrification and understanding that some component of that is inevitable.

But how do we balance that out, or how do we have some line of defense so that we are able to enjoy what we created? I think that that's really unique for this West Side neighborhood.

The MLK Fair Housing Exhibit Center is at 1558 S. Hamlin in Chicago.

Little Village: Three Stories

Yollocalli Arts Reach is the award-winning youth initiative of the National Museum of Mexican Art. Since 1997 they have offered free arts and culture programming—like street art, experimental photo, comics, zine making, and more—to teens and young adults. The three pieces excerpted here, published originally at Little Village Pilsen Portal, were created as part of the ongoing "Your Story, Your Way" class in storytelling, journalism, and radio production.

From Panda to Panda: The Power of Food in Our Streets

EMMANUEL RAMIREZ

There's a Panda Express on each end of Little Village's Twenty-Sixth Street, the second-highest grossing retail strip in the city. In between are street vendors, bakeries, candy shops, and taquerias, but this food is not of the community's culture.

Chicago is segregated, but very rich in culture. We go about our daily lives surrounded by people of our race, ethnicity, and culture. Do we branch out and seek out other cultures or do we stick with what we know? Using Little Village as an example, I set out to find out what the community thinks about whether integration is possible without homogenization, by focusing on food.

I interviewed civilians and business owners, starting with the basics, I asked: "What kind of foods do you buy and consume in the community? Are there any that you can't find in your neighborhood?" Most people that were from Little Village just shopped locally at La Ouachita or any other nearby grocery store, while Los Mangos owner Eladio Montoya stated, "I can't find Italian food, but then this isn't the place to buy Italian food. Just go a couple miles down and you're there."

I got interested in this question of homogenization after the opening of Sip 22. Sip 22 is a café that opened up on Cermak, in the northeast part of Little Village in 2017. Before it had opened, somebody spray painted "F*ck Yr Coffee / G.T.F.O.L.V." on the shop window. In an article in the *Chicago Tribune*, some community members expressed discomfort with the shop moving into the neighborhood, arguing that there were already cheaper places to get coffee like Dunkin' Donuts and McDonald's. During the construction of Sip 22, the owner planned to build a deck right in front of the shop, displacing a tamalera. The deck was never completed. Instead, Sip 22 now has public benches where people can sip coffee and eat tamales from the tamalera that still vends there.

Another new addition to Little Village is Sora Temakeria, a sushi shop on Twenty-Sixth Street. When I interviewed Sora Temakeria's co-owner, Jay Tanaka, on the vandalism of Sip 22, Tanaka said, "I'm gonna be honest with you, after that I was a little bit worried that perhaps something like that would happen to us over here, but so far [knocks on wood] nothing has happened to us."

Jay's approach to starting this Latin-infused sushi concept started with the location. "We found the real estate online first and then we actually kind of built the menu and the concept around the location." It's a sushi restaurant, he says, "But we incorporate some pepper, spices, and different concepts borrowed from, say, Mexican restaurants." Similar to Sip 22, Sora Temakeria is from a culture not of the community, but has incorporated the community into what the restaurant has to offer.

Community leader Vanessa Sanchez views the two restaurants differently. Sanchez values Sora Temakeria because "they're coming in to start a new business so I don't think it's an issue for them coming in or blending the two cultures for food." However, she believes Sip 22 entered into the community ignorant of its location and culture.

"It's full of controversy," she says. " I think that owner just came in thinking that they're entering this new trendy neighborhood in a spot that just happened to be open. I don't think they knew the history of the area. Especially that building that they moved into." Sip 22's building used to be the home of a youth Latino empowerment organization—Latino Youth High School. Alex Alvarez, the manager of Sip 22, says, "I'm more than willing to listen to people and have dialogue with them but not when the listening is only coming one way." Alvarez—who was born and raised in the neighborhood—made sure to point out that most of the people that work at Sip 22 are Mexicanos. When I asked another local business owner—Eladio Montoya of Los Mangos and Gordillas—if he thinks race plays a role in people's fears, he said they shouldn't. "I myself don't have a problem with it. I myself would go have a coffee right there [Sip 22 Cafe] because there's white people coming to eat in my place. So why am I gonna discriminate against a white-owned business when I have white customers? It just doesn't make sense. We have Asian customers, we have everything. I think it's good. I don't see any problem with gentrification."

For Sanchez, knowing the history of a place matters. Restaurants outside of the neighborhood's culture should do their research before coming in, she says, "and figure out what they can do to help the neighborhood before putting their business first, especially if they're entering a neighborhood that's on the cusp of gentrification."

Loving through Building:
The Story of Miguel Mendoza
ZIPPORAH AUTA

Why does Little Village have so much love? Why does the atmosphere change when you enter through the arch? Of course, the shops and cuisines draw people, but in order to feel the lively energy flowing through the streets, someone must have put it there; people must have put it there. Miguel Mendoza is one of those people.

Mendoza was born on September 7, 1958, in a small town in Guanajuato, Mexico; he has been an architect, painter, and contractor for his whole life. As a child, Mendoza grew up humbly. "It was a little difficult for me in those days," he says. I was a real poor guy and I grew up without toys. But I was so happy. We made our own toys." He has been creating things since he was a child. At the age of eleven, he started to paint and work with his father, who introduced him to the world of art and creating. When Mendoza grew older, he moved to the United States, where he began work as a painter.

"I started painting houses and little by little I started learning other things to do," he says. As time passed, he perfected his craft, and transformed into a general contractor.

In 2001, Mendoza moved from the North Side of Chicago to Little Village, and started to contribute to it almost immediately. Mendoza's favorite project in Little Village was the restoration of Universidad Popular, a nonprofit organization focused on education and community empowerment. But he was not satisfied with just using his talent to improve Little Village physically. Mendoza now takes youth from the neighborhood that are interested in learning about art and teaches them what he knows.

"I found that in the new generation, people are into alcohol or do drugs," he says. "I like to talk to them and try to help in whatever I can do." Many years later, some of his mentees have followed in his footsteps, becoming contractors themselves.

Using craftsmanship for good is a language Mendoza speaks fluently. "All my best, I try to give it to Little Village. Whether it's about my life, whatever I know, I like to show everybody. It's not necessary to be a painter, or to be a plumber, or an electrician. Try to learn something different because you'll need it in the future." Aside from his projects, Mendoza creates five-foot butterflies of many different colors, often of recycled materials, and gifts them to people that he has done work for, or that live in the community.

In the past, Mendoza has tried to explore Europe and work there, always admiring the artwork from far away. But due to a variety of barriers, he was never able to fulfill his wish. He has a dream of speaking to the Pope himself about him working in Europe. Miguel has many life stories, but the one thing he wants everyone to know about his life is his love for his late wife. Miguel's story is far from over, and when asked how long he thinks he will continue this work for, he responded saying, "Well, I think for the rest of my life. This is my job. I love my job."

How to be Neighborly in a Changing Neighborhood
GLORIA "NINE" VALLE

In the summer of 2017, I met my neighbor Rebecca Wolfram. Rebecca is an artist who has lived in the Little Village community for twenty-three years. I was neighbors with her up until the age of six. I remember her most from my childhood because of the museum setup she had installed in the front of her home. I always imagined she would be an interesting person, considering not many people have art installations attached to their gates.

The museum is known as the "Museum of Objects Left on the Sidewalk." Some things on display include toxic objects that are shown as an example of chemicals that harm the environment. Other items represent different ideas and concerns. It wasn't until I became friends with Wolfram and interviewed her that I learned the museum was set up in 2003 with the purpose of transforming nothing into something.

"I suddenly had the idea that I wanted to put garbage-like things or other things on shelves like exhibits," she says. "My feeling is like when you take something and you put in on a shelf and put a label on it, it kind of transforms into a different kind of thing. Instead of being a piece of garbage, suddenly it's something that you can look at."

This museum serves the community in different ways. It has a blackboard for people to pick up a chalk and express themselves through messages and drawings. There is also a gift shop where anyone can leave items or take items that have been left there. Quite the creative setup everyone could be a part of.

"People have really caught on to this museum. They like it. They participate. They put things in it, they take things out. They comment on it. Every time I think, well, I'm getting a little tired of up keeping this museum I realize . . . [that] people seem to really like it, so I have to keep being the director and curator of the museum," Wolfram says.

A few years ago she had it rebuilt, since it was falling apart. A neighbor across the street helped her build some solid shelves. "As the neighborhood changes, the types of things people will put in the museum are changing too and the comments that people write on the blackboard," she says. I find it amazing that she took the initiative to do something like this for the community. In a way, to me, it's sort of historical having seen this growing up; although the community is changing, it is lovely to see some things remain here. It makes her home look and feel welcoming, something that I love to see in the streets of my neighborhood.

The fact that Rebecca's home looks approachable is actually the reason why we met. During the summer of 2017, my cat Sunny went missing. I would normally let him roam in my yard, but one night he found a way out of the yard and he never made it back home. I was worried about his well-being so I made posters to pass around to whoever I saw in the area.

One night, I was walking home from work and I saw a cat who looked like Sunny hanging out on Rebecca's porch. I was afraid to approach him, but I decided to go in the porch anyway. He eventually noticed me and ran to the backyard, where I followed him. At this point, I realized I was trespassing, so I took a quick glance around the yard and got out immediately. Two days later, the guilt was bothering me, so I decided to give her door a knock and apologize.

"Hey! My name is Gloria and I live a couple houses away. I just wanted to apologize for sneaking into your backyard two nights ago. I thought I saw my cat in your porch so I followed him."

I did not know what to expect, but she calmly giggled and responded, "What does your cat look like? I might be able to help."

She was not bothered that I snuck into her backyard. We became friends and I began learning more about her charismatic life. I took the initiative to interview her for the Little Village Portal to learn in detail about what she does for the cats in my community and to share it with you all.

In 2008, Rebecca noticed how much the cats in the neighborhood were killing the rats, which are an issue in our area. At this time, two friendly young cats would often hang out in her back porch. She began to feed them and noticed that they didn't seem feral.

My inspiring neighbor has taken upon herself to help the community cats as much as possible. She works with the PAWS trap-neuter-release program, and has many different colonies living in her backyard. She even has three little houses there that are designed for feral cats. "They are extremely well designed," she says. "In the wintertime, the cats stay perfectly warm and cozy."

In the short amount of time I've known her, I have learned to admire Rebecca for the way she treats everyone and everything around her. Like with the cats, she is so detailed when she talks about them and I love it. These cats are just as important as anyone else in the neighborhood and she makes sure to not only acknowledge that but does something about it. Her museum setup is not the only thing she has gotten creative with.

One of the most beautiful and touching projects I've came across was an altar commemorating the lives and deaths of unidentified people who have been taken into the Cook County Morgue, created by Rebecca and two other artists as an ofrenda for the Day of the Dead exhibition at the National Museum of Mexican Art. Cook County has a website with the purpose of trying to identify some of the people, which at that time were forty-six people. Her voice shook as she explained that it felt good to try to commemorate these live.

"We thought maybe having this ofrenda in a public place also could conceivably help publicize the fact that the website exists and can help identify some of these people too," she told me. It took about five months for this piece to come together. The altar was donated to the medical examiner's office after and they have it in a big display case in a conference room.

Through Rebecca I have learned that everything is equally interesting. It all depends on how you look at it. Rebecca was able to turn a regular forgotten object into something special by acknowledging and providing a space for it through her museum. Rebecca has taken it upon herself to look past the identity our neighborhood cats have been given as pests. They are more than just street cats and she treats them as such. And she has taught me that everyone deserves to be someone regardless of the circumstances. Her commemoration of the unidentified dead proves that these people will forever be remembered, even without the regular social procedures that happen when someone leaves this world.

Where I am from, a lot of people feel like they don't belong here, as they have migrated away from their homeland. Those feelings come from the fact that not everyone looks at the big picture that we are all equal. We all breathe the same air and bleed the same color. It is foolish to degrade someone over social classes or because one comes from one side of the border. We are humans and we are all important. I want to inspire others to approach optimistic perspectives like caring and sympathizing for one another like Rebecca has sparked in me. Be open-minded and curious to shine light on things and ideas that we have been taught or have gotten used to keeping in the dark. It can be the change that we need.

SOUTHWEST SIDE

Garfield Ridge: Comeback Kid

SHEILA ELLIOTT

Prepositions best explain my connection to my old neighborhood, Garfield Ridge, on Chicago's Southwest Side. I've been *around* my old neighborhood a lot, gone *to* it, and gone *through* it maybe a thousand times since my teen years, when a pair of size six penny loafers were my primary mode of getting around its streets. I left in 1969, but I have sat through many traffic slow-ups along Cicero, watched speedometer times riding along Archer, and waited impatiently for red-to-green light changes on Interstate overpasses at Central and Harlem thousands of times since then.

Adulthood put distance between me and the neighborhood's neat and tidy streets, its villagelike friendship networks, its semi suburban ambience, far from Chicago's downtown. In the 1970s, '80s, and '90s, I was negotiating who I was and would become, and though I visited family for holidays and Sunday dinners, I barely noticed restaurant chains replacing once-favorite cafés, new business arrivals, or the bungalows and Georgians that seemed to balloon in size with second-floor dormer add-ons. What I did notice, though, was in the air above and around me. What was this disrupting the silence I recalled about home, these intermittent sound blasts? There—there was one—and then it was gone. After a while— another. Then it too would be gone.

Welcome to Garfield Ridge, a two-and-a-half-mile rectangular-shaped neighborhood on Chicago's Far Southwest Side, and one of a small number of American communities whose past and present is intertwined with transportation history. Welcome to the home of Midway Airport, which anchors its eastern edge. In Garfield Ridge today those blasts of sound from overhead are generally described as progress, a claim that's hard to contest when you have frequently rushed to make a flight or pick up friend or family. But if you were the 1960s teen who biked, walked, danced, talked, and dreamed in the neighborhood nearby, the neighborhood that always seemed more small town than large city, you'd see things a bit differently, or more accurately, hear things a bit differently.

In 1963, my parents purchased a brick bungalow, a building style that remains synonymous with the neighborhood today. One of my first recollections of life in the new house was noticing that we could no longer hear the rush of the "El" trains that had run a few blocks from the two-flat where I had spent most of my childhood. It took a night or two, but I got used to a place so quiet that you could hear the sprays of water from lawn sprinklers and the low growl of traffic blocks away. Garfield Ridge was something quite different, I began to think.

How many residents of aviation-rich neighborhoods can say their airport was once the busiest in the world? That it hosted the rich and famous—until they all flew away? That it became a ghost town, was written off as a technological dinosaur? That it slumbered for nearly twenty years before things began again to change?

In the 1960s and much of the '70s, Garfield Ridge was an area where teenagers spent listless nights taking long walks along the fences that protected the empty airport tarmacs. Colorful airstrip lights still flashed at night, but they cast their beams onto wide slabs of concrete rimmed by crabgrass. Lights still shone in a control tower, but the restaurants that once were filled with travelers had long since closed. An airplane guide light stood half a block from my parents' home, but as far as anyone in the neighborhood could see, its message was like that of a seldom heeded, old-fashioned lighthouse. That may have been a mistaken assumption, but it fit the mood created by an airport that, by its lack of activity, spoke more to the past than to the future.

The quiet at Midway Airport began around 1959, when Chicago aviation shifted to an up-to-date, more modern O'Hare Field. It was then that what had been the busiest airport in America entered a dormancy of more than two decades. If you were, as I was, among a throng of teenage girls waiting in 1964 for the private jet carrying John, Paul, George, and Ringo to their first Chicago concert, you glimpsed the Midway—and Garfield Ridge—I knew then and recall now: quiet, almost deserted, a place returned to the glittering spotlight if only for a moment. Not until the 1980s, when a slew of legal documents and decrees resulted in the deregulation of American airlines, did change come to Garfield Ridge again—not so much what could be seen, as what could be heard. The neat and tidy streets were all still there, but the near-suburban quiet that once characterized the place was lost to America's ravenous desire for affordable air travel. Little by little, flight by flight, Garfield Ridge's neighborhood airport was making its way back into the big time.

To get a sense of Midway Airport's past, think Lindbergh and Earhart, both of whom are said to have flown above its skies. If you recall the dramatic airport terminal scenes in Alfred Hitchcock's *North by Northwest*, you have glimpsed a bit of Midway in its glory days. Other famous names could also be entered into a story about the airport. Presidential candidates, famous writers, and notables of all sorts passed through its stolid terminal building from the 1920s until the 1950s, while American aviation was growing. It's unlikely, however, that any of them paid attention to the grassy fields beyond the hangars. In those years, when Midway, like Chicago itself, was flourishing, just a scattering of buildings stood in Garfield Ridge. It was an area that grew sluggishly to eventually jut west into the suburbs about ten miles west of Lake Michigan. A wide route famous for its angularity, Archer is Garfield Ridge's main street, slicing its way from the South Loop to the city's border. Situated on the edge of an ancient beach ridge, Archer follows a path forged by Native Americans long before European settlement in America. That Fr. Jacques Marquette and Louis Jolliet were among the first Europeans to venture into the Illinois wilds is common knowledge. Less known is that one of their first encampments, which would have been slightly north of where I drove that day, was a few feet north of Garfield Ridge, off Harlem. The year was 1673 and, according to their journals, the two Frenchmen found themselves facing an immense acreage of inhospitable muck, a miasma barely able to support their canoe. Later, once they had traveled through and around the swampy area to explore Lake Michigan itself, they speculated that a canal could give the area real potential as a trade center.

Later, after English became the region's vernacular, the swampy expanse they spotted was nicknamed Mud Lake and, by 1848, a man-made water route, the Illinois and Michigan Canal, had been thrust through the land near their old campsite. Fifty years afterwards, in 1900, a bigger, mightier, but more controversial waterway, the Sanitary and Ship Canal, cut a parallel route through the same area, which helped drain Mud Lake and make future development possible, and relegated the I and M to history's dust bin. Eventually, I-55 took a cue from the southwest directional pattern of both. By the early 1960s, three interstate exchanges were functioning immediately north of a narrow strip of light-industrial suburban park at Garfield Ridge's north border.

It's a history once overlooked in school books, though modern-day history caretakers have given the area greater attention. A striking sculpture commemorating Marquette and Jolliet's visit stands today in an unincorporated forest preserve a few hundred feet northwest of Garfield Ridge, near Harlem. It looms above the foliage, within listening range of interstate traffic, beneath the flight paths.

Recently, I stopped at a café, new to me, on—where else?—Archer, to eat. When I approached the register to pay, the cashier left for several moments. She couldn't locate my server, she told me. A few minutes later, she returned. My waitress, she said, was just spending a few minutes with the toddler of a coworker who had stopped by on her day off to say hello.

The cashier cast a knowing glance my way, telegraphing an unspoken message. "Friendships. Children. First things first," it said. I smiled politely; I understood. Some things in Garfield Ridge had not changed at all, I thought.

That interlude in the café was a reintroduction to the place I had moved away from long ago, but in an odd way had not left. If your old neighborhood has an airport, and you enjoy traveling, you get back to the old hood with some regularity, if only for expediency's sake. But driving slowly along Archer that day offered the chance to indulge in nostalgia. If local businesses were an indication, my old neighborhood had responded healthily to the intervening years. Names on the shops and overhead signs may have been different, but storefront vacancies were few. Vehicles filled spaces in the small lot outside a strip mall that replaced a burger joint, and the paper window signs advertising Polish and Slovakian food I recalled were nowhere to be found. Had there ever been a resolution to that favorite debate about which bakery made the best kolachky—was that question still unresolved? Perhaps so. I could find only two of the area's best-known bakeries that day. Maybe it was emblematic of any trip back to the old 'hood; memories revive the soft side and hard edges of everything, the sweetness with the salt. A ride along the most famous street in your old neighborhood may lead directly to memories long scuttled away, but it can also take you back to the reassuring facts of a place's history.

As in other neighborhoods, Garfield Ridge's newer names now fill the spaces on which many memories are built, which is no surprise. That the area retains the energy, vigor, and pride in homeownership that I recall is not unusual either. What's changed the most is its potential for aimlessness. An airport in its down time is a magnet for meandering walks around tarmac fences, past landing strip lights, even to the runway guide post that was once across the street. They are all still there, but more shielded now, protected from the bustle of regular arrivals and departures. Garfield Ridge has never been the only American neighborhood with an airport. But can another be called "Comeback Kid?"

Back of the Yards: Books and Breakfast at the Breathing Room

MIRANDA GOOSBY

A version of this article was previously published as part of Sixty's Envisioning Justice Residency (sixtyinchesfromcenter.org).

Food, like music, crosses all boundaries. It connects the physical and the soul. It honors the past and present in every human being's life. It is essential for survival. At the Breathing Room, a black-led liberation headquarters for arts, organizing, and healing on Chicago's South Side at Fifty-First and S. Bishop, Cherisse Jackson and I have been bringing a Books and Breakfast program to the space Monday and Wednesday mornings, from 7:00 to 9:00 a.m.

The program honors the black radical tradition and the Black Panther Party's Free Breakfast for School Children Program, which began in 1969 after the National School Lunch Program provided reduced-price, but not free, lunches for poor children, and the National School Breakfast Program was limited to only a few schools. Bobby Seale and the Panthers initiated the Free Breakfast Program at St. Augustine's Church in Oakland, California, with Fr. Earl Neil and parishioner Ruth Beckford-Smith, to address the need in that community. It quickly spread to multiple chapters and cites, helping to combat neighborhood hunger and fight poverty, flourishing thanks to local organizations, churches, and volunteers who donated their time and resources.

At the Breathing Room, the Books and Breakfast Program has, since August 2018, helped feed local community members, families, and children before they are off for their day. It provides a space of mindfulness, music, and calm, a library full of books, and a range of food. If one cannot stay for breakfast, fresh fruit, granola bars, water, and other foods are set outside the space and protected for anyone to take who passes by. Within the space, the Collective sources local vegetables from an urban farm two blocks away, offering fresh peppers, carrots, tomatoes, and fruit along with donations from the Collective's neighbor, Su Casa, a Catholic Worker shelter providing housing and meals for families going through housing transitions.

Su Casa's relationship with the Collective is one that highlights themes of collective accountability and community partnership. Many of the meals prepared within the Breathing Room and the breakfast program are made with ingredients donated by Ms. Freida, Su Casa's legendary meal creator for the last twenty-five years. Ms. Freida has helped Cherisse and me to understand who may come through and what everyone likes to eat. In the mornings, a consistent ten families, ranging from ten to twenty people a day, come to eat home-cooked meals and share the carefree, open atmosphere fostered for the children who attend and who bring their friends to decompress with music, drumming, and conversation.

The children who we feed range from toddlers to junior high schoolers, along with their parents, from the surrounding Back of the Yards neighborhood or nearby Englewood. Formerly home to Chicago's notorious Union Stockyards, the industrial and working-class neighborhood has suffered a great deal of disinvestment and neglect in the modern age. I have grown to truly enjoy making breakfast for the program each morning. It has taught me about the power of community, of caring for one another, and how combating hunger and poor living conditions through food may be simple but powerful.

Cofounded by poet Kristiana Rae Colón in 2014, #LetUsBreathe is an alliance of artists and activists working to reimagine a world without prisons and police. "The Collective was not originally a collective," says Colón, "but at first just the four or five people who were down—and through continued action the Collective was built. We hold an identity of abolition and we feel that the most important function in our actions lies within imagining alternative systems to the violent systems we wish to dismantle."

Painted on the gate of the Breathing Room is the mantra, "We are what we need." As Colón notes, "We believe that abundance is the natural law. Scarcity is engineered, and engineered scarcity equals capitalism. We ultimately want to break down the barriers of access to healing. The ingenuity of people is all we need. The generosity of people is everything we need. The abundance of the earth is everything that we need."

The Breathing Room now includes a Free Store, a library, a mental health and wellness lounge, and more. It hosts a monthly performance series, as well as art, yoga, and Reiki classes, and holds forums on the changing political climate. "I believe that the job of the artist is to challenge folks beyond what they can see in front of them, then comes the job of building the sh**," says **Colón**. "It is important that we provide resources for us to heal ourselves, because a lot of us come to activist spaces broken, looking for an outlet from their pain."

Right now the Collective is functioning at about half its potential capacity, she says. "We are trying to succeed where the Black Panthers failed. We hope to not capitulate to paranoia and internal drama and distrust. We are building the breakfast program, to stay open consistently, and to have more arts activism in Chicago. We hope to also launch studios for individual artists to launch their visions."

I have great hope that the Books and Breakfast program will continue; the Collective hopes to expand its days of operation and draw in more participants in order to assure sustainability and community participation. Understanding how important it is for children who attend nearby schools like Arthur A. Libby and Hamline Elementary to begin their day nourished physically and mentally is the driving force behind how the work must continue. We cannot do it without one another.

Englewood:
An Interview with
Tamar Manasseh, founder
of Mothers/Men Against
Senseless Killings

KIRSTEN GINZKY

Tamar Manasseh founded Mothers/Men Against Senseless Killings (MASK) in Englewood in 2015. The volunteer-driven group salves a range of social needs by providing food, childcare, and educational opportunities on "the block," two formerly-empty lots at the corner of Seventy-Fifth Street and S. Stewart Ave. Formerly one of the most dangerous blocks in Chicago, Seventy-Fifth and Stewart has now gone years without a shooting, as MASK's footprint has deepened and expanded.

Tamar Manasseh: I realized something this summer. One day, there was a lot going on. All these kids were running around, making so much noise, and they were purple, from the magnetic slime they made. I thought, *where else in Englewood would you see a sight like this?* There are black kids, white kids, rich kids, poor kids . . . all these kids, running around, having a great time. Where else would you see this, not just in Englewood, but in this whole city? Nowhere.

I think in places like Hyde Park and some places on the North Side, there's an artificial sense of diversity. It might be racially diverse, but not necessarily diverse in culture or background. You have to be able to afford to live there. If everybody is rich, it doesn't really matter if they're black or white, there isn't economic or class diversity.

On the block, we have kids from all different places, economic backgrounds, and they're just having fun. Their parents aren't paying anybody to have this culturally enriched, diverse experience. Everywhere else you go, if you want to see black kids playing with white kids, you usually have to pay for that.

Kristin Ginzky: When you were growing up in Englewood, did you have public spaces like the block?

Manasseh: All the kids in the neighborhood would just come hang out on the front porch. You really don't see people sitting outside like they used to. They're so afraid of getting shot, and all sorts of stuff. Before everybody had air conditioning, people would sit outside in the summer.

Ginzky: It seems like social spaces are disappearing. When I walk around, I spot places that used to be basketball courts.

Manasseh: Basketball courts are a resource, right? Somewhere your kids can go play, get exercise, and work things out. High schools were also a resource, and now they're gone. All the resources around Seventy-Fifth and Stewart have pretty much been zapped. The thing is, we're a resource. The people who come down to sit on the block are resources. Everybody wants to do something. It's a game changer.

Ginzky: You moved away from Englewood. Would you say you were "called" to go back?

Manasseh: Yeah. That's how it's supposed to be. You're from there, you get out and learn some stuff, and then you go back for the others. You don't just get out and stay out. You definitely don't watch it deteriorate, just because you're too good to be there now, and you're not part of that problem. If you have the tools to fix it, go fix it. I don't hate Englewood or resent it; I understand that it's a part of me, and I love it for the person that it made me. Do I like its condition? Absolutely not. But I love what I learned there.

Ginzky: What about the other MASK moms?

Manasseh: I love all of the people. I think the friendships are God's rewards for creating MASK. I would have never met these people otherwise.

Ginzky: The men, too! Did you expect that you'd have men jump on board?

Manasseh: Nope. I guess I hoped that they would, but they just started showing up in droves!

Ginzky: Do you know how they found you?

Manasseh: *DNAInfo* [a now-defunct local news outlet]. The idea was, if the press shows up one day, people will find out what we're doing and show up. People thought it would just crash and burn.

Ginzky: What changed?

Manasseh: The fact that we didn't go away. None of us were murdered, and we weren't just passing through—it was a committed effort. No one thought it would last this long.

Ginzky: Over the past four years, you've cooked out every day during the summer—that's almost your motto: "We do this every day that the kids aren't in school." That's changing?

Manasseh: Yeah. At this point, we're becoming a year-round, everyday party of the community. They wouldn't help us keep the schools open, so we said, "We'll just build our own school!" It gives MASK a greater sense of permanence. The kids can have a deeper attachment because they know, beyond the shadow of a doubt, that we're not going anywhere.

Ginzky: Where do you find the energy?

Manasseh: I was on a panel recently, and somebody asked, "How do you stay so positive and upbeat?" I don't. How do I not get burnt out? I got burnt out three years ago. I don't know what I've been running on since then. If I quit, bad things happen. If I don't show up, people will die. I can't let that happen.

Ginzky: How much do you think the impact of MASK reverberates beyond the block?

Manasseh: I think it's a lot bigger than we know. Seventy-Fifth and Stewart was terrible when we got there. What if people from Seventy-Fifth and Stewart were the ones in a lot of different gang wars and altercations, and they stopped doing that when we came around? The thing about shooting somebody is they'll come back to shoot at you. Who wants to bring that kind of danger to a block where moms sit on the corner and kids play? Who wants to be responsible for that? I think they've stopped participating in as many disputes as they were before.

Ginzky: You've had people turn over their guns?

Manasseh: Oh, yeah. Casual, like, "Here you go!"

Ginzky: You've gone four years without a shooting, yet CPD continues to dispatch more police?

Manasseh: Yeah, they said, "They sell drugs on that corner." You know why they sell drugs on that corner? Because they don't have jobs. I really used to think people who really want jobs can get jobs. They just make excuses. I started to drink that Kool-Aid. Those kids put all of their trust in me—I told them to stay out of trouble and go to school, and they did. Do you know how bad it hurt when I couldn't find them jobs, and they would end up in jail?

Ginzky: What jobs are there for the kids who go to school, graduate, and stay out of trouble?

Manasseh: I don't know. First of all, who's going to hire them? Second of all, some of them don't even have clean shirts to put on. They have so few resources. They don't have anybody to help them prepare for an interview. They don't know how to fill out an application or how to dress for an interview. Most of them don't even have bus fare to get to an interview.

Ginzky: You had a first phase where you were on the corner, and then you acquired the lot, poured a concrete pad and got some storage. . . . Now, you're creating something with a more permanent footprint.

Manasseh: Crazy, isn't it? Who says, "Fine, we can't go to that school? We'll make our own." We had to do it. The kids hang out there every day. They get to the block at 7:30 in the morning. They should be in school, but they hang around the gate all day. To watch the machinery, to watch the holes being dug . . . they are in awe of it.

Ginzky: Do you think they know, as they're watching, that you're building it for them?

Manasseh: They know. I overheard them talking about the subjects that they could help other kids with. "I can help tutor in math, and you can do this . . ." I'm so glad that they want to chip in and help with the younger kids. It's not like these kids are just selling drugs. They're tutors. They can do math. They are smart.

Ginzky: During the summer, they were already taking up the lead, serving food.

Manasseh: Yeah. All they want is to do something. Everybody wants to contribute, even if it's just putting some food on a plate. Normally, when people come and build things in neighborhoods like that, they're not building it for the people who live there.

Ginzky: Do you ever think of yourself as a kind of alternative developer?

Manasseh: I rarely think of myself as anything other than a mother. That's just it. Momming looks different to all of us, and this is what it looks like to me.

Ginzky: You've created something that people want to be part of, and they're proud to be part of.

Manasseh: You know, I think the whole city could learn from that. You can build community anywhere, and you need community everywhere. One can never be too wealthy for community. You're always going to need your neighbors—they're your neighbors.

Marquette Park: Members Only

GINT ARAS

My earliest memory of Marquette Park, a neighborhood embedded into Chicago Lawn—Sixty-Third to Seventy-First streets, Western to California—is from Liths Club, a lounge on Sixty-Ninth Street. This is circa 1979, and I'm about six years old. My father and uncle sit at the bar while I occupy a table with my younger brother. We slurp RC cola, chomp barbecue chips, and watch chain-smoking men play billiards.

Liths Club belonged to Lituanica Liths, an amateur (passionate, mad, oft-relegated) soccer team of the Chicago Metro League. The strip between Western and California, Lithuanian Plaza Court, was home to over a dozen similar bars, all of which I'd visit long before finishing high school.

Between the 1960s and '80s, the majority of homes in Marquette Park housed displaced World War II Lithuanian refugees and their children. The elders did not migrate out of economic interest or pursuit of romance; Lithuanians had fled Soviet occupation, and most ended up in America by chance. Earlier waves of Lithuanian immigrants to Chicago had set up infrastructure, naturally drawing new migrants. Certainly by 1960, though perhaps long before, Marquette Park had become the flagship Lithuanian neighborhood, boasting its own soccer team, newspapers, publishing house, bookstore, archive, teachers' academy, schools, theater troupes, opera choir, hospital, parish, bakeries, delis, and bars.

The bars were not just watering holes but community centers. Kids had their birthdays in the back rooms. Liths Club threw a Christmas party every year (I pulled Santa's beard at one to reveal my uncle's face), while another bar allowed an acting troupe to meet in the back for free, rightly assuming they'd buy a ton of drinks.

Because I was born to the displaced, neighborhood codes let me drink and smoke openly as a teen. Between the ages of sixteen and twenty, I spent the vast majority of my Saturday nights in sweaty and smoky bar rooms on Sixty-Ninth, where all but two bars had the same sign on the door: "Members Only, 3 IDs needed for entrance."

Obviously, I never produced any ID. Membership was coded in exactly the way small American towns code down-home identity, though perhaps with more pathos. When the bartender survived a bombing run with your grandfather, or he knew your father had been dragged across Poland by your grandmother—the rest of the family shot in some field or deported to Siberia—he'd pour you a damn beer. The American idiocy of "underage drinking" did not beat the bonds created by collective survival, those that determined neighborhood code and custom.

The neighborhood provided cohesive comfort; everything in walking distance, no practical reason to leave. The effort to maintain culture entailed a kind of sentimentality: amber necklaces and bracelets, wooden engravings of Lithuanian castles, colorful sashes on shelves . . . all things to confirm Lithuanian identity. That one was *true*. All other shades of identity, including whatever Americanness you might have gained by birth or in transit, was a side effect of war's aftermath, more a coating than a self.

Insistence on this version of truth naturally insulated Lithuanians. Cohesion's close cousins are skepticism of strangers and paranoia of the larger world. Interlopers could find themselves walled off. Some mothers, for example, did not allow children who didn't speak Lithuanian to attend their children's parties, no matter that the Lithuanian-American kids spoke mostly English among themselves. The system kept kids within fences, a long-term plot to discourage marriages to outsiders.

Perhaps the wanton teen drinking on Lithuanian Plaza Court makes more sense now? If the kids got wasted together in the safety of back rooms, in pubs whose regular drunks knew everyone's parents by name, hormones would do their thing in the safety of a controlled space. It was a variation of the arranged wedding, clannish without doubt, as Soviet occupation had this way of making you feel your culture was on the verge of being completely annihilated.

No world map showed your country—your culture existed almost exclusively to itself. When you told Americans your name was Feliksas, they'd change it in front of your face to Felix, deleting *your fucking name* for their own convenience. When you told Americans you were Lithuanian, they'd ask, "Is that like Russia?" You realized your family's murderer has successfully transformed you into himself in the world's mind. It left you clinging to what you had, as you anointed yourself protector, handling the trauma of war in the process, something inescapable in the Lithuanian consciousness, no matter if you were born in the States, in a refugee camp, or if your mother dragged you across Poland. Lithuanians did not treat trauma by lamenting their lot in the press, talking with shrinks, or popping pills. The antidotes were prayer and church, the occasional conversation with a priest, collective weeping at funerals, or midsummer singing in backyards, wartime laments delivered in harmony to an endless flow of vodka. The mission was not to express your culture or celebrate its tones. It was to keep from dying out.

Little of this registered to an outsider. Most people from outside Marquette Park, if they knew anything about its reputation, had heard it was a den of extreme bigotry, a flashpoint in the struggle for civil rights. The reputation is well-deserved.

Among the many inside jokes in *The Blues Brothers* is the satirizing of a Nazi march in Marquette Park, when Jake and Elwood announce they hate South Side Nazis and drive their rally off a bridge into the park's lagoon. In fact, fascists and racists of many stripes set up shop in Marquette Park, where various voices pronounced the neighborhood forever ethnically white, and where the Chicago Nazis had their headquarters on Seventy-First. Rallies and riots relevant to the history of class and racial struggle occurred in the park, including Martin Luther King's well-documented 1966 visit, which was met with massive violence. That was, of course, hardly the only incident. In 1976 the National Socialist Party of America gathered to confront a group of black protesters concerned with inequitable housing. The Ku Klux Klan staged infamous rallies, met by counter-protesters as well as cheering spectators, in the summers of 1986 and 1988. The latter turned violent.

By the 1980s, the fears of white flight fed ever-more frequent accounts of violent crime.

On a Wednesday someone's grandfather got attacked in his garage, his shelves looted of tools. The next Tuesday someone's aunt got beaten up, her purse stolen. A friend of my college roommate came to the neighborhood to drink in one of the bars and got shot in the face as she exited her car. Her survival was pure luck.

In every single one of these cases, the perpetrators were young black men. The stories made their way around coffee chats after church, discussed over Old Style at Plaza Pub and Gintaras Club, over cake at a *Lithuanian Futurist* fundraiser. The neighborhood was "being overrun." Blacks were "encroaching" from across Western Avenue, unable to remain where they "belonged." The violence wasn't a myth, or raw propaganda—a woman was, indeed, shot in the face, just as friends of mine were jumped and pinned down, thugs pointing guns to their heads, demanding everything from everyone's pockets and backpacks, including car keys, cigarettes, Led Zeppelin cassettes and a scapular, an heirloom inherited from an aunt. Residents saw real reason to fear what was happening, and no one could expect them to look to the history of American racism and housing rights to settle their dismay.

I cannot dismiss the violence in the neighborhood, though I need to stress something that bothered me in my youth, something I felt I was noticing all by myself. The diaspora Lithuanians I knew worried constantly about *them*, or *those ones*, or *juodžiai* bringing blight and violence, but it was rare to hear anyone express even vague concern over the presence of Nazis in the neighborhood—the very philosophy that had started the war from which so many had suffered.

Lithuanian racism was like an open secret. It always struck me, even as a schoolboy, that pointing out the obvious about bigotry in the diaspora often led to accusations of shock and outright denial. An uncle could go off at the dinner table, say something extreme—"Blacks should be burned just like the Jews"—but if you told someone he was a bigot, they'd gasp out, "No, no! What are you saying?" I learned racism wasn't wrong to feel. It was just wrong to admit.

I can't say how many Lithuanians carried membership cards for the NSPA or KKK, if any did at all. But let us remember that *membership* in the neighborhood was coded, abstract as the dividing line between the ghetto and Marquette Park, invisible yet ever real.

I had an experience in one of the bars that illustrates this. I must have been all of fourteen, a friend and I seated at the bar with men three times our age, our fathers among them. In the lazy buzz of barroom babble, the door creaked open and a few young black men stepped in. They did not get two yards past the threshold when all the men at the bar turned to them to shout, nearly in unison, "Members only!" The unwelcome guests left without a word, though I doubt they looked to sociological theories to quell their resentment. I learned another code that day, one of silence. There just wasn't any reason to wonder out loud: "Oh, so that's what those signs on the doors really mean?"

That mentality became a self-fulfilling prophecy. Neighborhood crime kept increasing: battery, robbery, vandalization, even murder. Some of the old timers looked at it as yet another invasion, another occupation, though others cautioned not to get hysterical, just to hold firm and avoid selling any homes to *those ones*. It proved impossible—not all neighbors were Lithuanian, and others just failed to feel identical shades of sentiment for the tribe. Whites fled. By the mid 1990s, the Lithuanian presence in Marquette Park was a mostly symbolic commuter culture, the delis gone, all but a few bars closed. I drank my final glass of beer on Sixty-ninth in the summer of 1996, a day before departing Chicago for a job.

Liths Club stood as a rather stubborn nostalgia act, though it was finally razed in 2013, something I learned from a Facebook status update, posted by a woman I'd neither seen nor spoken to for over a two decades. Laments sounded in the post's comments, including a memorable one from a Marquette Park expat, born in the early 1970s like me, a guy suffering from illnesses related to alcohol abuse, his mental health strained by the complex childhoods we all had growing up among traumatized refugees: "Better razed than taken over by them." He meant the non-members, of course.

I returned to Marquette Park in the spring of 2018. An artist visiting from Klaipėda asked to see the old neighborhood, whose story I'd told her, so we drove down on a whim. I was sincerely curious to see what it was now. Garbage everywhere, boarded up storefronts, barroom doors gated, their windows dirty with film. Every block had an abandoned building or two. The only active businesses, besides an old bank, were a food mart and clinic. The mart seemed primarily a liquor store, half-drunk men loitering outside, laughing and smoking. Yet with their paper bags and cigarillos, they seemed far from happy.

Wandering about, fielding unwelcome stares from the locals, we knew we were intruding, unable to claim membership to this street. Together, we sensed something we discussed on the drive home.

America—indeed, most of the West—is at a point that might be the culmination of the struggle for equality, an historical fulcrum that can see us collapse to extinction or be reborn with a new vision. The history of Marquette Park offers valuable lessons, perhaps best understood by outsiders, or those of us who have some distance from the passions.

Those of us who claimed opposite sides of Western Avenue shared much more than we could bring ourselves to see. The traumas of war and slavery are analogues, consequences of oppressive, dehumanizing philosophies that naturally leave their survivors feeling like victims. A curious note in the mentality of the victim is a sense of authority over a conflict, even a feeling that one is entirely good while others are entirely bad. Suffering can become its own drug, its own kind of indulgence, because feeling entirely good is far more pleasant than wondering what you've contributed to the madness before you. Even that question—*What role have you played in this?*—sets off snapping answers. None! I was not a slave owner. I was not a Soviet. And I am not a Nazi. I have no membership card.

The flashpoint of Marquette Park was a consequence of our inability to see both sides suffering from history's monster—families dismembered, identities rearranged, and bodies blasted across oceans. In fairness, the followers of Martin Luther King saw this with better clarity than did the residents of Marquette Park, primarily those that sympathized with the very energies that led to displacement. This aside, the question isn't who is more enlightened. The question is what codes do we want to use to determine membership to the same club. And does the survival of my club depend on a disaster befalling another?

Marquette Park used the codes of ethnicity and race. Its membership depended on a kind of paranoia that's based almost entirely on lines we're too frightened to examine. That's the lesson Marquette Park offers everyone on the outside, and the value of its history. We fear adding members to our club will kill the club's identity. That's to say, if I cannot be who I understand myself to be right now, it means I can't be anything at all. Perhaps it's time to have fewer small clubs on opposite sides of streets, but extend invitations to those who've suffered from history's monster. If we count up the members of that club, we'll find it's very large.

FAR SOUTHWEST SIDE

Ashburn: That's Amore

TIM MAZUREK

Growing up on the Southwest Side of Chicago, our lives were centered along Pulaski between West Lawn and Ashburn, though at the time I can't remember anyone using neighborhood names. We talked in terms of intersections or parishes—I grew up at Fifty-Ninth and Kedvale, my cousins went to St. Bede. Back then, the neighborhood was mostly Eastern European immigrants living in tidy brick ranches or three-flats contained by chain-link fences and protected by "Beware of Dog" signs. Block after block the pattern of nearly identical homes was repeated, which, when combined with Chicago's relentless grid, gave driving through the side streets a video-game monotony.

I lived on the top floor of one of the brick three-flats with my mom. My grandparents and great-grandparents lived in the flats below ours—four generations stacked in chronological order, a twentieth-century immigrant dream. My busha liked her garden apartment because it offered easy access to the vegetable patch, which took up a third of the small backyard. The rest of the yard was a blanket-sized patch of grass that I used to play on and that my mom used for sunbathing while planes landing at Midway cast sudden shadows over us. We were right around the corner from the original Dove Candies, where we walked for hand-dipped ice cream bars on humid summer evenings, their neon signs vibrating against the twilight sky.

My great grandparents had come to Chicago from Poland, like many people in the neighborhood, and held tight to traditions, especially culinary ones. Holidays meant pierogi, golabki, sausages, and sauerkraut, which weren't flavors that my childhood palate appreciated. Luckily the whole family had developed a taste for pizza by the time I showed up. Pulaski had a fair number of pizza parlors that we would pile in the car and drive to for a treat.

Trips out of the house, to the bank or grocery store or whatever errand I might be taken on, were a rare adventure—so much of my life took place in our three-flat or on our street. I felt stifled by the closeness of my family and the sameness of the neighborhood. Once when I was too young to be out of the house alone, I wandered out the front door and down the block. I don't know where I was going, but I was clearly looking for something. When my grandma found me, it was the only time she ever really yelled at me. I never did it again, though the urge persisted. Trips out of the house gave me an opportunity to look at other people and imagine—my first practice at desire. A common scolding during my early years was, "Stop staring, Timmy."

Trips out for pizza had the obvious added bonus of pizza, which, when combined with freedom and strangers to study, was an almost unbearable amount of pleasure. My favorite pizzas were at Vito and Nick's, which sat on the corner of Pulaski and Eighty-Fourth near my Auntie Bea's house. The neighborhood seemed nearly identical to ours, though there were fewer trees and Pulaski was more of a bully down there. Vito and Nick's was typical of a class of restaurants that were somewhere between a dive bar and a supper club. Hallmarks of these joints include glass block windows, wood paneling, a jukebox, light-up beer signs, and little league teams celebrating a win. Vito and Nick's linoleum-floored dining room was over-filled with tables and chairs, creating a disorder that seemed unresolvable. The walls were unpredictably covered in a plush brown carpeting, which adds a homey, if unhygienic, feeling to the space. Colored lightbulbs in the cut glass chandeliers provided the only real pop of color and a mottled, unflattering light.

Pizza for us was thin, cracker-crusted, tavern-style pie, which is the only Chicago pizza that I knew. I didn't have my first deep dish until high school when we went to some tourist spot off the Mag Mile. Deep dish was for North Siders, a class of people that felt as far away and foreign as anyone. Our pies were built on a thin cracker crusts, spread to the very edges with a sweet and pleasantly acidic tomato sauce and topped with a generous slick of cheese. The pizza was always cut into squares, designed for sharing. The imperfect cutting a circle into a grid—an edible version of Chicago—inevitably left four tiny, triangular pieces that I prized above all others, though for all the wrong reasons—they were cute.

But it wasn't the pizza that I most looked forward to at Vito and Nick's. It was the men making the pizza. They were neighborhood guys in their late teens or early twenties clad in tight white T-shirts and blue jeans topped by flour-covered aprons. They were tan and fit—all youthful biceps and bulges, glints of gold chains around smooth necks, too much aftershave. They probably went to high school together, or dropped out of high school together. In addition to their physical beauty, I was fascinated by their intimacy with each other. They laughed and commiserated, teased the waitresses, checked out female customers, shared private jokes, and landed friendly punches. They moved around the kitchen like dancers, aware of the space and each other, performing a carefully choreographed routine. Dough was rolled, sauce was spread, pizzas were loaded in and out of the hot ovens, wooden peels were tossed around. And all of this for me. It was beautiful.

The men in my family never cooked. They didn't do any domestic work, really. Once my grandpa put on my grandma's apron and did a pantomime of a woman for laughs. The idea of him doing housework was ridiculous to everyone. Gender roles were very clearly defined and difference was not celebrated. I'd heard people called "fag" enough in our neighborhood to know what was not allowed. Lucky for me, I was protected by the women in my family who taught me about cooking and gardening and taking care of things. My grandmother tried to assure me that I could do whatever I wanted and that famous chefs in Europe were often men. I gravitated toward domestic stuff, despite being aware that it wasn't expected of me. I think from an early age everyone knew I was different. My grandpa's attempts to play catch with me in the alley usually ended with me wandering off to help my grandma in the garden or asking to watch *The Dukes of Hazzard*.

The guys at Vito and Nick's stirred some nascent queerness in me. They were cooking and making it look good. They looked good. They were also showing me a closeness between men that I hadn't been exposed to as an only child with few friends. It was one of many early indications that things did not have to be like they were on Kedvale, that other worlds were possible. Those guys were an affirmation in the unlikeliest of places.

I still go to Vito and Nick's, though I have long since left the neighborhood. I drag my husband there once or twice a year for what I still consider to be the best pizza in Chicago. I will inevitably start reminiscing about the neighborhood with equal parts pride and cynicism. Not much has changed within the walls of Vito and Nicks, or if it has, memory smooths out any discontinuity. A new generation of guys are there making the pizzas, and I always feel a flutter when I see them in their T-shirts and aprons—the residue of desire from a previous version of me.

You never forget your first love.

Mount Greenwood: Growing Up In, and Reporting On, Chicago's Poster Child for Racial Tension

JOE WARD

Residents of Mount Greenwood use the phrase "South Side" interchangeably with the neighborhood's name. To many, they mean the same thing. Yet Mount Greenwood—which makes up the far-southwest border of the city—is not very representative of Chicago's sprawling South Side. Mount Greenwood is a largely middle-class area made up of cops, firemen, and other city workers; a blue-collar neighborhood of Irish Americans who still vote with the city machine that likely employs them—even if their national politics have shifted to the right. Its residents earn nearly twice the city's average household income. It is one of the safest neighborhoods in Chicago. And, as the *New York Times* has reported, it is a "holdout from a pre-white flight" era of the city.

To the rest of the city, Mount Greenwood is a throwback to Chicago's past, a place impervious to the demographic and political changes across the rest of the city. Its remoteness and lack of public transportation help give the neighborhood an insular feeling. Residents don't really have to venture out, and outsiders have little reason to venture in.

Its tradition is both what neighbors love about their tidy community and also why some outside the neighborhood look at Mount Greenwood with apprehension.

Like much of the rest of America, Mount Greenwood has a history to grapple with. That history collided with the present in the late months of 2016, when two white Chicago police officers shot and killed a black man in November of that year, sparking painful confrontations between black activists and white neighbors.

Watching the events unfold as both a journalist on assignment and as a native son, I saw neighbors confront an outside force—that is, criticism of its ways *and* literal outsiders, in the form of protesters—that the neighborhood has long worked to keep out. I also saw a neighborhood that was forced to confront its characterization as a hotbed of racism, a community that grappled with how it would present itself to the outside world now that, for the first time in a while, many eyes were on Mount Greenwood.

As a kid, my block felt like a universe to me. Irish American families no longer produce offspring like they did generations ago, but there were still plenty of children around when I was growing up. Rows of raised ranches with wide, pristine lawns were intersected by concrete walkways and gangways—striping for makeshift football fields and games of run the bases.

In sixth grade, a new family moved on the block. That was always big news, especially when it meant having new kids around. In this case, there were two, one of which was Will, a boy my age. His dad was a paramedic, his mom a nurse. They were the first black family to move onto the block in my lifetime and for some time before that. (Will's family moved to the neighborhood around the same time another black family in the area had rocks thrown through their windows.)

Will's introduction to the kids on the block came naturally. He spent a lot of his early days in his new home biking up and down the sidewalk. Not soon after, we asked him to hang out. When the school year came around, Will won over the sixth-grade boys by beating everyone in a series of one-on-one foot races against our class's fastest. (I was not in the competition.)

We were friends. We would walk or carpool to soccer games together and play video games in each other's houses. But even as a kid, I could sense something less than total acceptance of Will and his family by my classmates and my community. I knew what my dad thought, and I had heard the racist jokes of peers, and gleaned what they might be thinking. Will was one of two black kids in a class of one hundred at our Catholic grammar school. I knew it must have been difficult. I wondered if I did everything I could to make that experience less tough for him.

It was my first time thinking about what it's like to feel out of place, to feel even a tinge of resentment from neighbors and peers. But, as an eighth-grade boy, I found it easy to compartmentalize the shame and self-questioning. I filled my head with the dramas, emotions, and excitement that come with that time. As eighth grade wrapped up, Will moved away. I was shocked by his sudden departure. Then I started high school.

News of Joshua Beal's death spread quickly, after he was fatally shot on November 5, 2016, by two off-duty police officers. The shooting came as Chicago—and the rest of the country—was grappling with multiple episodes of police brutality and the use of deadly force.

Almost exactly a year before Beal's fatal shooting, protests roiled the city and made national news as activists denounced the shooting death of seventeen-year-old Laquan McDonald at the hands of police. By the time Beal's death made headlines, Chicagoans were hardened in their views, many weary after a year of protests and political unease. Still, what happened in Mount Greenwood following the tragedy shocked the city, political activists, and neighbors.

About a dozen young black activists came out to 111th and Troy for the first protest after Beal's shooting. They were met by hundreds of counter-protesters carrying Blue Lives Matter flags who yelled at them to leave. Barking German shepherds were brought to the scene. I saw officers confiscate a baseball bat.

I arrived early and found a large crowd of police supporters gathered at the corner of 111th and Kedzie. A man was pacing in front of the group with a loudspeaker, and I asked if he was with any of the neighborhood groups. He saw a cell phone in my breast pocket and accused me of filming him. I said I wasn't, told him I was a reporter but that I was from here. He asked me to prove it. Later, as I was actually filming, a man shoved me and grabbed my phone, accusing me of trying to set him up.

A protest two days later—on election night 2016—proved to be bigger and more chaotic.

Earlier that day, many people had finally registered their voice in a presidential election that was more divisive than any in recent memory, one that unfurled along racial and social lines more than many others before. At the rally, people were angrier, more dug in, more charged up.

This time, more Black Lives Matter activists came out than for the previous rally, but they were drowned out by an even bigger counter-protest. A planned march got about a quarter of a block before the marchers were effectively boxed in at the intersection, where hundreds of counter-protesters lined the corner and a group of bikers revved their engines to drown out the protesters' chants. Profanities and demands to leave were hurled at the marchers.

Police worked to keep the parties separated, and ultimately brought in a city bus to the crowded intersection. Officers tried to get the activists on the bus, and the plan was to drive them around until the crowd dispersed and they could return to their cars. The activists were furious at the request—furious that they felt they couldn't express their right to protest, furious perhaps at the hatred strewn at them. Most walked to their cars amidst a heavy police presence while white counter-protesters—men, women, and children—screamed at them.

I was looking through a dusty box full of rubber-band-bound stacks of family photos, shortly after my dad died my freshman year of high school, when I found something curious.

It was a photo of my mom and I and my dad's many brothers and sisters, except my dad was not there. We are pictured at a race track, celebrating my dad's birthday—except, as I later found out, he didn't show up because his sister was dating a black man.

Even as a sixteen-year-old, it was naive of me to be shocked by this. My dad, a union pipefitter like his father before, was a rough man—rough in his demeanor, rough in his language, rough in his line of work, and rough in his way of life. My dad's biases, and views on race, were not a secret to anyone who knew him.

After his death, I began thinking more about my dad's impact on my life. Which of his traits did I inherit? Of those traits, which were a matter of biology, and which were foisted upon me by surroundings and circumstance?

These questions have stayed with me for some time.

Then, while reporting on the Beal shooting and the racial tension surrounding it, I came across a 1992 *New York Times* story about Mount Greenwood and nearby Roseland, both Far South Side middle-class neighborhoods divided starkly by race.

The story paints a devastating portrait of Mount Greenwood before the neighborhood became a stand-in for the city's problems with racial segregation.

At the end of the piece, the reporter quotes William Knepper Sr., who would be my eighth-grade math teacher ten years after the story was published. He gives an empathetic take on racial conflict that was comforting and unsurprising. It immediately put me back into his classroom, where the jovial Mr. Knepper showered us with M&M's for correct answers and kindly helped you after school if the lessons weren't taking.

"From my experiences with them, they're like us," he said, of black Chicagoans, in the story. "They have the same goals, the same aspirations, the same fears. When they blame something on racism, I tend to agree with them."

I began thinking about the other people in my life who, like Mr. Knepper, led quiet, upstanding lives. People who might not show up on either side of the protests gripping the neighborhood, but who show their true colors in how they live and treat others.

There were many of them. There was my mother, who quietly showed me there was another way of thinking and living than what my father displayed. There was Fr. Marty O'Donovan, who forcefully rebuked the earlier rock-throwing and other racist incidents. There was Mr. Knepper, whose kindness and understanding seemingly informed his everyday manner and his views on race.

These are the people who truly represent Mount Greenwood.

After the election night Mount Greenwood protest ended, I quickly filed my article and drove home while listening to a radio report that Donald Trump was on his way to a shocking win over Hillary Clinton.

The news of his victory and the images of what I had just seen in my hometown made it hard to comprehend both events simultaneously.

It was not lost on me, however, that Mount Greenwood's history of racial resentment crested with Trump's win. The emergence of both events sparked a national conversation about what caused them and what they mean about us. Three years later, I'm not sure there's a consensus—or a comforting—answer.

For one, the investigation into the fatal shooting is ongoing as of April 2019, according to the Civilian Office of Police Accountability, which investigates the police's uses of deadly force. The pain of the event, meanwhile, continues to reverberate. For the family of Joshua Beal, many of whom saw the twenty-five-year-old die after being shot eight times in broad daylight. For the officers, who await their professional and perhaps legal fate after the split-second confrontation in the middle of the street. For a neighborhood and city that still has so many unanswered questions about its treatment of its black citizens.

Three years after Beal's death, life in Mount Greenwood is outwardly back to normal. The community dinners and neighborhood forums on the topic have ended. No visible signs of the ugly confrontation remain. The community conversations about race relations have left the school halls, church basements, and neighborhood meetings. They've returned to the home, to the front porch, and the sidelines of kids' sports games.

My hope is that those conversations include someone like Mr. Knepper or Fr. Marty, whose quiet dignity and upstanding demeanor can be more influential than one might imagine.

Beverly:
How To Integrate a Chicago Neighborhood in Three (Not So) Easy Steps

SCOTT SMITH

Here's what it takes to racially integrate a Chicago neighborhood.

You have to be a black real estate agent in 1971 who brings families who look like you into a white neighborhood even when neighborhood associations ask you to stop and someone throws a Molotov cocktail at the front door of your house.

Six months later, you have to be a white guy who stands up in front of your similarly white congregation on a Sunday morning in 1971 with a set of poster boards which say things like, "Integration is inevitable."

And you have to be willing to be the only black family on your block.

Then you have to spend the next forty to fifty years acting in fits and starts as black and white residents strive to live among each other, not just with each other, in a city so poisoned by segregation that neighborhoods with black populations higher than 40 percent stop growing economically.

At least that's the way it's been in Beverly/Morgan Park, a racially integrated area of the city roughly bound by Eighty-Seventh Street on the North, 107th Street on the South, California Avenue on the West, and Vincennes Avenue on the East.

According to the most recent census numbers, Beverly is 55 percent white and 35 percent black. Residents with tight-lipped midwestern smiles forgive outsiders who believe these tree-lined streets full of historic architecture are some Oak Park-ian suburb.

In fact, Beverly, along with Morgan Park (66 percent black and 29 percent white) and Mount Greenwood (86 percent white, 4 percent black, and 6 percent Latino) make up the Nineteenth Ward on Chicago's Far Southwest Side, one of the last strongholds of the legendary Democratic machine. It's a community that rallies and fundraises when one of its own needs help, whether it's a family displaced by a fire, local police in need of bulletproof vests, or a young child stricken with cancer. Its strongest businesses—in stark contrast to the big-box stores in the suburbs next door—are small and unique, from decades-old stalwarts like Top Notch Beefburgers, County Fair Foods, and Rainbow Cone, to newer establishments like Horse Thief Hollow Brewpub, Belle Up Boutique, and Tranquility Salon, which is a hairstyling business in the front with occasional live music in the back. The South Side Irish Parade is still a Western Avenue tradition, but so is an annual neighborhood art walk started in the last decade, which features a multiracial coalition of artists and changemakers.

Though nearby Morgan Park had some racial integration in the first half of the twentieth century, the *Encyclopedia of Chicago* tells us this didn't occur "on a large scale" until the 1960s. Meanwhile, Beverly was 99 percent white in 1970.

By 1980, Beverly would be 15 percent black.

None of that change happened naturally.

The years in between were when Frank Williams, Pat Stanton, and Audrey Peeples entered the picture. None of them were looking to make history, nor did they know each other at the time. Their stories are merely representative of what happens when ordinary people don't act in ordinary ways.

Frank Williams will tell you he's a fighter. But he got kicked out of high school for being a lover.

In January 1971, Frank opened a real estate agency at Ninetieth and Ashland in Beverly. Soon after that, he began showing houses in North Beverly to black families who wanted to live there. This did not endear him to some of the neighborhood associations there and they asked him to sign a consent decree, promising not to show homes there.

He refused.

It was not the first time white people tried to persuade Frank to act counter to his interests.

Frank was on the high school football team when he lived in segregated Flint, Michigan. He was dating a girl named Joanne, who was white. The school was not happy about it and Joanne's parents sent her away for a time. The principal of Frank's high school sat him down and asked him to promise he would not date another white girl. Frank said he could not make that promise.

Kicked out of school at eighteen for this refusal, Frank went to work in a factory, which he hated. Eventually, Joanne returned to Flint and the two decided to get married and move to Chicago. Frank found work, first as a mail carrier, then as a realtor in 1966.

When asked if he was purposely trying to bring black families into predominantly white Beverly, Frank doesn't mince words: "All my life I've attempted to do that."

"I always believed I—and my children—had a right to live and play everywhere, in all communities."

Ask Frank what the reaction of the residents was to his efforts and he laughs. "Oh, you know, heh, heh, heh," he says before begrudgingly admitting, "I was not welcomed with open arms."

This is Frank's way of saying the windows of two of his real estate offices were broken. Someone bombed the front of his house with a Molotov cocktail, too. Frank seems to consider this the price of doing business the way he wanted to do it.

"We lived our lives on a daily basis. No, we didn't like it. But I've always been a fighter. And I fought. And I told those folks, 'No, I will not sign a consent decree that I would not solicit in Beverly.'" So that was that.

Incidentally, Frank and Joanne have been married for fifty-nine years now.

Frank doesn't have much good to say about the neighborhood associations of the time, suggesting they weren't much concerned with anything other than "the niceties" of a community until black people started to move in. "They would do things such as integration management, integration maintenance."

He describes the practice this way. "The strategy was that no more than two or three so-called minorities on a block [was] acceptable. Once you get to that fourth person, that's the tipping point. That creates flight, that creates the exodus from the community."

Just so we're clear, Frank means "white flight."

There's a long, sordid history of white flight, panic peddling, redlining, and other government-sponsored segregation through housing nationwide. Chicago plays a particularly odious role in it. Ta-Nehisi Coates's *Atlantic* magazine article, "The Case For Reparations," is a good place to start if you're new to the topic.

To Frank, "integration management" was just another form of segregation. To the neighborhood associations of the time, it was smart urban planning, which brings us to the Beverly Area Planning Association and a white guy named Pat Stanton.

Laurence "Pat" Stanton was an advertising man, comfortable winning over people in a pitch. The one he delivered in the summer of 1971 would change the community of Beverly for decades.

A resident since 1959, Pat saw what was happening in Beverly with black families moving in and had a very simple view: "Integration is inevitable."

A member of the Human Relations Committee at Christ the King's Catholic parish in North Beverly, Pat and others had some success with anti-solicitation efforts aimed at keeping panic peddlers out of the community, but they were looking for ways to have a broader impact.

So Pat wrote a ten-page plan and presented it to the board of C-K, which felt that before it could endorse the plan, it would need the congregation's input. A couple weeks later, Pat found himself in front of the C-K congregation, a layperson standing at the pulpit—unheard of for the day—delivering a presentation off flip charts.

On July 11 and 12, Pat would deliver his sermon at five different masses. A low-quality recording of one of his presentations was made surreptitiously by a parishioner.

"We call this presentation 'Beverly Now.' And 'Now' should be underlined three or four or five times because now is certainly the moment for coordinated action in this community."

Rather than stirring oratory calling upon the higher ideals of those assembled, "Beverly Now" is often mundane, with facts and figures about housing migration and real estate prices. Pat's words sound pragmatic at best, even though they likely sounded radical for the time.

"Let's face up to it. Change is beginning to affect our community. And that change will continue. There's nothing to prevent it. There are thousands of blacks who want homes, they can afford homes and certainly they deserve to live where they can afford to."

"Beverly Now was for realists," Pat says on a Sunday afternoon forty-seven years later. "It wasn't a do-gooder approach. I certainly had strong feelings about what was right, but you don't convince people because it's right, you convince them because it's practical and it's right for the community."

During his presentation, Pat made it pretty clear he anticipated pushback and where those folks could go.

"There will be a certain percentage of people—let's hope most of them have already moved away—who won't want to live here because there are blacks in the community. . . .

"Fight the panic peddlers and the blockbusters . . . let's insist that if blacks are going to look in this community, they look throughout the community."

Pat explains this approach years later. "The South Side changed block by block. The secret, we thought, was that you have to convince the realtors, if they have black prospects, to show them houses throughout the community and not to the obvious place where blacks have recently moved."

Had Frank been in the pews that Sunday, he may have objected to this. But Pat, ever the ad man, knew his audience and how to craft a message that got them to buy. In fact, the majority of Pat's "Beverly Now" presentation is less a call for racial integration in housing and more a verbal white paper, a holistic program of urban planning which includes improving the schools, supporting local businesses, promoting the area's historic architecture, and talking up the local arts center.

Pat says a handful of people told him they objected to his plan and a few people interviewed for an article in the *Southtown Economist* (now the *Daily Southtown*) said so, too. No broken windows in his case, though he does note that two realtors quickly moved their offices.

Most importantly, Pat knew the most important color in the discussion was green.

"The genius was 'And Christ the King will contribute $15,000 toward the implementation of this plan,'" the older Pat says. "For the life of me, I can't think of what sparked that thought." Nevertheless, the pastor of C-K committed the money. At this point in the telling, Pat leans in conspiratorially. "Years later, he got in deep shit with the Cardinal."

Within a month after Pat's "Beverly Now" presentation, the decision was made to fund an expansion of the Beverly Area Planning Association. At the time, BAPA was a small organization without much clout, concerning itself primarily with real estate and zoning matters. BAPA became an organization charged with managing not just integration but small business, real estate, beautification, and safety concerns. It still carries out this mission to this day, though its dedication to integration has waxed and waned, depending on its leadership.

But hard-charging real estate agents, advertising men, and planning associations are only part of the solution. It also takes residents willing to risk being the first black face on a white block.

Audrey Peeples moved to Beverly in 1972 from what is now called Bronzeville. In Beverly, she and her husband were the only black family on the block.

"They would try and show us a place in Morgan Park or Washington Heights on the other side of the railroad tracks," she says. She specifically instructed the agent to show them homes from Ninety-Seventh to 103rd, between Wood and Western. Beverly proper.

Like Frank, Audrey's husband believed "people should live where they want to live." He wanted to live in Beverly because the older style of architecture and hills reminded him of Haverford, Pennsylvania, where he grew up.

Audrey says they moved to Beverly in May, over the Memorial Day holiday. It was hot and they had the windows open. Someone driving by yelled the N-word and "get out of that house." In another incident, a kid from the neighborhood rode by on a bike and yelled a slur at Audrey, who was pregnant at the time. Her husband jumped in the car and drove to the kid's house to inform his mother. "Oh I'm sure it wasn't my son," she said. It was. Most everybody in Beverly then knew where everybody else lived.

"It wasn't real friendly," Audrey says.

Still, a white neighbor invited them to a "welcome to the block" party. Audrey remembers a Protestant friend of hers saying she fit in better with the neighborhood because, unlike her friend, Audrey was Catholic. She says she didn't experience any bigotry within Christ the King when she started going to services there in 1977. Over time, she found more acceptance. Integration, after all, was inevitable. Many years later, Audrey would chuckle to herself and say her lighter skin may have helped.

"I've been in situations when people say 'What are you?' And then I say, 'Why do you ask?' and then they don't know why they asked."

Ask her why integration took hold in Beverly and Audrey brings up a point not mentioned by Frank or Pat. Interest rates were going up at the time and white families who might otherwise have been tempted to leave and sell their homes would not have been able to get as much for them as they would have liked, nor would they have been able to get as much home in another neighborhood.

Once the only black girl in her Girl Scout troop, Audrey would go on to be an anti-racism trainer with the YWCA as well as a board member with the Chicago Community Trust.

Unlike some families of the 1970s, Audrey says today's North Beverly families accept integration as a given: "Diversity is who they are." Beverly has, in her words, "settled down." "It takes dialogue and conversation. Can we have a quiet dialogue and not make people feel guilty?

"I bring it up at every opportunity."

Underlying all this is that question of the tipping point and whether BAPA and others were right to try and spread the integration throughout the community rather than expecting it to occur naturally, whatever that means. If the government can try to manage it negatively through redlining, can't others try to manage it positively? Doesn't that ultimately help the economics of a community?

Natalie Moore addresses this in her 2016 book *The South Side*. In writing about Bronzeville she says, "no infusion of capital and amenities followed when new black middle-class homeowners bought into the neighborhood, therefore confirming the theory that green (as in money) doesn't trump black (as in race)." She goes on to cite a 2014 Harvard University study that found economic opportunities halted once a neighborhood became 40 percent black.

By 1990, Beverly was 24 percent black. It's 35 percent now and often shows up on "Best Places to Live in Chicago" lists. Its residents have a significantly higher than average income and crime is low, especially compared to surrounding neighborhoods.

Frank, Pat, and Audrey's efforts all predated the Harvard study by forty years, but the questions are the same. Is this how you keep integration from becoming segregation? Was this the right approach? Is it now?

Whether the Beverly/Morgan Park of the 1970s has settled down in the 2010s is perhaps in the eyes and ears of the beholder. No broken windows or porch bombs, certainly. But a few times a year, a racially charged controversy will erupt publicly over slurs at a local bar or ballfield, or Nazi graffiti that appears overnight on a garage or wall. Other racial issues simmer beneath the surface in schools or local businesses, ever ready to break through.

On the other hand, a local artist recently took discarded lawn signs from political campaigns and repainted them with messages like "Multi-Racial Unity" and "Black Lives Matter." Residents send her their addresses via Facebook and, under cover of night, the signs show up on front lawns. Sometimes they get stolen. The artist always makes more.

As for Frank, he's still showing homes in the area and was recently given the Gale Cincotta Community Visionary Award by Neighborhood Housing Services of Chicago.

Pat spent the early 2000s as a columnist for the *Villager*, expounding on the history and the present of the neighborhood. Last year, BAPA gave Pat and his wife Lorraine an award for all their years of volunteer service to the community.

Audrey still lives in the same house she moved into back in 1972. She just started her second stint on the board of the Beverly Area Planning Association, too, still starting conversations.

Depending on where you stand, the neighborhood of Beverly can seem either of another time or slowly embracing change.

There are always a few ordinary people working on the latter.

SOUTHEAST SIDE

Roseland:
They Killed Him and His
Little Girlfriend

RAYMOND BERRY

I. *under a starless sky*

     1.
he, dead on scene
shot in the head

a documented gang member
police said to explain

his death, an affirmation
that people don't change

an armed robbery conviction
one year ago, released

from jail he planned
to change his life

a former classmate killed
just two weeks prior

Drake enrolled in college
because of his girl

he wasn't a thug
with her beside him

*On August 6, 2015, William Drake, 20, and Briona White, 22, were shot and killed on the 500 block of West 109th street in the Roseland neighborhood.

2.

she,

gasping, fighting bullets
in her chest
riddled with ash

black, the sky
concrete beneath them
where they lie

under the moonlight
she beside him
hands almost touch

3.

she visited him
despite her family's
warning to leave
Roseland, known
once for fertile
land and flowers
now nothing grows here

violence reaches
its peak, weeks before
her senior year
the couple shot
in an alley
her man first
she next, alive

just long enough
to gaze at a starless
sky, releasing her
last breaths, she learns
that those who love

---

*White was a senior studying orthodontics at Kansas State the year she was killed.

the men here
lose their dreams too

II. *they didn't look like thugs*

jumping into a small yellow car
to flee the scene
of a double homicide
inopportunity the true culprit
the once jewel of the south side
vacant lots and empty factories
teens raising children

who take lives without remorse
a mother hands her daughter a blade
to kill another girl
over a Facebook dispute
Drake's classmates shot the couple
who could've been college kids
but they were born across the track

III. *the whole neighborhood, a memorial*

of fallen teens
miles from museums and skyscrapers
an army of foot-high stones
Blair Holt first
then Arthur Jones,
a ten-year-old who went to get candy
in a neighborhood
where residents bolt iron doors

*In 2007, Diane Latiker started a stone memorial in Roseland at 11627 S. Michigan Avenue with the
names and ages of Chicago's teen victims of violence

and latch window shades
no one sees the spray of bullets
two blocks here, or there
574 names on stones
now 500 more
as shootings continue
across the tracks
mothers gather around crime tape

IV. *these kids have so much hatred*

I'm not a stereotype; I'm not somebody else's version of who I am.
—Toni Morrison

thugs for low riding
or wearing a hoodie.
police take them out.
for minor offenses.
black lives don't matter.
zoning and redlining
contained them on the south side.
they'd create their own
enterprise, over drugs
and turf, they shoot

their own. eyes reflect
others' versions of them.
watching a white girl
pummeled on the blue line.
because she's every white
who scowled or cringed
in passing. fists retaliate.
since a clean heart isn't enough
they turn off their humanity.
like any person would.

V. *why is my child lying on the street?*

1.

we must collect evidence
before removing the body
an officer tells her
after calling the media
to report another murder
her son, exposed
behind the crime van
officers walk around him
confirm his gang status
to reporters
leave the area soon
they brush past her
i'm sorry, they whisper

2.

dusk becomes night
Drake's mother paces
the crime scene
her boy, defenseless
she'll protect him now
because in life she couldn't
so she rips the tape
confronts officers
taking pictures of her son
covers him with a sheet
calls medical examiner herself

his body, unrecognizable
she informs relatives he's dead
the crowd gathering
he wasn't in a gang
his pink and black Nikes
a final gift, she refuses
to let officers leave the alley

---

*Forensics services officers photograph a body at the scene of a double fatal shooting.

until every witness interviewed
the crime tape, fluorescent
red ribbon
a bloom in her hands

VI. *where is Jesus?*

*Then I bathed you with water, washed off your blood from you and anointed
you with oil.*
—Ezekiel 16:9

1.
where he's always been
before a soul turned black
the heart,
of every teen
who stepped against the light
on the other side of the tape
now a warning
for the innocent
to remain on the right side
the price if we don't

2.
a white truck
hoses his blood from the street

a fault line
drifting toward his mother

before spilling into the sewer
body in a bone white bag

no anointing here,
blood giving back a life wasted

---

*Police detectives and officers wait for a body removal service while standing near the body of
William Drake.

even in death
no one's past washed clean

VII. *black butterflies*

I am still alone, broken and small, butterflies fighting for life in the grass.
    —Marie Lu

    1.
people stare at them
flying Cockroaches
too dark to be beautiful

invisible in the night
they creep
to the other side

having never learned to soar
they're caught with nets
life span short

like a bee before it dies
no stinger, but a shell
thin legs, thick thorax, bulging eyes

children point out their ugliness:
"mommy, there's another one"
it's just black; it'll go back to where it came

from another part of town
where flowers wilt,
petals closed

they migrate to where the sun is
but even in the light
nothing blooms for them

2.

if they could,
they'd scorch our wings

a flare tossed up
to watch us fall mid-flight

wings ablaze
they burn to ash

before we hit the ground
caterpillars again

the hope in us
cracked wide open

Pullman: Ideal Communities in Chicago, the Rust Belt, and Beyond

CLAIRE TIGHE

I. LIGHT

I'm obvious, driving slowly down the residential side streets on Chicago's South Side, looking left and right at the Victorian-style homes in Pullman. Though I have lived in Chicagoland all my life, I am seeing this neighborhood for the first time. There's a beauty and unfamiliarity to the homes and row houses in this special neighborhood. The architecture stands apart from the typical brownstones, graystones, and courtyard buildings dotting the city. The sky is late-April overcast. It's "spring," but winter can end late in Illinois. I've seen snow during this week of April. Despite the calendar, I'm cautious.

While I look for a place to park, the neighborhood's classic buildings peek into the sky. There's the stately Hotel Florence, the old Arcade and market buildings, the Green Stone church, and of course, the workers' cottages and executive mansions. This is Pullman—the famous neighborhood founded in 1880 by George M. Pullman as a commercial center for his new business, The Pullman Palace Car Company. This land held the industrial district of the company and the residential community for Pullman's employees. Today the neighborhood spans North to South from East Ninety-Fifth street down to 115th, with Stony Island Avenue to the east, and Cottage Grove along the railroad tracks to the west.

I park on a side street across from a set of brick row homes, around the corner from the historic Stables building, now a gas station. The church steeple rises behind the trees to the east; the building's stone is a gorgeous emerald green. There is hardly any ambient noise, aside from the occasional car passing and the Metra train rumbling by on the elevated tracks to the west. I'm less than fifteen miles south of downtown Chicago, but between the Arcade Park, the quaint commons of green space, and the square, brightly colored homes, I feel miles from the city.

It's a Sunday and despite President Obama's recent designation of Pullman as a National Monument, I seem to be the only tourist wandering about. I'm surprised—thinking that now tourists would be coming in droves. There are plans for a new visitor center to replace the current cinder-block building. Will the new status change the neighborhood's sleepy vibe? Would tourists descend despite the media's portrayal of Chicago, and the South Side, as a monolith, a violent and forlorn place? Would the public come to see its complexities, its beauty?

It was Obama's proclamation that drew *me* to Pullman, finally. I blazed through the Sunday traffic on the Dan Ryan, heading south. From the highway, you wouldn't know Pullman was there. The historic clock tower barely peeks out from behind a giant Walmart sign and a new building, the Method Soap Factory. And then, tucked right off the highway, Pullman, the 150-year-old community that played a key role in the industrial, labor, and civil rights history of America.

A neighbor stands in front of one of the homes facing north, across from the Arcade Park and old stable building. He's watering his lawn with a garden hose. Flowers blossom from every corner of his garden and porch. As I pass, he turns his gaze toward me.

"Been here before?" he calls out. Like I said, I'm obvious.

No, I tell him. I've wanted to visit for a while, but this is my first time. I had heard that Pullman was one of Chicago's hidden secrets.

Without prompting, he tells me he owns the house, that he loves living in Pullman, and that it's a Chicago neighborhood unlike any other.

"Welcome," he says with a nod. "It's hard not to love."

In the visitor center, I get a photocopy of a hand-drawn map of the most notable historic sites. But to focus only on the landmarks would be to miss the essence of the neighborhood. I look for the small stuff: the square mailboxes for residents staying at the Hotel Florence, the painted trim of the workers' cottages, the manicured lawn of the square.

And then there it is, facing the traffic on East 111th. A mural. It poses a question rooted in the rich history of Pullman: "WHAT IS YOUR VISION OF A CONTEMPORARY UTOPIAN COMMUNITY?"

The white lettering is fitted over what looks like black chalkboard paint. If there had been chalk readily available, I would have tried writing an answer. No chalk, but the question imposes—daring me to come up with an imaginative response.

II. DARK

In 1879, George Pullman purchased 4,000 acres of land fourteen miles south of the city that would house his railroad car factory and company town. After gaining some success as a Chicago businessman, Pullman founded his eponymous neighborhood at a time when national eyes were on city. Chicago was growing at a rapid pace, becoming more prosperous, crowded, and filthy by the year, writes Carl Smith in *Urban Disorder and the Shape of Belief,* his 2007 book about the Chicago fire, the Haymarket bombing, and the making of Pullman. Pullman the neighborhood was supposed to be the city's foil—a quiet place that was planned, clean, orderly. A utopia, of sorts, though by Pullman's paternalistic, capitalist definition.

Pullman the place was a solution to the problems of a modern city. Pullman the man offered amenities to his tenants unavailable elsewhere: indoor toilets, running water, trash collection, backyards, paved streets, and sidewalks. The neighborhood became a symbol of progress for the modern age. It "seemed to demonstrate that it was possible to have a healthy, humane, prosperous, and productive urban order," writes Smith. The town was praised in the national press and gained attention as a symbol of economic prosperity. Pullman was a man, a neighborhood, and an idea. An experiment, a symbol: of capital, industry, labor, of possibility.

In 1883, Reverend David Swing, a friend of Pullman's, dedicated a new library in the Arcade Building. In a speech, he praised the man and the neighborhood, suggesting that the United States look to Pullman for a solution to the problems of the modern city. "What a country shall we have," Smith quotes him as saying, "when such an example shall be imitated in all parts of the land." Pullman hosted guests at the Hotel Florence and invited visitors from the 1893 World's Columbian Exposition.

But Pullman was far from utopian. Pullman's requirements for his residents went against American ideals of basic freedom. Workers could not own their homes. They could be inspected and evicted by the company on short notice. Their daily behaviors were monitored and there was little freedom of speech.

Despite his attempts at creating an alternative to the woes of the city, "Pullman himself hardly aimed at lending his name to the cause of racial or social justice," wrote Ron Grossman in 2015 in the *Chicago Tribune.* "He was a control freak, dedicated to being the absolute master of every element of his enterprise." Later criticisms of Pullman highlighted the racial hierarchy in hiring black laborers to serve white customers of the Pullman railroad cars.

In 1884, journalist Richard Ely visited Pullman the place. Unlike many of the other early public assessments, Ely was skeptical. His subsequent article in *Harper's*, "Pullman: A Social Study," asked a number of important questions about the town. "Is Pullman a success from a social standpoint? Is it worthy of imitation? Is it likely to inaugurate a new era in society? If only a partial success, what are its bright features and what its dark features?" Ely pointed out the lack of basic freedoms afforded to residents and questioned the positioning of the town as ideal. "The conclusion is unavoidable that the idea of Pullman is un-American," he concluded. "It is not the American ideal."

Pullman lost momentum in 1894 after the labor strike. The influence of the town, on the history of the labor rights movement and the legacy of African-American workers, lives on. The question of Pullman as an idea remains: What does it mean to envision an ideal community?

III. VISION

It's December. For eight months the mural has haunted me. It's a few days before the New Year and the city feels quiet. I'm in the Loop with a few hours to spare. Pullman calls. I drive south. I want to see the mural.

This time I'm bolder. I drive all around Pullman again, attracting the glances of passersby.

It's only the afternoon but the early winter darkness descends quickly. An inch of hard snow is on the ground from the days before. When I slam the car door, a few flurries dance around my head. I tuck my scarf into my coat, pull the zipper up to cover my nose, pull my hat down over my ears, and flip the hood over my head.

While this Chicago winter layer adds a noticeable weight to my walk, I love the obscurity I gain behind a hat, a zipper covering the bottom half of my face, and a hood covering the rest. This time, no one greets me. It's too late in the afternoon on a weekday before the holiday—the museum is already closed.

But there it is: its looming question, really more of a call to action than a query. WHAT IS YOUR VISION OF A CONTEMPORARY UTOPIAN COMMUNITY?

At this point in Chicago history, people are fleeing in droves, the economics and inequality becoming too much. South Side billboards advertise the benefits of moving to Indiana. While the city's institutions fail to meet the needs of the entire city, communities insist on keeping it alive. What is our vision of an ideal community? The answer may still lie in Pullman.

The sun is setting and it's time to head back downtown so I don't get caught in traffic. Before getting back on the highway, I take one last loop around the neighborhood to drink it all in. I slow down as I pass a new café. I can see someone in the window, wiping the counter with a towel. There are no obvious customers to be seen. Outside, the winter air fogs up the glass.

For fifty years, Pullman neighbors organized to make their home a national landmark. They remind us: figure out what we need and demand that lawmakers deliver. And they continue to lead by example, their community a constant symbolic reminder of the work of neighbors together. The historic district prompts us to imagine what an ideal community could be, for this city, the Rust Belt, and the country.

Americans displeased with the results of the 2016 election looked to the Midwest and to the Rust Belt, asking, "What happened?" As in, "How could you elect this leader? How could you do this to us?" instead of looking deeper and inward, at our collective history as a nation and as American people, and asking, "What are we capable of doing together?"

In the 1880s, George Pullman attempted to build a utopia. The nation wondered, "Could this thing really work?"

In 2019, what can Pullman, Chicago, and the Midwest tell us about ourselves as a nation?

What is our vision for an ideal community, as Chicagoans, the Rust Belt, and America?

To consider what is possible, first we must begin to dream.

Hegewisch: Pudgy's Pizza

JOSH BURBRIDGE

Bob Zajac is special. This is his place, and he fits it—as tall as the floor-to-ceiling wood-paneled walls, homey as the faux brick and cutesy signs covering the front counters. His red T-shirt, drawstring lounge pants, and glasses—not to mention the worn baseball cap and beard that distract from the white ponytail extending six inches down the center of his back—bely his status as Hegewisch's foremost ambassador. Lovable, infectiously charismatic, nice, caring—whatever is the opposite of cold or insular—Bob emphasizes words to drive home his points. He has a gift of making you *believe*. The owner of Pudgy's Pizza, at the edge of the Baltimore Avenue commercial district, he *is* Hegewisch.

A baby boomer, Bob grew up at the peak of the American steel industry, when Hegewisch, even more isolated from much of Chicago than its sister steel-producing neighborhoods, felt like a modest, yet proud, small town. Tucked in the center of a collection of rivers, lakes, marshes, railroad tracks, industrial sites (alive and dead), other city neighborhoods, other *cities*, and even another state, Hegewisch, Bob notes, "is kind of a lost little area here." Other parts of Chicago seem a world away.

"I remember I would watch television as a kid and they would talk about the South Side of Chicago and they'd be at Comiskey Park at Thirty-Fifth Street," Bob says. "*What you mean*, South Side?! This is the South Side! That's way up north! You know? And not even understand how *massive Chicago was*." To most locals, Hegewisch, which begins around 126th Street or so, was not really even in Chicago. "No, no, never. I'm in Hegewisch."

By the mid-twentieth century, about half of Hegewisch's residents were either born in Poland or, like Bob, the descendants of immigrants who flocked to Hegewisch from Europe following its founding in 1883 as a rail-car-producing company town. Polka thrived there, as did the Catholic Church and parochial schools. Pudgy's even still sometimes sells a popular Polish sausage and kraut pizza, advertised with a red and white sign echoing the Polish flag. On Fat Tuesday, Bob heads to bakeries in Calumet City and Lansing, Illinois, to purchase paczkis—the pre-Lent Polish pastries that are extremely popular throughout Chicago—for his customers. Meanwhile, even as the neighborhood's population skews increasingly Hispanic, with Mexican taquerias and markets popping up here and there, it is often forgotten that the community's founder, industrialist Adolph Hegewisch, was himself Mexican.

When he was growing up, Bob says, "You didn't have to leave Hegewisch for a thing. You had lumber yards. You had bowling alleys." Most storefronts on Baltimore and Brandon were occupied with grocery stores, clothing sellers, and other services. Bob's father's family once owned a meat market up the street where Opyt Funeral Home stands today. In the 1920s, a market owned by a Polish immigrant who later worked as a mill foreman occupied the current Pudgy's space. But one type of business stood out even then, says Bob: "You had taverns up the ass, you know?" It's true: Hegewisch, with its heavy industrial past, has always been home to more taverns per capita than almost anywhere else in Chicago. In the early 1900s, there were reportedly at least twenty-one. Many were within steps of the old rail car factories, in buildings that surround today's Pudgy's, where immigrant workers cashed—and drank—their paychecks.

"At one time I had three aunts and uncles that owned taverns," Bob says. His mother's family ran a tavern called Krupa's at 134th Street and Avenue O in the eastern section of Hegewisch known as Arizona. The tavern operated under the name Georgie's for many years, and recently it reopened as Uncle Bobby's, a comfortable place where you can occasionally get Polish food and maybe even still hear some polka. Bob's mother, Flossie, along with his grandmother, Ma Krupa, and his father, John, later owned another tavern just one block north of Pudgy's called Flossie's Club. They served fried fish, shrimp, and frog legs on Fridays. Bob has a black and white snapshot of himself as an infant in a pram stroller pushed by his *busia* outside the club. "It was *so cool*, you know? [Hegewisch] was a *beautiful*, beautiful area to grow up in."

And soon pizza would play a large cultural role, too, first introduced to the community at Milan's Snack Shop on Baltimore. "Pizza was kind of in its youth, you know, in the late fifties, early sixties," says Bob, who was then attending St. Columba Grammar School in Hegewisch. Aside from the Southeast Chicago institution, Pasquale's, where Mr. Pasquale's cigar ashes were a secret ingredient, and John's Pizzeria on Calumet City's sin strip, where his aunt, co-owner of the namesake Blondie's Lounge, took him to eat "ground meat" pizza, Bob's heart was in Hegewisch. "Mama D's, mother pie to Pudgy's, was *great*. Ann's, which was almost right across the street from Mama D's, tremendous pizza. Another was Sam's, and that was on Brandon and that was a ground meat pizza," Bob says. "Kind of like John's. Same thing, only different." There was Snookie's, too, run by a former employee of Mama D's and the sister of the original owner of Pudgy's. All of these places are now gone. One other longtime pizzeria, Doreen's, anchors the northern end of Baltimore, but an empty storefront halfway between the two shows the remnants of a pizzeria that closed just a year or so after it opened.

"And there was also another one called Bus Stop Pizza," Walter and Marge Bokowy's pizzeria at the corner of 133rd Street and Avenue O. Wally, as Bob referred to him, had relatives who had worked in both the Western Steel and Ryan Car factories in the early twentieth century. "That's where I hung out as a teenager," he says, "in my developing youth," while attending Chicago Vocational School. A red, white, and green awning advertising the latest of Bus Stop's failed successors, Pucci's Pizzeria, adorns the building today. But the southbound 30 South Chicago CTA bus still stops directly in front of the building.

"Of course, I was like the world's worst student," says Bob. "No doubt about it: the world's worst student." It didn't matter: even if the rail car factories were gone, jobs were always available in the mills. His father worked until retirement as a steelworker for Youngstown Sheet and Tube in nearby East Chicago, Indiana. Through ups and downs, heavy industry has been crucial to the social and cultural character of Hegewisch, a feeling captured by the community's current most noteworthy musician, a paint-speckled, work-jacket-wearing white hip hop artist who raps endearingly about hard, blue-collar work and surviving day by day. Like Bob, CoJack could only come from Hegewisch.

After somehow managing to make pizza in Vietnam out of canned tomato rations, bread mix, and dehydrated cheese, Bob went to work at Republic Steel, a mill that once occupied a massive lot between Avenue O and the Calumet River, and where ten union demonstrators were killed by police in 1937. For decades, local collective memory of the "Memorial Day Massacre" played a crucial role in labor-management relations. A patinaed plaque honors the strikers–"martyrs—heroes—unionists"—at the site of the former Local 1033 union hall, just across the street from the eerily vacant Republic site. Through many economic booms and busts, generations of families in Southeast Chicago depended on the mills for financial stability. "I worked in the seamless tube mill, and that was supposed to be forever. 'Oil exploration! Man, we got orders to last us for twenty years,' which would have got me to my pension, you know? And, that went downhill."

After Bob left Republic, he found more heavy blue-collar work with an industrial contractor. "It was dirty work. I mean, *filthy* work, and it was OK—money was fantastic—but I wasn't happy with it. I'd get up in the morning—four o'clock in the morning—get dressed, go to work.

"I would come home at six or seven o'clock at night, and Pudgy's was here." He lived in the century-old blue frame worker's cottage immediately visible from Pudgy's front door. "They were here for about a year and a half. I'd call from across the street, order a pizza, and ask them to deliver it, because I'd jump in the shower. About the time I got out of the shower, I'd throw on a pair of shorts and a T-shirt, my pizza would get there, and I'd answer the door. I'd have my beer in my hand. Eat my pizza, go to bed, and do the same routine, same routine, same routine."

By the early 2000s, all the mills in Southeast Chicago, including LTV, the successor to Republic, were gone. Many families left town. Those who stayed needed to find other avenues to make ends meet. Bob had already found his—as the Pudgy's delivery guy.

Later, after becoming partners with the founder, Pudgy herself, Bob made small promotional innovations like sending pizzas, always accompanied with a menu, at no charge to local taverns. Another change was even more crucial. "My first year into this," he says, "this place had no sign in front. And I happened to be down at Aniol's Hardware. You familiar with that? About a block away." Run by a World War II veteran and her son, Mike, Aniol's has served Hegewisch for decades.

"Mike and I played little league ball together. We're the same age. And some guy Mike was taking care of said, 'Who is the guy in the next aisle?' And Mike says, 'That's Bobby Zajac. He's got Pudgy's Pizza.' And the guy said, 'Pudgy's Pizza. Where the hell is that?' And the guy was like six doors away from it! That's how distant this place was."

"And I said, well," Bob laughs. "Gotta get a sign."

"And, you know what, it was one of those things that was good because this was the first business I'd ever owned. I have no *business skills*. I have *no* college education. All I know is hard work. That's all I know. I know hard work, make people happy, give them a good product. That's all I know! And if I make dollar on it, too, god, that's great!"

For Bob, buying Pudgy's was "just an opportunity to do something I *dreamt* of. It was an opportunity to be someone I worshiped as a child that was a hero, a business owner, in this tight little community," he says. Bob appeared on television once when, to his surprise, Pudgy's was voted the number four pizzeria in Chicago on WGN. "I don't know how many times my mom called," he says laughing. "I'm sure it was a lot, you know?" Bob reflected as he pointed at the beautiful framed photograph on the wall, placed perfectly above the table at eye level. "That's Mom in her car," one she had long dreamed of sitting in the driveway of her modest, but well-kept home.

"When my mom got sick—you know, got the big C—with my wife's blessing and almost her insistence we bought this car," a burgundy 1951 Buick Roadmaster. Cancer rates in Southeast Chicago, byproducts of the area's industrial pollution, are well above the national average. "And we got about a year and a half, two years with her before she—we lost her. And every time I got a chance, I'd pick her up and went for ice cream or if there was something going on at the VFW—she was in the ladies auxiliary—I would pick her up and that's how she would arrive. The license plate was, her name, Flossie. F-l-o-s-s-i-e. She *loved* coming in here."

As the night gets busier and busier, Bob juggles more and more responsibilities, all with a sort of sixth sense. He answers the phone when Donna, his wife, cannot, monitors his cell phone to communicate with drivers, and directs kitchen traffic. Heat emanates from two well-used deck ovens just behind the register, one decorated with random refrigerator magnets (a pizza slice, a Bears football, an American flag, and one that says "Keep God in America"). Wooden rolling pins, metal pans, and a sifter hang on the wall, lightly dusted with flour, above a handful of busy stainless steel prep stations. "By the way, the Green River, they still got 'em five for five over at Jewel's where I shop," a statement that could only happen in the Chicago area, was overheard. Bob and Donna both cut pizzas—thin crusts in squares, thick pizzas like pies—and box them for carryout or delivery.

Both delivery drivers wait either at the tables or in the window, where stacks of red canvas Velcro hot bags were ready to go for long orders. They cover a significant area and diverse terrain that might give a typical Chicago delivery driver pause. One of the drivers, Scott, decked out in a green stocking cap, glasses, and a Carhartt, asks about an order, and Bob responds with detailed knowledge about the customer at a local industrial workplace. "He'll be at the front. He will be there. Usually is working the scale." Industry still surrounds Hegewisch, like the Ford Chicago Assembly Plant, an anchor of the community since 1924. A calendar on the wall—for a concrete drilling and sawing company, reached at the phone number 574-CUTTING, in similarly secluded and heavily industrial Whiting, Indiana, home to one of the nation's largest oil refineries—also highlights this fact. Next to it hangs an old map of Harbor Pointe Estates, the only trailer park in the city of Chicago, or what is left of it. 850 families once lived there. Most were bought out for a new housing development that was abandoned just after the 2008 crash. And if there is any doubt as to the natural geography of the Calumet Region, all one has to do is drive on Boy Scout Road through this area. Tall grass and thin trees flank a bumpy and potholed road. It floods, but Pudgy's delivery drivers and other locals are undeterred.

"Our customers are very local," Bob says, including the surrounding communities like the East Side, Cal City, Burnham, and North Hammond, right next door. Some come from all the way from Valparaiso, Indiana. "Now these were former Hegewischites, as we call them, that will come into Hegewisch, and they'll call a couple of neighbors and say, 'I'm picking up Pudgy's. Do you want some?'" says Bob. "They will order, like, five or six pizzas, and we'll have to mark all the boxes 'cause this is getting dropped off for this one, or this is getting dropped off for this on—" almost like they're trying to find something they have lost.

Bob himself moved about thirty-five miles away to a subdivision in St. John, Indiana, a few years ago. "It's tucked away. You have to be totally lost or totally know where you're going to find this. You're never just gonna happen upon it, you know?" Key characteristics, of course, of his true love; a love that has always drawn him back. "I'm all about Hegewisch. That's home. I'm so *rooted* here it's pathetic!" he says, laughing.

"When my mom and dad passed, I thought, would I lose my taste for here? Would I lose my connection with it? Would I lose my love for it? Nah. I still have the memories, you know? In the summer, getting up in the morning, taking my bicycle going to Mann Park and going to Wolf Lake. Playing in the swamps. Playing in the dump. Made it home by four o'clock before Dad got home from work. My mom had *no idea* where I was all day, and it was cool, because it was fun to grow up here."

"But when I was a kid, the tallest building in Chicago was the Prudential Building. We would drive down the expressway and at a certain point you could see the Prudential Building. *Wow, dude.* Now you can't even find it. It's just so dominated. But, again, things remain the same here, as they seem to just change all the way around us," he says.

Just a breath later it goes the other way, hinting at an underlying uneasiness about the community's future while remaining positive: "I wish it were [the same]. I wish it were. I try and keep my part of this world exactly the same as the way I grew up. And by that I mean being a part of the community that I love. I love where I do business. I love the people I do business for. You support the community that supports you. If I can't give back to the community, I've got no business doing business here. I should be out of here."

Hegewisch returns the love, too, every time it walks through the front door. There's the twenty-something daughter of the owners of another legendary Hegewisch business, Drago's, or DragoBob's, a grocery and food carryout business with a secret shish kabob recipe. Her Croatian immigrant parents purchased the store on Baltimore Avenue in 1983. After over three decades, they sold the market and moved to Northwest Indiana, taking the family recipe with them. "You tell the boys I said hello, would ya?" Bob says as she leaves with her pizza.

There's the upright, quietly confident Latino teenager, a regular customer that Bob chats with about hockey. "How's that Hawks gonna do tonight, man?"

"They're gonna win," the kid replies.

There's the husband and wife having a get together across the state line at which Bob's pizza was to be the star. "Everybody loves them. Don't have no good pizza in Indiana," the man laughs. There's the twenty-something Hispanic woman who seemed a little shy on what seemed like maybe her first visit. Bob welcomes her: "Howdy! How are ya? Whadya have?"

Then there are those most honored. "Hey, what's up, buddy?" Bob says to a man, at least in his seventies.

"Pick up my sausage sandwich."

"How you been?" Bob says. "Five dollars with your veterans discount." A new veterans memorial, with a tank that echoes Hegewisch's wartime production, sits directly south of Pudgy's. There are veterans, including Bob's father, on the wall, too.

Some favorite customers are gone, like Wietold Sielchanowicz, a native of Poland and survivor of Auschwitz, who came to the United States in 1949 and found safety, opportunity, and community in the then-growing Hegewisch. Victor, as he was affectionately known, met Bob's parents during the Flossie's Club days. Whenever he walked in, the crew greeted him loudly by name. "He is missed," Bob says.

It is just another Friday night. Another glorious Friday night in Hegewisch. "I couldn't give this up. This is where my heart is."

Bob did hang up the apron, in late 2017. He sold the business to a husband and wife who promised to keep the business exactly the same and promised to continue supporting the community. Hegewisch honored him with a big party to say goodbye. Pudgy's Pizza lives on as his legacy, serving the community he loves, hopefully forever.

East Side: Something about the South Side

MARE SWALLOW

On a weekday morning in a corporate office in Northbrook, Illinois, twelve new managers are sitting at gray desks organized into pods. Resting on those desks alongside their training manuals are small, soft toys—squishy balls, eggs of Silly Putty, and rainbow-colored pipe cleaners—all placed there by me, their instructor. If you give adult learners something quiet to fidget with, they'll stay engaged with the lesson.

Today's lesson is a discussion about how aspects of your culture—where you grew up, how you were raised—influence your leadership style. I launch into the well-worn, but effective, example from my own life:

"For instance, the way I was raised, you got a job, any job, and you were *grateful* for that job. If the boss said you were working overtime, you didn't question it. You're there to work, not to make friends. If you complained—about anything—it was 'Stop whining and get back to work.'"

The last sentence is barely out of my mouth when a hand shoots up in the back.

The owner of the hand points at me and asks, "South Side of Chicago?"

I ask, "How did you know?"

He says, "'Cause I grew up with the same thing."

"He" was Martin Fernandez, a new manager I'd had in workshops before. I liked him. At the lunch break, I say to Martin, "I can't believe you picked up on that."

He shrugs and says, "It's such a South Side mentality."

I never thought of it as a "mentality"; it was just what I grew up with. But that's the thing about growing up in any family: Whatever you see, hear, or do, is normal.

My "normal" was shaped in a neighborhood misleadingly called "the East Side." When I tell people I'm from "the East Side," I usually get,

"That's impossible! If you go east you hit the lake," as a response. Despite the name, the neighborhood sits on the Southeast Side of Chicago, just under Lake Michigan, right before you hit Indiana. If you've ever driven the Chicago Skyway, you've passed the neighborhood where my culture and values were formed.

In my family, hard work was the expectation. Laziness was sneered at. When my mother suddenly found herself without a husband and with two toddlers to care for, she took a job, any job, doing secretarial work at Republic Steel. My sister and I were expected to go to school, get good grades, help clean the house, do yardwork, install screen windows, work hard, and earn money as soon as we were able. We were also reminded, regularly, that we were going to college and we had no say in the matter. The phrase, "I expect you to . . ." began most of my mom's admonishments.

I expect you to help around the house.
I expect you to get better grades.
I expect you to set a good example for your sister.
I expect you to go to college.
I expect more from you.

When I was ten, my mother informed me I would be cut out of her will if I didn't attend college. No surprise that one of our few family vacations was a week at Cornell University where families would live in the dorms, eat in the cafeteria, and attend college classes. I signed up for drama class. The instructor had a last minute emergency and didn't show. Her replacement was a Method-acting magician. We alternated between learning simple magic tricks and pretending to be cheese.

Before I was old enough to stay home alone during the summer, my sister and I spent summer days on Ewing Avenue at our grandmother's house while my mom worked at the steel mill. Those days at Gram's house had their own sort of productivity. We made friends with the Skibinski sisters next door, who were a few years older than us. Sometimes my sister and I would help them on their paper routes, and they would pay us a dollar or two, which would be quickly spent on penny candy at the Ben Franklin five-and-dime. Sometimes we set up lemonade stands on the then-bustling Ewing Avenue. We always made money. I recall my mother being happy with those pursuits. Then there were the non-money-making days when Gram would teach us how to play poker, or to garbage-pick through the alley and restore our newfound treasures. My mom grimaced at those last two activities.

In my family, the worst thing you could be was not an abusive parent or a wife-beater—because we had those. No, in my family, the worst thing you could be was *unemployed*. Being out of work was *shameful*, and if you were unemployed, it was to be kept hush-hush. Whenever a family member lost a job, we would be informed of this news in a stage whisper, usually on the way to a holiday dinner: "Uncle Jim got laid off again. But don't say anything." We'd arrive at our Aunt Kathy's for Christmas, never saying a word about who lost what job. We acted like everything was normal—because it was.

I don't recall anyone telling me I had to work. I just knew it was expected. At thirteen, I babysat the little kids next door. At fourteen, I worked the local newspaper drives, earning $2 an hour at a time when minimum wage was $3.35. At fifteen, I secured a work permit so I could tend the locker room at my local pool. At sixteen, I became a lifeguard during the summer and waited tables nights and weekends during the school year. It didn't leave a lot of room for scholarly excellence.

I do recall one Saturday afternoon, when I was sixteen. I was at the library, working on a paper. Over the loudspeaker, I heard my name, followed by, "Please come to the front desk." I jumped, assuming I was in trouble. What I possibly could have done, I didn't know, but we were Catholic, so everything was always my fault, and I was always guilty. "There's a phone call for you," said the woman at the front desk.

It was a local city official. One of the city-run pools was short a lifeguard that day, and they wanted me to fill in. I had to be there within an hour. The guy had called my house, and when my mom learned the purpose of his call, she told him that I was at the library—and he could find me there. Heaven forbid she tell him I wasn't home. Heaven forbid I miss an opportunity to make money.

Chicago native and author Shel Silverstein once said, "In Chicago, I feel guilty if I don't wake up every morning at nine and carry a lunch bucket. . . . If you don't go to work you are a bum in this city and that's all there is to it." Thanks to my upbringing, I felt that way no matter where I lived.

At age twenty-three, I moved to San Francisco to pursue my dreams of writing and acting. I ended up working in Silicon Valley, where you could wear shorts and sandals to work, and the silent mantra was, "It doesn't matter *when* you get your work done, just get it done." No one was watching—and nobody cared—if you were really at your desk by 8:00. The new culture I found myself in was so foreign to me. I never could quite adapt. It was like putting on a fun dress that didn't match my personality, a dress that I never got used to. For the first time in my working life, the boss wasn't reprimanding me for being five minutes late. After a dental appointment that ran long on my lunch hour, I raced back to work, tumbled into my boss's office, breathlessly announcing, "I'm sorry I'm late! I didn't mean to be gone for so long!" My boss looked up and said, "You were gone?" Lunch dates with my co-workers always ended with me panicking that we weren't back at the office at 12:55. They couldn't understand why I was in such a hurry to return to *work*. They would roll their eyes at me and tell me to relax, because it wasn't a big deal if we weren't back by 1:00. I'd silently clench my jaw, thinking, "*Yes! It! Is!*"

The friends I made in California were all West Coast natives who embodied the same "whatever" attitude I saw in my coworkers. I was struck by the contrast between our respective values—and lives. When my friend Randy was laid off one June, he took the summer to travel through France, Germany, Austria, Switzerland, Italy, the Czech Republic, Belgium, and the Netherlands. My friend Sarah, an attorney, spent the summer before law school backpacking through Thailand.

Their travels amazed me. *Three months in another country?* It seemed irresponsible. Why didn't Randy spend his summer looking for a job? Why didn't Sarah spend her summer waiting tables so she'd have some money for law school? Back in Chicago, we would *never* take such a long, expensive trip (especially without a job!), unless we had saved up for at least a year or four. I wondered how they were able to pull off such fantastic travels. When I got out of college, I did what any good South Sider would do and got a job—any job. While my California counterparts were exploring the world, I was asking customers at the Calumet City Chi-Chi's, "Chicken or Beef for your burrito?"

I once asked Sarah how she was able to pay for three months in Thailand. She nonchalantly said, "I just took it out of my student loans." My inner South Sider thought, "You can't do that! That's money for tuition and books! What if you got caught?" I was stunned. She was unfazed.

I later found out that Sarah hated her job at a law firm, but she kept the job to pay off her six figures of law school debt. I recently heard from Randy, who told me he does not enjoy his job—but he has a house and a family to look after. He asked me what I was doing for a living. I told him I started a literary organization and also had my own consulting business. He said, "Wow! It sounds like you are in control of your own destiny."

My destiny offers no health insurance or retirement plan, but, yes, I am doing things I enjoy that pay the bills.

I'm not saying one way is wrong and the other is right. I think my work ethic contributed to the moderate success, five-figure salary, and TJ Maxx wardrobe I enjoy today, but I will also tell you I wish I had traveled more in my youth.

As a teenager, I studied French for four years and became fluent. Once I was out of college, I immediately let those skills go to waste because it was too expensive to travel to Europe. Or, for that matter, even Quebec.

At age thirty-eight, I found myself with something else my culture taught me to value: a savings account. This was another mantra pounded into my brain: always have a savings account, with a huge chunk of cash, in case you're ever unemployed.

By that time, though, I'd had it with saving money, working hard, and staying in Chicago with French language skills I used only to order *croissants.*

What good is money—and work—if you can't use it to enjoy life?

So at thirty-eight, I finally said "fuck it," and planned a vacation to France with my husband.

We did all the cliché touristy things. We walked along the Seine and drank wine straight out of the bottle. We ascended the Eiffel Tower on a foggy night. We didn't care that we couldn't see anything. At the Louvre, we laughed at the flock of tourists clamoring to photograph the *Mona Lisa.*

And during the entire ten days we were there, not a single client called to see if I could drop everything and get back to work.

SOUTH SIDE

South Shore: Between the Lake and Emmett Till Road

AUDREY PETTY

these are my people & I find
them on the street & shadow
through any wild all wild
my people my people
—excerpt from "If They Come for Us," by Fatimah Asghar

From the outset, we knew a big house wouldn't do. Togetherness was the whole idea, but we'd need separate kitchens, bathrooms, and front doors with their own locks for the arrangement to last. We were on the lookout for at least three stories.

Hyde Park-Kenwood was our starting point in the search for a family building. After all, my brother-in-law worked in the neighborhood; my sister Jill and I had grown up there, and my husband Maurice had, too. For decades, my father had made his home in Kenwood with my mother, who'd died a few months before we embarked upon our search. Her illness had brought me back to Chicago from central Illinois. The comfort of the familiar was profound. What had sometimes been tiresome about being back in the old neighborhood was suddenly balm. Within close reach were those who would claim me, those who could remember when. To my initial disappointment, the Hyde Park survey went bust quickly. Three-flats were few and far between, and prices were steep, so our search spread to North Kenwood, Woodlawn, Bronzeville. The search lasted two seasons.

Early on, we visited a new construction on Kimbark, due south of the University of Chicago. How I hated that one at first glance. Narrow, newfangled, formed of split-face concrete block. What passed for its decorative front was faux stone veneer, straight-up ugly and soulless, resistant to any change. From the inside, the building made okay sense.

The floor plans met our needs. The kids could grow up there. I could see it all when I closed my eyes.

We'd move on to consider a pricey and decrepit red-brick six-flat on Ellis—the light there barely light at all, but its backyard was doublewide immense, promising. We toured an imposing graystone in Bronzeville divvied into odd-shaped units, near-kitchenettes. We lingered long inside a three-flat on Langley, bordered by an empty lot, and stripped down to the studs. So many prospects we encountered seemed viable to me, but, fortunately, we were a five-headed, deliberative body, weighing each listing quite carefully. My father, who drove the hardest bargain, encouraged us to consider ditching him at every turn. "You all should do what you need to do. I'll figure my own thing out." We wouldn't move without him.

We finally arrived at our family building on the day my dad took his time on the walk-through—when he strolled each floor instead of making a clean exit, detouring to wait for us in the car. To be sure, the summer drive from Hyde Park to South Shore—to Oglesby Avenue—had set the stage for our unanimity: Lake Shore Drive, past the museum, the beach house at Sixty-Third, around the bend at Jackson Park Harbor, the public golf course running along our passenger side. We paused to admire our future building from outside. Elegant, made of true brick and stone with craft and with care. Quoins flanked the sides of its stories, and crowning the building was the emblem of a ribbon—festoon—near center, and a concrete urn on the far left.

The interior of this one had been nearly entirely reworked. As Redfin revealed, the sellers had purchased the residence, erected in 1922, on the very cheap, in a tax sale. Now these sellers were flipping it, aiming to bank a nearly eight-fold profit; this was a pattern amongst the many buildings we'd seen, a phenomenon of what realtors dubbed *the post-crisis bottom*. To my eye, so much of precious value at Oglesby had been excised by *rehab*; that the sellers were white *and* faraway added insult to injury. They'd stripped place out of the place, scrapping sconces, tilework, and, likely—from the looks of our neighbors' buildings—leaded windows and chandeliers. In return, they'd been heavy handed with recessed lighting and cheap, domed fixtures. They'd installed faux fireplaces run by remote control.

Still, somehow (how?), by day's end, the building was what we all wanted. I suppose we thought as much of what could be as what had been, in making up our minds. And I sought out vestiges upon our second-look visit. Polished hardwood, a set of French doors, crown molding in the dining rooms. "From my floor, I've got a treehouse," my father told us from the first-floor unit. He stood in place for a while, peering out at lovely, lively Hasan Park.

We moved into our place in the late fall of 2012. We met neighbors in the family buildings on either side of us, three generations deep, in South Shore for decades. And Hasan Park was soon our front yard living room, no matter the miserable temperatures. Ella, five, and Malcolm, six, climbed, slid, and raced with their rambunctious set while we paced and shivered with fellow caregivers. We'd become acquainted with more folks at community organizing meetings, brought together by multiple crises. O'Keefe was our nearest elementary school, and its entire staff had been fired and replaced. Fermi Elementary, about a mile to the west, was one of fifty neighborhood schools slated for permanent closure. Our local Dominick's would also be shuttering, leaving the closest full-service grocery two miles away.

Soon I'd meet Sylvia. A mom and grandmother and former eighteen-wheeler trucker, she made a living as a registered CNA and a part-time caterer. This work was balanced with organizing and creating events for nourishment and fellowship in her neighborhood of Park Side, an area of South Shore where many people displaced by the demolition of high-rise public housing relocated. Sylvia organized Peace Fests, gospel concerts, and movie screenings in abandoned lots; she cooked an annual Christmas buffet that was accompanied by a gift giveaway. She also prepared enormous feasts in the warm months, making the occasion for what she calls Community Feeds. Sylvia's grandparents had migrated to Chicago as young adults. Her mother's people came from Louisiana. Her father's people came from Tennessee and Mississippi. As a girl, Sylvia lived in Wentworth Gardens, then and now public housing. And this is where she first learned about community gardens. Southern folks came up with this know-how, she told me, and at Wentworth Gardens, their gardens once thrived.

Sometimes we'd head out after dinner, just the three of us, scaling the wall bordering the sidewalk at Sixty-Seventh and the public golf course. Atop that wall, we'd inch towards wild mulberry, with Maurice holding Ella steady and high. As she grabbed and tasted the sweetness, I made peace with rose-purpley stains, the only price for what my husband called *goodney*. From there, we'd pass across the tended lawn, saluting the golfers we'd startle, and then it was on to the tangle of bramble, on to the edge of Lake Michigan. Ella was strong and confident enough to take her own stony path safely down to the water. Back then, we called the place Turkey Burger Beach. The slabs of red-brown slags were our roomy perches before the lake. Quiet beach. Unofficial beach. Free of flags and unattended by lifeguards. The north skyline Oz-like. To the south: the smokestacks of Gary Steelworks. Straight ahead: lake and sky melded. That first summer the beach was magnetic. *Can you believe it?* Nearby and magnificent, still grieving the death of my mother, the lake was my tonic. Choppy or still. Arm's length away. Numbingly cold and piercing and wondrous.

We'd measure our time in South Shore by the hidden beach's changes. The second summer would be the summer of thick dragonflies hovering. There'd be the summer of the coyote dashing away from the brush. And, of course, the near constant occasions: those many weeks of high *E. coli* count and keeping bacteria test strips in my shoulder bag. We'd meet regulars. A trio of middle-aged Polish women from the Southwest Side, always sunning and swimming for entire Saturdays with a transistor radio, folding chairs, and small overflowing picnic basket in tow. At dusk on weekdays: a young man in a white Thobe and turban, praying on a limestone ledge.

When a visiting friend from Atlanta made the stroll to the beach with us, he'd ask how we could afford all of this beauty. My husband and I would try to explain Chicago-style white flight and the Black Belt, and how Chicago segregation persists—how we'd come to know and feel the city's ironclad segregation. If a Chicago neighborhood was black enough, it would stay black, we'd attest. This seemed as certain to us as the lake being east. What we didn't acknowledge was Black Chicago was rapidly shrinking. Maurice and I were children of the second wave of the Great Migration. Ella and Malcolm arrived in the time of the Great Exodus.

In 2018, as summer was ending, we scaled the wall at Sixty-Seventh and South Shore Drive with Ella and her friend and classmate, who's also our neighbor. It had been over a month since Chicago police had shot and killed Harith Augustus, a neighborhood barber, on busy East Seventy-First Street. The mulberry tree had already yielded its fruit. The golf course was vacant, pristine. On the beach, Ella and Cosima were boisterous, skipping rocks and tapping the lake with their fingertips. In the weeks since we'd last been there, the shoreline was changed. Many slabs were disappeared, swallowed. The few that remained had been shoved aside by currents, the biggest of them all hosted green shoots. Maurice marveled out loud at the power of the lake, while we studied a strange iron bracket at the shore's edge. Whatever it meant to contain, it was going to rust, loosening, on the cusp of drifting out. The beach wasn't our final destination that day. I'd been meaning to finally visit the Nature Conservancy behind the South Shore Country Club. I was well overdue.

The next day, early morning, Ella and I headed to our favorite bakery, seeking a large cake, a pie. What we found instead was a case full of miniatures: sweet potato pies and peach cobblers, pecan bar slices, key lime squares. We asked for two of everything, and while we waited, we breathed the sweet air deeply. I tried to convince Ella that smelling cooking butter and sugar was halfway to tasting dessert for free. She disagreed, and, to my surprise, declined my offer of any choice of treat. "Gift?" the clerk asked as she set our box on the counter. Nervously, realizing my nervousness, I paid.

Pulling up to Sidelines Studio, I noticed the red and white sign in the window.

"HIRING LICENSED BARBER" it announced. Ella carried the box and I held the door. We said hello to everyone in the shop as we entered. One barber was sweeping. The other finished trimming the beard of a young man whose gaze was fixed on the TV overhead.

"We're your neighbors," I told the sweeping barber, whose face I recognized from the news. He'd organized the vigil. "We wanted you to know we've been thinking about you." I tried to find the words as I introduced myself. "We want to share our condolences. For Snoop. For Harith. We've been thinking about him. We've been thinking about you all." He hugged me tightly and then he bent down to Ella. "What's your name, little sis?" he asked as they reached out to each other.

Woodlawn:
Memories of Obama

JONATHAN FOILES

Reminders of President Obama are everywhere you look in my neighborhood of Hyde Park and the neighboring communities of Kenwood and Woodlawn: you can order from the Obama menu at Valois, see the barber chair he used to sit in enclosed under glass at the Hyde Park Hair Salon, visit his favorite classroom at the University of Chicago Law School, even see the spot on the curb in front of the old Baskin-Robbins where he and Michelle shared their first kiss, now memorialized with a plaque. But the biggest one of all will be going up soon to the south in Woodlawn, and not everyone is happy about that.

Within the next few years the Obama Presidential Center is set to be built in Jackson Park. A number of other locations were considered for the Center, from other cities with some significance to him to other sites within Chicago, but it feels right that the Center will call the South Side home. Some local residents have concerns over the chosen location of Jackson Park, a green expanse near the lake originally designed by Frederick Law Olmsted, which will now be radically reshaped by the forthcoming Center. Far more, though, are concerned that the Center will transform their community and, in the process, force them out.

Residents of Woodlawn have formed a coalition calling for a community benefits agreement with the Obama Foundation. These residents want a guarantee that the new attention brought to their neighborhood will result in jobs for the community as well as safeguards to prevent them from being priced out of their neighborhood. Thus far the Obama Foundation has made some gestures in that direction, but has resisted forming any enforceable agreement with their soon-to-be neighbors.

Woodlawn has been through this before. The University of Chicago has been slowly creeping southward, and construction is underway for a new Woodlawn Residential Commons built to house 1,200 students just a few blocks to the north of the Presidential Center. The press announcements for these developments talk of supporting minority-owned businesses and job creation, but many residents still agree with James Baldwin's 1963 observation that "urban renewal means Negro removal."

Hyde Park is mostly white, Woodlawn mostly black. Despite the fact that mere blocks separate the two, the median household income in Hyde Park is almost two times higher than that in Woodlawn. The University of Chicago, the biggest landowner and employer in the area, has a student body that is just 4 percent black. Property values are rising around the location of the Presidential Center even before construction begins. Some nearby landlords have begun raising rents, and more are sure to follow suit. What is promoted as growth often feels like an invasion to those whose homes are threatened.

Woodlawn is a neighborhood with a rich history. The aforementioned Jackson Park was home to the 1893 World's Fair. Lorraine Hansberry was a resident and set *A Raisin in the Sun* there. Nearly every major figure in jazz played in one of the clubs that used to dot the neighborhood. Aside from its cultural significance, it's home to thousands of residents, many of whom may be sacrificed as the neighborhood is forced through another transition.

Obama moved to Chicago to become a community organizer in Altgeld Gardens, a housing project located on the far South Side. Now he finds himself on the opposite side of a struggle to preserve a community and a way of life in an oft-neglected area of Chicago. Perhaps some young community organizer will trace their political awakening back to the struggle to maintain a Woodlawn recognizable to those who now live there.

Hyde Park: Quarks and Quiche on the Midway

JOHN LLOYD CLAYTON

Depending on the day, he'll tell you his name is Marcus, George, Raymond, or Lamont. He lives and works at the Garfield Red Line Stop at the intersection of Fifty-Fifth Street and the Dan Ryan. He's a very, very educated man. And he'll tell you so himself.

"I'm a very, very educated man," he says, before launching into his spiel, whose script never changes. In two days time he's starting a new job after a year of unemployment. It's been a rough year. He's not going to waste your time with details or with begging; he hates begging. It's beneath him. It's *humiliating* for him to be out here doing this. But it's not about him: he's not going home until he has enough scrounged up to feed his daughter. For her, he'll do anything, even get out here and do *this*. And if they can just make it until Monday, then he'll be off the street and will never have to be out here again. He looks at you with large, puppy-dog eyes, bright yellow from jaundice. His right hand shakes, but palm up and open, is at the ready.

Though he's highly educated, his memory isn't that great; he doesn't remember that he's been telling me about this job "in two days' time" for the past three years, every time I take the Red Line. By now, I just keep moving; fool me once, shame on you. Fool me twice? He blinks, sighs, and then moves on down to the next batch of marks getting off the bus. Heading down the stairs before I board the train, inevitably I see some *newb*, probably a freshman, face gaunt from hearing of such plight, concern ready to save the world, dismayed about the depths his fellow man has reached. I see hard cash change hands as the train door slides shut.

Thinking about Hyde Park, everything comes out like this: a series of vignettes. Images and snapshots, points of impact that stick out and that don't organize themselves easily. Things aren't always like this for me, though; when I lived out in Oak Brook in the western suburbs, everything was more unified and a clean, clear thesis guided all the diverse threads: middle-aged white business executive goes shopping for Canali sportcoat. Wife spritzes large-sized bottle of Jo Malone; they eat overpriced quinoa salad at the café while waiting for the buttons to be sewn on.

Not so with Hyde Park. It's random and it's disjointed. Hyde Park is "eccentric," the kind of description your family used for Great Aunt Sally, the one who wore taffeta ball gowns, drove a champagne Cadillac, and ate cat food. Really, she was just plain crazy, a lifetime of random incongruities, except she had a lot of money.

The injection of cash that keeps up decorum in Hyde Park is the University of Chicago. It's the heart and soul of the neighborhood, and the primary economic driver. Unique in Chicago or anywhere else, it is perhaps the only place where Marcus/Raymond/George/Lamont can exist side by side with a nuclear physicist, where a cheap neighborhood liquor store can be a stone's throw from a multi-star French bistro. It's a neighborhood that tries desperately to gentrify, but fails. It's a neighborhood whose optimism and patience know no bounds, always with modernization in view, but that fails again. Like the Yucatan jungle after the fall of the Mayan empire, the vines always win out and infiltrate the pyramids. Hyde Park does, however, keep up a battle of attrition that's sort of interesting to watch from the sidelines and yields interesting side effects. For every three or four years, the warring parties are replenished and refreshed, as much of the population moves in and moves out. Students matriculate in September, survive three quarters of "Classics of Social and Political Thought," and graduate in June. Faculty members win big prizes and move off to Harvard or Yale, the Sorbonne or Cambridge, or a cabin out in the Maine woods. Like its "eccentric" character, Hyde Park is a little bipolar, with a short regenerative memory that defies clean distinctions, clear lines, and any sort of unifying thesis. It's definitely not Oak Brook. Instead, Hyde Park is a neighborhood of multiple universes and multiple personalities, each existing side by side, sometimes coming into contact, but often just revolving around each other at a safe gravitational distance.

There's J. M. Coetzee, for example. He's won just about every literary prize on the planet. He's quiet and shy and doesn't really take part in the social scene, but every spring he used to fly into Midway, taking up residence in a wood-paneled office off the main quadrangle. While there he taught a graduate class on Proust. When they gave him the Nobel, the King of Sweden called him a guy who, "in innumerable guises portrays the surprising involvement of the outsider." But on a particular Thursday, he is just another fellow who likes gourmet cheese: I bump into him, literally, when our shopping carts collide at the grocery store off Lake Park Avenue. I look up and see this quiet, thin genius of the printed word with a wheel of brie in his hand. He looks at me; I look at him. I move left, he moves right until he's flat up against the refrigerated cooler. Our moment passes. I continue on west to the milk; he moves east to the bags of fresh salad.

There's Harold's Fish, Chicken, and Pizza Shack in a strip mall on Fifty-Third Street. I recommend the half white with mild sauce (salt and pepper). They also have fried perch, chicken wings, gizzards, pizza puffs, and deep-fried pies. You can get soda from a vending machine on the far side. There is no restroom. The only renovations in decades are an extra coat of Signal Red paint over the wooden walls, and a door cut into the far side that allows entry to the small store next door that sells scratch-off lottery tickets. Your order prepared, you pick it up in a small revolving door in the bulletproof glass. Open up the bag and reveal some of the world's best chicken, crispy and succulent and served hot enough to scorch your tongue; on top is a single slice of Wonder bread to soak up the grease, and a side of coleslaw no larger than a sewing thimble.

There is Powell's Bookstore, one of the largest in the nation, on Fifty-Seventh near the Metra tracks. Inside you'll find both volumes of Sartre's *Critique of Dialectical Reason* and a coffee-table book of Lichtenstein serigraphs. The owner is gruff, dislikes you, and has no time to answer questions. Inside are university faculty and philosophy undergrads that squeeze down the narrow aisles alongside street peddlers who have found books for free at local libraries and try to sell them for cash. A ratty, worn paperback of Stephen King's *Rose Madder* is hardly what the owner knows will sell, and he sighs and just says, "NO."

Rinse, repeat—minutes later another comes sauntering in and up to the counter, this time with an ex-library copy of Alvin Toffler's *Future Shock*. It's missing the dust jacket and has pencil underlining from cover to cover. Again sigh, head shake, *no*.

To the east the neighborhood meets Lake Michigan. To the west is Washington Park, strictly off limits after sundown. I'm told tales of brave Ulysses, mugged for his iPod and his pocket money. He was carjacked while trying to start his gray Honda Civic. I'm also told that the university has one of the largest private security forces in the world. Press any one of the dozens of emergency buttons affixed to neighborhood telephone poles, and within thirty seconds an officer will be dispatched to your location.

Even in its heyday, Hyde Park was still a neighborhood unique in its character, trying to figure out where and what it wanted to be. In the late 1800s, it was one of the swankiest neighborhoods in town. Just south of campus were the Midway Gardens, one of Frank Lloyd Wright's largest public projects. The World's Columbian Exposition opened there in 1893, bringing millions of visitors to the eastern part of the neighborhood, over by the lake. And into this John D. Rockefeller injected a huge supply of cash to form the university, which was born as a premier research institution. It didn't grow and develop and finally find itself at the top after years of intense struggle, like the College of New Jersey that slowly morphed into ivy-tinged Princeton. Instead, like Athena, sprouting from the head of Zeus fully armed, the University of Chicago gave to Hyde Park its own neo-gothic romance, staffed with the greatest minds in the world, and at salaries that couldn't be beat. T. S. Eliot taught there. Heisenberg gave lectures there on quantum mechanics. There are quarks and gluons and memories of the first nuclear reaction on a squash court near the dorms. John Dewey developed an entire philosophy and, right on campus, put it into practice. But by the 1950s the swank had escaped and moved north to the Gold Coast; those who moved in weren't exactly listed on the social register. Midway Gardens closed and was torn down, replaced by a dismal expanse of empty greenery bisecting the campus that they called a "Plaisance." I even heard a rumor that they'd considered moving the university, whole cloth gothic romance and all, out of Hyde Park and west to Colorado. But they stayed and continued fighting it out; at Harold's you can see the class struggle in action. A CTA bus driver in his uniform will be next to a man who hasn't bathed in days and smells like Mad Dog 20/20; a young woman in scrubs from the stem-cell research division steps up to the glass with a scholar of Assyrian poetry. They each inhale the glorious hot sauce and move on.

This list of images and vignettes is endless. Here are the Prairie-style houses, lovingly preserved. There are the modernist condos slowly falling apart. Here are Starbucks and bodegas and stores that sell African clothing in bright colors and imported fabrics. There's a Walgreens. There's a hospital with two of the world's finest neurosurgeons and two floors down a new trauma center that sees a half-dozen gunshot victims every single night. There's a silver Jaguar parallel parked behind a Chevy that has no wheels. The Obamas' house is right up the street, cordoned off behind fences, Secret Service barriers, and dense green foliage.

There are all of these things and more in Hyde Park, a place of constant optimism despite never really being sure quite what it ought to be.

Side by side, here the students learn and the professors teach. Two streets over, the workers service and the muggers steal. And through it all, the one universal constant, a panhandler with a great story just trying to get through the weekend, ready to siphon off a little more of what daddy sends every month for making the Dean's List.

Bronzeville:
Black Metropolis

ALEX MILLER

"You ever think we'll make it out of this?" My friend Terry asked this question a lot. On the South Side of Chicago in the early nineties, what else was there to talk about?

As usual, I nodded my head, hopeful: "Yeah, probably. I bet we will." Didn't matter. He was shot dead the next week in a mistaken identity drive-by. We were nine. I grieved for Terry in the best way I knew how: by staying alive.

This was commonplace in projects like the Chicago Housing Authority's Robert Taylor Homes. I realize now how unfortunate it was to name these projects after a man so great—Robert Taylor had been a very influential black social activist and architect who worked in Chicago for years. The collection of twenty-eight buildings erected in his name were supposed to be planned communities to rival suburbs, but just for low-income families, post-World War II. So many people got less than they bargained for in this so-called Fair Deal.

But things weren't always so bad. From the 1920s to the 1950s, Chicago's South Side was the center of African American culture and business. Known as "Bronzeville," the neighborhood was surprisingly small, but at its peak, more than 300,000 lived in the narrow, seven-mile strip.

For a time, Chicago's black population stretched from Twenty-Second to Sixty-Third Street between State Street and Cottage Grove. The epicenter of entertainment, the true Mecca of arts, belonged to Bronzeville, and was located at the corners of Thirty-Fifth and State Street and Forty-Seventh Street and South Parkway Boulevard (later renamed Martin Luther King Jr. Drive). When I was growing up, those were great places to get shot.

Bronzeville was well-known for its nightclubs and dance halls. The city's massive impact on jazz and blues, which cannot be understated, developed with the migration of Southern musicians. In the 1920s, the New Regal Theater opened its doors and immediately attracted the wealth of the nation's most talented black musical artists.

Bronzeville was also home to such all-black businesses and institutions as Provident Hospital, the Wabash YMCA, the George

Cleveland Hall Library, and the Binga State Bank, the city's first black financial institution. Named after Jesse Binga, the banker who bought up property from whites and sold it to blacks desperate for a place to live, it crashed during the Depression and its founder died earning fifteen dollars a week as a janitor. But these were more than alternatives to racially restricted establishments downtown. They were shining pillars, perfect examples of strong community and the potential African Americans can have when they are upwardly mobile.

Key figures and residents associated with the area included Andrew "Rube" Foster, founder of the Negro National Baseball League; civil rights activist and journalist Ida B. Wells; pathbreaking aviator Bessie Coleman, and R and B legend Sam Cooke. Naturally, I learned about these people as a kid, but hardly understood the significance of where I lived. It's exceptionally difficult to look at the successful past when your present is as bleak as a storm cloud. They called it "Black Metropolis" and that just blows my mind, to think that I could have been a part of such a rich, magnificent, beautiful thing.

I just happened to be born too late: 1986, the same year as the Challenger Shuttle disaster, a nuclear meltdown called Chernobyl, and, on a positive, the year the champion Chicago Bears toppled the Patriots in Super Bowl XX.

Like every other place in America, the Black Metropolis was not immune to white flight. That phenomenon, redlining, and racism are primarily blamed for the decline of the racially restricted housing. Beginning in the 1960s, upper and middle-class residents (mostly Poles, Jews, and Italians) in the areas surrounding the Robert Taylor Homes saw the opportunity to move away from the community, as more and more blacks filtered in. But that's nothing new. Sadly, these things happened right in the midst of the cultural revolution of the Civil Rights Movement.

This is what had become of the great Robert Taylor's legacy. Projects. The most devastating aspect of my youth.

And the architecture sure did make this seem like an experiment, a project, and we were the subjects. Chain-link fences zigzagged along the sides of the building, like a maze for a rat, where walkways showed proof of how distant the rest of the world was from sixteen stories up. I would place my hand on the fence, much like a gerbil testing its glass prison, and I'd stare out at parts of the city I'd never been to, would likely never see. Playgrounds. Chain stores. Ice cream trucks. I could leave anytime I wanted to, but I knew I'd always have to come back here, to my cage, be a good little guinea pig. Or monkey. Maybe that's how the government saw all of us . . . some simple creatures foolish enough to accept the inadequate conditions our experimenters provided. They did not care how many of us died. Or got transported to a more secure cage. As long as they had more subjects, as long as they could continue the project, harvest data, let us run wild inside two square miles, what did it matter?

Government-issued food was always fun, too. Ridged cans of pork and beef had silhouettes of the animal you were about to eat in that same, government-issued lettering in that same, government-issued font. I remember someone once trying to describe Pig Latin to me while we handled a can. "Yeah, man," the kid said, "it's just like English but it's like how pigs talk. The Three Stooges use it all the time!" It's true, those three little piggies hilariously spouted off their gibberish language while smashing into lampposts or gouging each other in the eyes. Because, as we all know, that stuff the government sent us was not really food, but more like a cheap, government-funded route to a heart attack. Not much was funny about whatever substance the government had prepared for us in those cans. It was great for keeping black people nice and fat, just like the pictures suggested.

Prostitutes, yes, even here. Usually sweet-candy-crack-smoke wafted into the hallways outside their apartments. Instant enlightenment about what you were about to get yourself into.

And winos. Oh, the winos. Their routine was fairly predictable. But most intriguing about this group was how similar they looked in appearance. They would drink, drink, and drink. Some would get up to stagger along the fence adjacent to the abandoned playground, a once-beautiful escape for street children that had sadly become littered with every color of excrement and despair. Others would stumble toward the gangs, or the stick-up kids with pistols at the ready, and get heckled, or have the canvas of their faces beaten until the colors of red, blue, and orange brilliantly decorated what once was blank. And as they paid obeisance to the god of forgetting yesterday today by clinking a toast with their forty-ounce bottles of liquid-gold, the winos, one-by-one, made some sort of half-statement/half-malapropism to the memories of the recently deceased.

Gunshots at nighttime. Rapes in the daytime. The things I've seen and heard. It wasn't hell on Earth, no. This was hell inside hell. The fearscape of Satan's nightmares. One image has never left me: a man, arms wide as if to hug a large person, leaned forward as if slumped over a railing. His upper body was bent at the hip at this weird, forty degree angle, with his eyes closed, as a string of drool pulled away towards gravity—yet never touched the ground. His poses were reminiscent of a Shaolin master—contorted, overly-exaggerated, deeply at one with self. He was at peace all up until he got stomped out by a group of thugs. Once the violent jerks of his body ceased, the sloppy "thwacks" of flesh being mashed into pavement, his pockets were raided. He really should have known better than to be so doped up outdoors. There was no mercy.

They blew up the Robert Taylor Homes between 1998 and 2007. Forty years of suffering, demolished in nine. Nine: the age when my first best friend died. I say good riddance. But, and there's always a but, what they did next was even more of a kick to the gut of a community already wincing in pain. Now Bronzeville is home to high-rise buildings of a different kind—gaudy monstrosities of wealth and elegance strode in on the red carpet known as gentrification, transporting the problem of poor, desperation, despair. Not solving it. Just hiding it away somewhere else. Gentrification, the bug that every neighborhood seems to be catching these days.

New building "projects" pop up nearly every day in Bronzeville, but they're not for the poor. Despite Chicago's urgent need for low-income and affordable housing—in 2017, 282,000 Chicagoans applied for housing assistance, including nearly 16,000 homeless residents—plans to change the policy of displacement have yet to reach their goal.

Lessons should have been learned from the city's public housing past—including the negative effects that expanding gentrification, and displacing tens of thousands of people as buildings are razed, has on a society—but no, amnesia is much more lucrative. These new moves have, however, emboldened Chicago's citizens with community organizations, action groups, and developers committed to revitalizing neighborhoods and expanding affordable housing through innovative strategies and collaborations.

Now, black heritage tours guide visitors to the phantoms of architectural landmarks that remain. It breaks my heart, the history of the twenties so many people forget, that shining Black Metropolis.

I've mostly blocked out the worst parts of my childhood. Well, I think I have. But now that I live in Harlem, and I see some of the projects around the neighborhood, oftentimes a mist will fill my eyes. Something tells me there's a little kid looking out the window questioning whether a brighter future is possible. This kid will be one of many who'll never see freedom. Like Terry never did. Sometimes I wish those projects had never existed, that I'd never met Terry and had never lost him. Sometimes.

NEAR WEST SIDE

Bridgeport: The Community of the Future

ED MARSZEWSKI

For the last twenty-five years, I have lived and worked in and out of Bridgeport. Once this place was known as a rough and tumble neighborhood—the home of the Democratic Machine and the legendary Eleventh Ward Democratic Organization, the power center of both Mayor Daleys. It was a staunch working-class and politically connected place, where every third person you met was working for the city, county, or state government, or at a construction or trucking company. Living here has taught me what segregation can do to a city, as Bridgeport's prejudicial reputation went way beyond the neighborhood boundaries. Back in the day, if you were a black or brown person, you probably felt the white power vibe from some of our more vocally cretinous residents. Luckily, things are quieter on that front now, and when they aren't, neighbors are even readier to fight back (myself included). So now here we are. Living in the Community of the Future.

Today Bridgeport has become one of the most ethnically diverse neighborhoods in Chicago, due mostly to the migration patterns of Chinese and Mexican American families, as well as some mutant artist and hipster communities. Over the past decade or so, the neighborhood has shed most of its small-town vibe and embraced the twenty-first century! Halsted south of Twenty-Sixth is now basically Southwest Chinatown, with a dozen or so restaurants. Cultural amenities like coffee shops, bars, locally sourced restaurants, art galleries and studios, and even a microbrewery are popping up, mostly around Morgan south of Thirty-First. Almost everything you like about living in Chicago—mass transportation, proximity to downtown, great food, nice parks, affordable housing, nice people—can be found here. Bad things like corporate chains, bro-bars, no parking zones, and too many white people are not found here. There is space. There is quiet. But there is still danger!

This guide to Bridgeport is biased. I founded, work at, or own three of the locations in this list. All of the venues mentioned are places I bring friends and visitors to eat, drink, and play. If you are in the hood for the day, stop by and say hi to my mom. Let's start with her place.

Maria's Packaged Goods and Community Bar / Kimski

Maria's (once known as Kaplan's Liquors) was a stereotypical dive bar serving shots and beers to late-stage alcoholics for decades. In the last few years it has been chosen as the best bar in the city by *Chicago Magazine*. Maria's is a testament to the hard work of my mom, the legendary Maria Marszewski, whose stubborn entrepreneurial life force overcame all odds. She still oversees the bar, hosting guests in one of the most ethnically and class-diverse places in the city. Maria's now features over forty craft beers on draft, and has an expansive spirits menu and a killer craft cocktail program. We also sell packaged goods to go and are home to Kimski, a Korean/Polish street food joint helmed by Chef Won Kim.

Bridgeport Coffee

"What the hell is a fancy yuppie coffee shop doing over 'dere' on Morgan Street?" I would hear some of my customers say while sipping a shot of Rock and Rye and an eight ounce glass of Old Style at Kaplan's Liquors. "We already got a Dunkin' Donuts." True, Bridgeport's main coffee shop was Dunkin' Donuts, but Mike Pilkington of Bridgeport Coffee knew this little corner was the perfect place to ply his own roasted beans to the artists and dreamers. Bridgeport Coffee may have been the first nail in the coffin of old xenophobic Bridgeport. Mike brought some sanity to the corner of Thirty-First and Morgan and a refuge for those needing space to meet, drink, and use Facebook. Today Mike's award-winning coffee shop has three siblings throughout the city, and his roastery and astute mentoring have helped spawn dozens of other local coffee brands.

Co-Prosperity Sphere

In 2006 a bunch of artists and weirdos (including myself) moved out of Wicker Park and into this building. We planned to create an "Experimental Cultural Center" modeled after the legendary Mess Hall in Rogers Park. The Co-Prosperity Sphere was one of the first contemporary art spaces in the history of the neighborhood, and has since become one of the largest independent gallery spaces in Chicago, hosting emerging artists and socially engaged art projects. Co-Pro also became the headquarters of *Lumpen* magazine, *Proximity* magazine, and other publishing projects under the umbrella of Public Media Institute, a 501-C3 nonprofit organization. The space played host to two biannual festivals for over a decade and produced hundreds of performances. Today it's still an exhibition venue and performance space, and also houses WLPN-LP (105.5 FM), a low-power radio station. From our base here at the Co-Prosperity Sphere, we continue to provide resources and platforms to keep the weirdness flowing.

Martinez Supermarket
My favorite bodega has been around for decades. Located on Morgan Street, Martinez is always a good place to grab groceries and household odds and ends. But it's also known for having some of the best Mexican food on the South Side. Their three-pound burrito is a hit (but try the torta "Rudy Style" too). Weekend specials, housemade chorizo, and more are made in their on-site butcher shop and food stand.

Zhou B. Center
In 2006, the Zhou Brothers, longtime resident artists, purchased this remnant from the Spiegel Catalog Factories Complex and turned it into a crown jewel. The once abandoned building became one of the first studio complexes in the neighborhood, offering affordable space to dozens of artists. The building still hosts the Zhou Brothers Collection and is a popular event space. Their Third Fridays open studio event brings thousands of people to the neighborhood each month.

Duck Inn
Housed in a pre-Prohibition era tavern, the Duck Inn is a neighborhood gastro-tavern located at Loomis Street and the Chicago River, a stone's throw from the state of the art, Studio Gang-designed Eleanor Boathouse. The Duck Inn takes its name from a Depression-era lunch counter at Ashland and Thirty-Fifth, run by Chef Hickey's great-grandmother. This joint is an homage to that history, and a major culinary contribution for the community of the future. Hickey, a sixth-generation Bridgeport guy, serves his eponymous whole duck for two alongside other delicious fare. Great cocktails and good beer round the menu off quite nicely.

Min's Noodle Shop
As Bridgeport's Halsted Street continues to develop as Chinatown South, we find ourselves enamored with the Chungking noodles served by this

relative newcomer to the neighborhood. Chungking is a popular spicy and mouth-numbing noodle that originates from Chongqing municipality and is popular in most regions of China. You can order your noodles with different types of proteins, but feel free to order anything on the menu too, like the baos and bing sandwiches. There are also non-spicy options for those not into the spice game.

Gio's Cafe and Deli

You would think a neighborhood known as a historic South Side Italian enclave would have great Italian restaurants. Well, there wasn't much for the last few decades, until the BYO Gio's opened. It's basically an Italian dry goods store with a bunch of checkered tablecloth tables in the middle of it. The owners are expats from Rosebud, and they make some quality fare. Plus, old school residents are always eating here, so you know the price is right.

McGuane and Palmisano Park

One of the best things about Bridgeport is this park complex. McGuane is your usual Chicago Park District Park with a baseball field, trees, pool, and kids zone. But across the street is the twenty-seven-acre Palmisano Park. Once the century-old Stearns Quarry and dumping ground, Palmisano lay fallow and dangerous from the seventies on, until some intrepid leaders from the Eleventh Ward transformed it into one of the most interesting green spaces in the city. Take a stroll to the top of Mount Bridgeport, check out the skyline, and meander down to the quarry pond. You'll see why this is one of the neighborhood's favorite places to bring families.

Ricobene's

Ricobene's is a neighborhood institution, and you may as well surrender to it. Not only is it one of the first pizza parlors in Chicago, but these guys own the breaded steak game. If you want to have a signature sandwich that all of us South Side fatties eat, then do it. Do it, and know that it will feed an army. Do it, and know it was voted one of the best sandwiches on Planet Earth. Personally I like their Sloppy Joes.

Jackalope Coffee and Tea House.

Speaking of coffee—lifelong Bridgeport resident January Overton and her beau, John Almonte, opened their coffee and tea house mere yards from the OG coffee hut, Dunkin' Donuts, proving that people need good coffee more than they need bad donuts. Jan and John run a great spot, filled with quirky art by locals and local quirks that like art. The Jackalope is your prototypical punk rock coffee shop that makes you feel like society isn't crumbling.

Phil's Pizza

Pizza is political here in Chicago. Picking your favorite place sends signals to onlookers, friends, and family. You get judged, and if you admit to liking so-called "Chicago-Style Deep Dish Pizza," you might just get punched (or worse). Here in Bridgeport, we host "Get Sliced," a contest where a panel of judges and an audience of ravenous pizza lovers decide who makes the best pie in the hood. Last year, Phil's won the People's Choice award. Their tavern style (the *REAL* Chicago Style of pizza) is a staple, and a regular diet for thousands of Bridgeportians. For about fifteen years, I had no idea they made Italian beef sandwiches. Then I tried one. The beef with mozzarella cheese and giardenera is dipped, and then toasted in the oven. It can come with a side of red sauce if you ask nicely. It's better than all the beef sandwiches anywhere. In fact, Phil's won the People's Choice Award for Best Sandwich in the annual Bridgeport's Got Beef contest. There is a pattern here.

Bernice's

Steve Boudaskas runs this bar with his brother Mike. It's named Bernice's, after their mother who recently passed away. If you want a glimpse into a timeless Bridgeport bar that's a little too cool because there is a lot of art on the walls (some by Steve himself), then here it is. This neighborhood joint is the real deal, serving Polish beer, cheap macro beer, and stiff drinks. If you want to see a great mix of the neighborhood vibe then hit Wednesday STINGO nights, where Steve hosts and emcees a weekly bingo game.

Bridgeport Art Center

The other big art dog in the neighborhood is the Bridgeport Art Center. Occupying a much, much larger building within the original Spiegel Catalog Factories Complex next to Bubbly Creek (the south fork of the south branch of the Chicago River), the center is a testament to the visionary work of real estate magnate Paul Levy. Paul, an arts patron and supporter, had used the space for decades as a storage facility and then slowly started letting artists rent studios. Over time he has completely renovated the space and built out hundreds of thousands of square feet. He built a large community ceramics studio, and hosts a nonprofit arts organization for outsider artists, serves as a fashion industry incubator, and has one of the best rental rooms with a view in the city. A coffee shop anchors the beautiful courtyard space and should be the first stop to investigate this massive complex, where small manufacturers commingle with the Chicago Maritime Museum, antiques showrooms, and much more.

Filbert's Old Time Root Beer

This fourth-generation soda plant is ninety years old. They made beer before Prohibition but made the switch to their famous draft root beer short after the twenty-first Amendment came into effect. Filbert's warehouse is closed to the public, but you can always drop by and ask to buy a case of one of thirty varieties of soda pop from Ron Filbert, the current owner and independent Soda Czar.

Marz Community Brewing

Okay, so technically it's not in Bridgeport. But it's just on the other side of Bubbly Creek in the Central Manufacturing District, on a road that only exists in name for a few short blocks. When we relaunched Maria's, we fell in love with craft beer and, betting on the potential that small manufacturing could have in developing the neighborhood, we went for it. Four years ago, a bunch of misfit artists, homebrewers, and lumpens started brewing out of a storefront on Halsted and Thirty-Third. With hard work, perseverance, the advice of some great local brewers, and the help of hundreds of friends, we grew with the craft beer and small manufacturing movement around us and moved to this big ass place. The brewery has a taproom and kitchen serving sandwiches and snacks. People who are interested in our beer and other in-house non-alcoholic beverages can see, eat, drink, and breathe firsthand the fruits of the labor of a community of artists, designers, activists, and culinary freaks. When we say Bridgeport is the Community of the Future, Marz is one of the results of that thinking.

Heart of Chicago: A Sketch

DMITRY SAMAROV

I used to live in the Heart of Chicago, but when I'd tell people that, no one knew where that was. The official boundaries of the neighborhood are the BNSF railyard to the north, Ashland Avenue to the east, Interstate 55 to the south, and Western Avenue to the west. If you're approaching the Damen Avenue exit on 55, you might notice the small brown Heart of Chicago sign—doubtless mounted there by proprietors of the Italian restaurants on South Oakley Street—but it's pretty easy to miss. More often than not, I'd just tell people I lived between Pilsen and Little Village.

When I moved to Twenty-Fourth and Western in 2004, I felt like I'd pulled a fast one. Coming from a hyper-gentrifying Wicker Park, this felt like an oasis of calm. No sushi joints, no sports bars, no quickie condo conversions; just single-family homes with a few four or six-flats sprinkled in. The houses on the streets in the neighborhood are below street grade, dating back to when central plumbing was put in and city planners raised the streets rather than having to dig deeper below existing housing stock.

The residents were primarily Hispanic—my landlords came from Uruguay in the seventies—but there was a mix. Bill Duvall, Robert Duvall's nephew, opened a coffee shop and tango cafe on Twenty-Third Place for a time. There was also a short-lived tapas joint on Oakley. Hoofprint printmaking studio landed in a former funeral home at the intersection of Twenty-Fourth Place and Oakley, but when I walked the neighborhood recently, it was gone and the funeral home was up for sale.

On Oakley, there were several Italian restaurants which have been here for decades but look like they have been here for centuries. Every summer the blocks between Twenty-Fourth and Twenty-Sixth Street are closed off for a Taste of Italy block party, complete with a singer belting out Sinatra and more cannoli and Italian ices than you could ever swallow. Tayahua, the Mexican spot across Twenty-Fourth Street from my apartment, introduced me to the earthy taste of huitlacoche, and Miceli's Deli on Oakley was good for a homemade ravioli lunch five days a week. I used to see city workers from Twenty-Sixth and California in there all the time. The alderman's office was across the street.

A dilapidated building at Twenty-Fourth and Western, demolished around 2008, is now a construction site after sitting fallow for a decade. On Cermak near Leavitt, in the space which was the longtime home of the Egg Palace—a restaurant where chain-smoking elderly waitresses used to drop off omelets a shade of yellow not found in nature—El Taco Azteca serves some of the best tacos I've ever had in Chicago. On Twenty-First Street, in a residential block, inexplicably, there is a brand-new outpost of the Gino's East pizza chain.

The neighborhood is easily accessible via the Pink Line, the 49 Western and 60 buses, but it's difficult to tell if it will go the way of Pilsen into full-on gentrification. A couple of the old Italian joints are still hanging on but Miceli's is closed for good. On a hot summer afternoon the streets are nearly deserted. It's hard to imagine this quiet place, a flyover between the bustle of Pilsen and Little Village, will ever match them in commercial activity, but weirder things have happened.

The Heart of Chicago used to be a closely-held secret of a place. Whether its secret will be revealed and whether it yields treasure is not for me to say.

Pilsen:
The Quietest Form of Displacement in a Changing Barrio

SEBASTIÁN HIDALGO

"The Quietest Form of Displacement in a Changing Barrio" was first featured in the "Lens" blog of The New York Times. *It has since been published at* Roads & Kingdoms, Chicago Tonight, *ABC's* N Beat, Voyage Magazine, *the* Politico *What Works Series, and* City Bureau. *It was also exhibited at United Photo Industries Photo Ville and is part of the permanent collection at the National Museum of Mexican Fine Art.*

Pilsen—the largest Mexican American community in the Midwest—is a 2.76-square-mile neighborhood in the heart of Chicago. Gentrification has left deep emotional wounds here that are often invisible to newcomers. Places that once held deep meaning, painstakingly created by immigrant mothers and fathers, have morphed into what *Forbes* now lists as one of the "12 coolest neighborhoods around the world."

According to a study released in 2016 by University of Illinois at Chicago professor John J. Betancur with Youngjun Kim, Pilsen experienced rapid development between 2000 and 2010, and more than 10,300 Latino residents left, 41 percent of them families with children.

"I'm seeing more and more different buildings being torn down and built up as condos and being rented out by all these 'happy' Anglo families," says Phrito Cruz, a twenty-four-year-old born and raised in Pilsen. "It's not anything bad to see them happy. It's the backstory that's frustrating. Like, oh, they feel comfortable here, when I'm over there wondering where my neighborhood went—I just don't see it anymore."

In 2018 the city of Chicago announced a new "community-based strategy" to preserve the Mexican American culture of Pilsen and Little

Village. The ordinance will require that 20 percent of all family-size apartments in new developments in the area be preserved as affordable housing. Developers can opt out of the ordinance by paying fees of as much as $175,000 per unit.

Many consider the pilot ordinance to have come too late, as plans to begin construction of a bike trail connecting the two neighborhoods are expected to begin sometime in 2019. Comparing it to the 606 trail in Bucktown and Humboldt Park where property values have risen sharply, many hold their breath, worried that the new developments will only displace more families and strip away their sense of home.

It wasn't that long ago that newspapers highlighted Pilsen's gang conflicts and shootings instead of new development and condos. A 1988 article in the *Chicago Tribune* said, "It seems that not a night goes by anymore without shots being fired on 18th Street. The latter part of the summer, not a week has gone by without someone being wounded. Eleven people were shot in the last three and a half weeks of August."

Those who grew up in these previously unsafe streets learned the importance of hyper-vigilance—avoiding spaces marked by gang graffiti, ready to react to the unsuspected rumbling of a car or the pop of a firework. They remember a different Pilsen, now finding it difficult to build relationships with newcomers who don't understand its history.

Francisco Pantoja, fifteen, learned to avoid running into local gang members on certain Pilsen streets. In his short life, he has lived in three different apartments in the neighborhood. Earlier in 2018 his family was forced to move a thrity-minute bus ride south, because they couldn't afford to stay thanks to rising rents.

"There's a lot more new places opening up down Eighteenth Street— lots of gentrification that's happening," Pantoja says. "I remember this one time somebody that recently moved into the building we live in once asked me for directions. I told him to go down here, here, and make a left here. He was like 'but isn't it faster to just go down this block?' I told him he could do that but it's getting a bit late and it's gonna get dark soon so you're going to put yourself in danger. I didn't want to explain it to him, I told him to just trust me, it's the best way to go—that's what I think I envy about the changes. The diversity and different backgrounds that don't share the same story."

Anthony Macias plays Jesus Christ during Pilsen's annual Via Crucis. The role of Jesus is highly sought after in the Catholic community of Pilsen. Macias second language is Spanish, he committed to the role and practiced for months. During Via Crucis, he performed the entire procession fluently in Spanish.

A young girl relaxes in the stream of water released from a fire hydrant during a summer day in Pilsen.

Residents care for Jason Patlen after he was wounded August 14, 2017, during a gang conflict on Eighteenth Street.

Jezebel Patlen hears the news that her older brother had been hurt after police have arrived on the scene.

Students from a range of schools from Pilsen gather at Dvorak Park, showcasing their creations among hundreds during the Day of the Dead parade in 2016.

Jose Salgado walks into his family business, Angel's Tire Shop, on July 18, 2016, where hundreds of new tires are labeled and stored for customers.

Thousands gather along Pilsen's main strip, Eighteenth Street, to see the low-riders parade for Mexican Independence Day.

Residents write "Don't Brooklyn Our Pilsen" on the freshly painted gray walls of the once beloved community center, Casa Aztlan. The building was bought by a developer who erased the iconic murals that once displayed Latin American political figures.

Greektown/Maxwell Street/ Little Italy: UIC, Chicago's Past and Future

ANN LOGUE

The University of Illinois at Chicago campus is ugly. Let's just get that out there. It is a nightmare of brutalist architecture and some buildings don't have bathrooms. (You read that right.) It does not have the lakefront views of Loyola or Northwestern, and it lacks the ivy and gargoyles of the University of Chicago. Yet it stands out in a city of endless brick bungalows, limestone two-flats, and story-and-a-half wood frame houses. It is clean and quiet, unlike few places in this city.

More than any other place in the city, the University of Illinois at Chicago is Chicago. As the tenth most diverse college in the United States, according to *US News and World Report*, it is one of the very few places in this very segregated city where people come together.

The campus is strung along the southern edge of the Eisenhower Expressway and the CTA Blue Line. The West Campus (Illinois Medical District stop) is the home of the University of Illinois hospital and UIC's extensive human health programs. Everything else is located on East Campus (between the Blue Line's Racine and UIC-Halsted stops). The highway, the "El" extension, and the campus were central features of Mayor Richard J. Daley's urban renewal projects in the 1960s, which scraped off nearly a century's worth of homes and businesses. But as with the coyote (we have coyotes in Chicago), the great ethnic neighborhoods will not be held back by a little concrete.

I've taught finance at UIC since 2001. I am usually assigned the large introductory courses and I see the diversity. The students in front of me are military veterans, Occupy activists, and frat boys. People who speak multiple languages. Students whose names don't match the name on the roster—maybe they prefer a more Americanized version, or maybe they are transgender. Students who take the train from the suburbs, who live on campus, who drive to campus after they drop their kids off at school.

Some show up at class after working overnight at UPS. Others skip because they are sleeping off fraternity pledge week or too much time at the bar the night before. I have seen Orthodox Jewish men and veiled Muslim women in the same class, Cubs fans and Sox fans sitting next to each other, kids who could get into any university in the country, but whose parents expect them to live at home and work in the family restaurant.

Why, UIC is so open to diverse ideas, I even had a student keep the respect of his classmates when he gave a presentation on the advantages of the ownership structure of the Green Bay Packers. And if there is one creed that any true Chicagoan must swear to, it's that the Bears rule and the Packers suck.

The main tourist site on campus is the Jane Addams Hull-House Museum at 800 S. Halsted. Jane Addams won the 1931 Nobel Peace Prize for creating the field of social work, and the open spirit on campus is her legacy. When Hull House was built, the neighborhood was a fashionable suburban getaway. Following the Great Chicago Fire of 1871 and massive immigration from southern and eastern Europe, the neighborhood become a slum, and the Hull family gave the house to Jane for her experiment with settlement work.

Addams wanted to help Chicago's new arrivals settle successfully in the city, and she approached the work scientifically. Rather than simply hand out food or set up a shelter, she researched the needs of the people in the neighborhood as well as the results of different programs that she and her colleagues tried. They would live in the neighborhood to experience the same issues that the residents did. At the time, it was a revolutionary approach to philanthropy. It also marked the nonprofit sector of the economy as a place where educated women could make significant contributions to public life.

Hull House itself is a charming red-brick building that may or may not be haunted. To the right of the entrance is an exhibit on the history of the settlement's work. There's a relief model of Hull House and its buildings as they were in Jane Addams's time, and you see how much of the area has been turned over to the campus and to cars. The area was razed, piece by piece, for the construction of the Eisenhower and the UIC campus, with Hull House and the residents' dining room being the sole survivors of the complex by the time the campus opened in 1965. After all, Chicago is a city that is not in thrall to the past, even when it perhaps should be (see: the UIC Campus's atrocious architecture).

The settlement house movement had a profound effect on American life. As the second industrial revolution took hold, some Americans were coming into untold wealth, and a large middle class was emerging. There were plutocrats with money to donate and a lot of women (often the plutocrats' daughters) with education and drive; around the country, programs modeled on Hull House were established and staffed by the likes of Eleanor Roosevelt and Mary Astor. Our economy still relies on volunteers, usually women, to support cultural, charitable, educational, and civic life.

UIC began life as the medical college in 1896, an affiliate of the main University of Illinois campus in Urbana-Champaign. After World War II, veterans in the Chicago area wanted to attend college with their GI Bill benefits but didn't want to relocate downstate. In 1946, a temporary branch campus was established at Navy Pier, and enrollment quickly overwhelmed the space. It was clear that Chicago needed a public research institution, and after years of searches (and political wrangling), the site at Harrison and Halsted was selected. UIC opened for business as a full-fledged university in 1965.

UIC was conceived as a commuter school. People would show up, go to class or work, and go home. But the campus has since become a thriving institution with some residential students; in 2017, one of the parking lots was given over to the construction of a dorm. Depending on the day and time you visit, you can see rotating art exhibits at the African American Cultural Center, an amazing mural at the Latin American Cultural Center, student plays at the theater, and UIC Flames basketball, baseball, and soccer games, and concerts at the UIC Pavilion.

Surrounding campus are the remnants of the ethnic communities of Addams's time: Greektown, Maxwell Street, and Little Italy. To the north of campus, across the highway along Halsted, is Greektown; two fine places for lunch are Artopolis Bakery and Meli. You should also take a peek at the Athenian Candle Company at 300 S. Halsted, a family-run business founded in 1922 that continues to supply light to Chicago's churches.

Little Italy is mostly along Taylor Street these days, south of UIC, but there are two culinary gems that are practically on campus. Fontano's Subs, at Polk and Carpenter, just south of Vernon Park Place, started stacking meats and cheeses in 1950. It has fueled those people driving bulldozers for the urban renewal, operating cranes for the campus construction, cramming for midterms, and rushing back to the office to write another memo.

A little further west on Vernon Park, across from a huge campus parking lot, is Tufano's Vernon Park Tap. One legend has it that lemon chicken Vesuvio was invented there. Another has it that it escaped demolition because it was a favorite spot of the first Mayor Daley. No matter the truth, you will find some seriously old-school Italian food here—excellent quality, affordable prices (cash only), and efficient service.

To the east of campus is the neighborhood formerly known as Maxwell Street. The area was once the center of Chicago's garment trade and the home of a freewheeling open-air flea market and blues festival. It's now a sterile combination of UIC dorms, chain stores, and highway. A remaining scrap of the old neighborhood is the White Palace Grill at 1159 S. Canal, open twenty-four hours a day every day since 1939 and serving traditional American diner food.

Although the best food is off campus, your last view of UIC should be Student Center East, which is just north of Hull House. This is the main hub of the undergraduate campus. The ground floor houses the bookstore and a bowling alley, and there are usually student groups with tables promoting something. Upstairs is the Inner Circle food court, a space surrounded by ledges where you can sit and soak in the future of America, in all its multicultural, multi-perspective glory. It gives me hope.

River West: Counting Cranes

JEAN IVERSEN

The paint guy at the Home Depot on North Avenue said that one sample-sized jar of Behr Marquee should do it.

It was the final project on my list: transform my ancient, peeling bathroom vanity cabinet into something that potential homebuyers might mistake for new. On trend. Or at least, not so hideous. Only one jar of semi-gloss paint in Moon Quake and a set of brushed-nickel drawer pulls stood between my stressful existence in River West and a peaceful new place to live.

Armed with supplies, I surrendered a Saturday night to painting in the confines of my Jack and Jill bathroom. As the dark gray paint settled in the roller tray, I flicked on the exhaust fan—not so much to suck up the fumes, but to fill the space with white noise as yet another "family gathering" unfolded in the upstairs condo. I suspected this would happen. The midday drone of a vacuum over the hardwood floors above me had become a reliable predictor of an evening party with a few dozen adults and children who were clearly not asked to please leave their shoes at the door. For over ten years, I endured these nights with increasing frequency. This had to be the third or fourth time this month.

I dipped the roller in the tray. Don't oversaturate, I could hear paint guy say. That's how you get drips. My aching, stiff hips protested as I crouched down to apply careful, smooth strokes. Would potential buyers be duped by my ten-dollar DIY job?

Children stampeded above me while I worked, chasing each other at speeds normally reserved for fleeing crime or impending death. In my mind, my upstairs neighbors insisted their guests only wear heavy work boots and chunky high heels. I cranked up Soundgarden on my iPod and started a second coat. Even with the accompaniment of the whirring fan, however, it was no match for the cacophony overhead.

Then, there it was, right on cue at 11:00. Boom! Boom Boom! One of the other reasons why I was squatting on a stepstool on a Saturday night to sand and paint a cheap piece of bathroom furniture.

Thud! Thud! Thud!

My jaw clenched as the restaurant next door morphed into a 3:00 a.m. nightclub.

"They're allowed to remain open until 3:00 a.m., ma'am," the City of Chicago's Department of Buildings employee had spat into the phone. As though I was the one who deserved to be reprimanded.

Ten years of stampeding children and a revolving door of neighboring restaurants and nightclubs that never made it to their second year in business. Boom! Boom Boom! My cabinets started to rattle. I couldn't take one more year of noisy neighbors, nightclub owners, or the angry bicycle-versus-car war that now raged outside my door on Milwaukee Avenue. This latest 3:00 a.m. Goliath was the last straw. I was too tired, too unequipped, to fight.

Back in 2006, I found myself shopping for a new home in the same seller's market that spurred me to unload my starter condo in Wicker Park. If I had only waited a few more years, of course, my equity would have bought me a post-bubble dream home. Lacking in any type of crystal ball, I instead frantically orbited my desired neighborhoods with a real estate agent, staring in despair at stamp-sized bedrooms and shoddy rehab jobs. As we scoured the 60622 and 60647 ZIP codes, my lengthy wish list was whittled down to "decent place to live in my price range."

I finally set my sights on a loft on the Milwaukee corridor in River West. Nearly every inch of it needed updating, but it had high ceilings and a rooftop deck with a stunning skyline view. Still, even my friends who were born in Chicago asked me where my new neighborhood was. One train stop away from the Loop, I explained, bounded roughly by the Chicago River, Grand, and the expressways.

The first night at my new place, my friends and I devoured some Leona's deep dish on the roof. How ironic, I thought, as I breathed in the view. My first job in Chicago was around the corner on Halsted in an old factory that had been converted into loft offices. I thought working in a building with exposed brick and timber beams was super cool, even if there were dealers and prostitutes on the corner. I never would have guessed I'd buy property just down the block.

Yet here I was, fifteen years later, the proud owner of a fixer-upper in a former warehouse of sorts, built sometime around the turn of the twentieth century. As we devoured our pizza and guzzled our beer, my friends and I counted the Polish churches zooming skyward all around us—churches I would eventually be able to name with authority. The glass high rises bounced gold from the setting sun before giving way to a glittering skyline. We inhaled the aromas from Blommer's chocolate and Gonnella bread factories and admired the majestic Prairie Concrete plant, which posed dramatically against the sky.

Sure, there were no parks or grocery stores yet in River West, and buildings up and down Milwaukee were vacant or boarded up. Potential, potential, I chanted. Besides, I'd only intended to stay two years, the time it would take me to fix the place up and double my equity. Some paint, a stainless-steel appliance package, and boom. I would cash out for a bigger, better, nicer place. In 2006 one could make statements like this out loud and genuinely believe them.

I eagerly set to work painting over my loft's brightly colored walls with trendy neutral tones that my just-around-the-corner buyer would certainly adore. With a kitchen and bathroom to remodel, I drooled over design magazines and became one of those people who browsed Menard's for fun.

2008. A blur of bubbles bursting, markets crashing. Hospitals, breathing treatments. Becoming intimately familiar with a disease called COPD. A job layoff, just days after my father passed, my boss unable to look me in the eye as she delivered the news.

Excursions to Menard's were replaced with hardship letters to my mortgage lender. Hardwood flooring and mosaic backsplash would have to wait as I scraped by on erratic freelance work and honed the art of getting clients to pay past-due invoices. My hard-won equity from my starter condo wasn't doubling; it was evaporating as my loft's value plummeted. But I was determined to grab on to my investment and not let go.

I measured the economy by the number of construction cranes sighted from my roof deck. From 2008 to 2010, I counted zero. The old General Office Furniture building at Grand and Halsted remained a boarded-up ghost town, taking up an entire block. Still no grocery stores or parks anywhere in River West. I signed petitions that the city buy one of the many vacant lots in our neighborhood for a community garden. A small park. Anything. Just a place to rest, convene, decompress. River North and Noble Square outsourced their parks to me while I waited.

As I stubbornly settled in on Milwaukee, I realized there were pockets of wonderful, unpretentious establishments all over my newish neighborhood. I discovered French 75s at Matchbox, a narrow biker-meets-classic-cocktail bar at Milwaukee and Ogden. I found refuge at 694 Wine Bar on Milwaukee, where the owner offered generous pours and decadent cheese plates with zero attitude. D'Amato's on Grand transformed my bad days with buttery Italian cookies and fresh focaccia baked in one of the city's last coal-fired ovens.

I took long walks along the river around the old Montgomery Ward warehouse, now a warren of offices and condos. Respite was found at Montgomery Ward park in River North, where I sat and watched toddlers chase geese while architectural boat tours drifted by. "This was once the Montgomery Ward catalog warehouse." Duh, I'd mutter under my breath. I could recite the tour in my sleep. I hated leaving that park, since once I did, I knew I'd be back in River West's cannon of crisscrossing highways, impatient cement trucks, and six-corner intersections.

2011. A newfound full-time job in a new field. Quartz countertops were still on hold; now I had a few years of accumulated debt to obliterate.

The neighbors above challenged my nerves on a daily basis with their apparent choice to raise their children in the living room. None of my complaints registered, not even the night their younger daughter stomped so hard on the floor above me that my track lighting was knocked out of place.

I scanned the sky for cranes. Nothing. It's okay, I sighed, as Kars 4 Kids towed away my old, scarred Honda. I told myself I was being a good citizen, donating my car to charity. Deep down I felt they were doing me a favor.

Zipcar came to my rescue with two carshares in the lot next door. I was so excited to have some wheels, if only for a few hours a week to haul groceries. My downtown office was a mere ten-minute commute away. Mom had moved to an assisted living facility accessible from the Blue Line, and I spent more time with her than I had since moving out. Life was good.

As the economy sputtered back to life, I updated my two-year flip. But my post-bubble self was more cautious than my pre-bubble self. Every single dollar was carefully evaluated for strategic upgrades—upgrades designed for an anonymous future buyer, not me, the poor schmuck who only lived, worked, laughed, and cried in the damn place for eleven years. Each year-end bonus, each tax refund squeezed out new window treatments here, a closet organizer there. Appliances were replaced one at a time, and only if they exhaled their last breath and defied any chance of recovery.

Finally, there it was, like the first robin after a long winter. A crane. Then another. New bike lanes were striped on Milwaukee. Less cars on the road, I exclaimed with glee. But it meant new lane configurations and the elimination of all parking on one side of Milwaukee. My neighbors and I scratched our heads.

Bicyclists cascaded down Milwaukee at warp speed, as though unleashed from their cages, screaming at anyone who dared inch onto their new turf. Frustrated drivers had no choice but to creep into the bike lanes to view oncoming traffic and screamed back. One day, as I was recovering from surgery, I crept across the bike lane on crutches to my idling Uber. A biker nearly slammed into me, apparently annoyed by my slow pace. My ensuing shriek to "Slow down!!" incited him to stop, dismount his gearless ride, and walk toward me to say, in a weird, creepy voice I will never forget, "Excuse me, ma'am, but I'm gonna need you to shut the fuck up."

In my mind, I draw back my crutch and hurl it at him like a spear with marksman-like precision. It knocks him smack in the chest and renders him unconscious, a motionless figure in the middle of the bike lane.

Instead, I sized up this heartless prick and decided my physical capabilities were no match for his wrath, or mine. Trembling, I flash froze my boiling blood and waited until he got back on his bike and rode away. I hobbled to my Uber, hating myself every step of the way that I didn't, couldn't, do anything to defend myself.

Bikers weren't the only villains on Milwaukee. I avoided the Ogden and Milwaukee intersection after nearly being clipped by a car racing for the Kennedy on-ramp. Ghost bikes appeared on Milwaukee and Elston. Horns blared. Middle fingers saluted. Road rage became the norm. Italian baked goods and neighboring parks weren't enough to cool me down.

2014. Property values were on the rise, but mine still hadn't reached its 2006 value. I was going to leave River West with my original down payment if it killed me. I watched in anticipation as businesses started to fill long-vacant spaces on Milwaukee and the gray ghost town was set for demolition. The toddlers upstairs were now kids roller skating and riding scooters above me. Nostrils flared as my neighbors and I went head to head in heated email exchanges. *I'm so sorry we can't help you with YOUR problem.*

Petitions for a community garden were rejected and weed-choked lots became five-story mixed-use developments with parking. I lost my job after medical issues cropped up and returned to chasing freelance gigs at home. The kids upstairs had regular play dates and sabotaged my efforts to make deadlines.

A so-called gastropub moved into the building butted next to ours, pumping a loud sound system through my walls. Customers arrived in limos and trolleys, not choppers and Schwinns like the rest of River West. The raw space behind their building became an outdoor patio that crawled with twentysomethings who enjoyed a good beer tub, nothing like the neighborhood regulars who sipped Rob Roys at Matchbox or stood in line for an Italian sub at Bari's. Even though I hadn't planned on staying for the long-term, I suddenly felt protective of the old-school, unpretentious River West.

2016. More cranes. The gray ghost town became a soulless high-rise residential development featuring a dog run and yoga studio. Two-bedroom units fetched $2,500 a month. Duran, my beloved European café on Milwaukee, closed after the landlord doubled the rent. 694 Wine Bar suffered a similar fate and it, too, closed. Still no parks, still no grocery.

Our building received regular notices from law firms about new developments within 250 feet. I used to ignore them; they never came to fruition. Ten years into my two-year flip, I pounced on them and attended neighborhood association meetings held in the basement of St. John Cantius.

"Is anyone opposed to this proposed development?"

A few years earlier, I would have declared my unwavering support for expansion, growth, improvement. Now I panicked at the alarming rate of real estate development that caused congestion without any regard for quality of life. I defiantly raised my arm.

"Any comments?"

As I opened my mouth to say something about the lack of green space, I spied the alderman sitting two seats down—the same alderman who ignored our building's complaints about the gastropub's music and who was now rubber-stamping any development proposed in his ward. I choked and said nothing. That year I counted thirteen cranes within a half mile of my house.

Gonnella bread factory was torn down for a residential high-rise, soaring thirteen stories into the air. According to a 2017 article on *Curbed. com*, nearly 3,000 new housing units were either completed, under construction, or planned for on the stretch of Milwaukee from Grand to Logan Square.

Still no grocery, still no park.

The battle with the upstairs neighbors escalated to nuclear warfare when they decided to remodel their duplex. Six months of nonstop hammering, drilling, fumes, and dust. A seafood restaurant claimed the now-defunct gastropub's empty space, and a big-budget, long-term buildout commenced next door. The beautiful pear trees in their back lot—the only green outside my windows—were cut down for an outdoor patio with a tacky nautical motif.

There was no relief from construction, inside or outside of my home. No oasis from biker versus car, or stampeding children, or ongoing construction up and down Milwaukee. No wine bar or café to escape to, only Montgomery Ward Park on loan for the price of a two-mile walk. The flock of cranes were telling me: it's time to sell, it's time to go.

After eleven years, I finally sold my condo. I barely broke even on the deal, though I knew some friends who were still underwater on their mortgages, still in holding patterns, waiting for property values to recover.

I moved to a tree-lined residential street of single-family homes several miles north of River West. At first the quiet was so unsettling I couldn't sleep. I flinched the first time a neighbor said "Hello!" and the sound of construction still makes me jump. But I'm able to write in peaceful silence and entertain the radical notion of relaxing on my deck. Nothing above me now but the rising moon.

About three months after I moved, I received a message from a former neighbor in my condo building. The 3:00 a.m. nightclub burned down last night, he texted. The attached photos of smoke and flames towering into the air, just inches from my old loft's bedroom, sent me into an emotional tailspin. "What if I had stayed? I could've died!" I cried to anyone within earshot. Weeks later, my thoughts turned: What if I had stayed? And survived? My main nemesis, the nightclub, was destroyed and demolished. . . . There was no permanent damage to my unit. . . . The kids upstairs were getting older, things may have started to calm down. . . . My property value could have skyrocketed. . .

My newfound quiet leaves wide open spaces in my mind to obsess over the years I tried to make River West my home. Even amongst the whisper of trees, I search for peace.

CENTRAL

South Loop: Michigan and Harrison

MEGAN STIELSTRA

1995

I'm at the Harrison, a diner in the South Loop on Harrison Street between Michigan Avenue and Wabash. This place has vinyl booths. It has bottomless coffee for a buck twenty-five. The waitresses are in their fifties; they smoke and wear orthopedic shoes and if you're rude or tip like crap, they give you a look. *Think about how you treat people,* it says. *Think about the kind of person you want to be.* One of them calls me "Honey." She has bleached hair high with Aquanet and she's chewing hot pink bubble gum. In my memory her name is Flo, but I was twenty then, and I'm forty now, and when I was six I watched that show *Alice* with my babysitter, so it's possible I'm thinking of Polly Holliday.

"Here you go, Honey," she says, refilling my coffee. I like it when she calls me that. Makes me feel like I'm her girl, like she's watching out for me. Lord knows I need it. I pour in sugar, a faucet-like stream from the dispenser. When I think of myself then, alone in a new city with all my desperate dreams, the first thing I remember is coffee, thick and heavy, too-too sweet. I remember the backs of my thighs sticking to the booths. I remember Flo looking at the stack of books in front of me and asking, "You a writer?"

"Yes," I say.

It's the first time I said it out loud. The first time I believed it.

I came to Chicago for college, my third in three states in three years. I studied journalism and hated it, then English Literature which was better, but still not me. I wanted to write stories, but you can't go to school for that, right? Where I was from in small-town Michigan, you majored in education or agriculture or nursing—steady salary and 401(k). Still, when my sophomore-year boyfriend[1], said he wanted to move to Chicago, I went to an internet café and punched *creative* and *writing* into Yahoo. An art school came up in the South Loop, the corner of Michigan and Harrison. Its fiction program was housed in the School of Performing Arts,

1 * I don't know what happened to that guy.

which seemed so totally radical, a place that treated writing like theater or painting or music. I applied, got a transfer scholarship, and showed up for orientation in the blistering sauna of summertime Chicago.

I remember coming up from the underground at the Red Line stop at Harrison: asphalt, sidewalk, brick. Tangible humidity, a baking blanket spread over the grid. Straight north was the Chicago Public Library with its massive red walls and sculptures looking down from the roof—owls, I'd later learn, for knowledge. I walked east between parking lots and graffiti and iron fire escapes hanging precariously off the sides of buildings eight, nine, ten stories high towards a vertical slice of open sky: Michigan Avenue, Grant Park, the lake. I passed kids smoking on the sidewalk, kids with tattoos and books and cameras. They were women and men and both and neither, old and young and *how can you tell?* Later, in class, I'd learn about their lives: Vietnam vets and single mothers and recent immigrants and dumb, scared kids like me. We were, most all of us, broke. We had two or three jobs. We worked hard and partied hard—some of us harder than we should have—and we crashed and burned and got back up, but above all else, we made things.

It was my place.

I was there for twenty years.

It's different now, of course. They gutted the Harrison. There's a fast food-style counter in its place; Styrofoam cups, get it 'n go. I'd pass it on the way to my office and watch the college students through the windows.

2000

I'm at George's, a rat trap of a dive bar on the corner of Wabash and Balbo. It butts up to a parking lot. It's open 'til 4:00 a.m. It's small—Five tables? Six? Five or six stools at the bar?—and felt exactly like sitting on the inside of an ashtray. This was years before the Smoke Free Illinois Act banned smoking in public buildings. I didn't smoke, but five minutes in George's was a full-on contact high. You could feel the smoke in your pores, taste it in the baskets of popcorn from the free machine in the back, smell it in your hair and clothes and nails for days.

How else to say it?—this place is *perfect*.

I come here after class to shut down my brain. I'd line up my quarters and play "Barracuda" on the jukebox until the bartender promised me shots if I stopped. When I think of myself back then, working days in a brunch restaurant, taking three night classes a week towards my MFA plus student teaching, the first thing I remember is bourbon—with coke, with ice, with nothing. I remember the dull, fuzzy buzz and no sleep. I remember sitting at the bar and talking about books. Everything was books. I could tell you about Lorian, Ohio, where Pecola lived in *The Bluest Eye*. The Isle of Sky in *To the Lighthouse*. Sunset Park in *Last Exit to Brooklyn*. Macondo and Robledo and Asgard and Lothlorien—places that live only in our heads.

"But what do you know about here?" asks the bartender. He's an older guy, his accent thick. He opens his arms like he's showing me the world. Or maybe he's showing me the city. Or maybe Congress to Cermack, Lakeshore Drive to the Chicago River, this neighborhood I come to every day and don't know shit about.

What do you know about the place where you live? Where you work, go to school, where your kids go to school?

The next morning, I went to the library and read about the South Loop: its history as the country's railway epicenter, the Midwest's largest printing district, its experiments in urban planning. It housed waves of European immigrants, shipping magnates in their mansions, and Chicago's version of a vice district, brothels both drug-addled and couture. I read about the Fort Dearborn Massacre during the War of 1812. I read about Pacific Garden, the "oldest, continuously operating rescue mission in the country." I read about gentrification and the part I played in it, the beginning of an ongoing conversation I have with myself about what it means to contribute ethically to a community, a city, the world.

In a recent interview, I was asked to name the most important thing I learned in graduate school.

I thought of that night at George's.

They tore the place down in early 2016 to make room for high-rise apartments, which, according to the developer, feature "amenities and floor plans tailored to the needs of today's Millennial renter." He declined to say how much they would cost.

Do me a favor. If you're ever near the corner of Wabash and Balbo, give a little whisper: "Hey, George."

It's not a place that history will remember. The least we can do is wave.

2005

I'm at Gourmand, a coffee shop on Dearborn just north of Polk. It has mismatched couches from thrift stores. It has open mic poetry readings. It has giant chalkboards with the day's specials, weird[2], local art, and weird

2 * I like weird.

local artists writing and drawing and meeting and scheming. I like the energy, the accountability. If all these people are working, then I have to work, too. I get coffee and camp out in a ratty velvet chair, reading student writing. I have adjunct gigs at colleges in the South Loop and Hyde Park and I teach writing and performance in community organizations around the city. When I think of myself then, running from classrooms to libraries to living rooms, the first thing I remember are folders of stories, people putting their hearts on a page and handing those pages to me. I read about growing up young in Chicago, female in Chicago, black in Chicago, queer in Chicago—the joy and the fear and the fight. Everything I do has been influenced by those stories; how I write, teach, parent, vote.

Thank you for trusting me.

"Megan?"

It's a student, here for a meeting. She'd asked if we could talk in my office and was surprised when I said I didn't have one. I get it. When I was in her shoes I didn't know that some of my professors didn't have an office or, for that matter, a salary. I didn't know that 48 percent of college teachers in this country were part-time; no benefits, no job security. I didn't think about how that would affect my education. She sits on the ratty velvet loveseat and we talk about what she's reading. We talk about what she's writing. We talk about what she's scared of writing—it's too personal, her parents can't know, if he finds out he'll get mad, no she doesn't want to go to the police, she's having nightmares, panic attacks, can't breathe.

This is not the first time a young person has come to me about sexual assault. It is not the last.

The specifics of our conversation are not mine to tell, but it ends with her asking if I'll go with her to the college's counseling office. We bus our table, pack our stuff, pile into sweaters and scarves. "Can we talk about something else?" she asks as we walk. "Please? I don't care what, I just don't want to think about it for a minute." I start saying whatever comes into my head because it's a thing she asked of me that I can do even though what I *want* to do is cry. I point up at the twelve-story clock tower at Dearborn Station and tell her how I first read about it in *The Jungle* by Upton Sinclair. I tell her how they block off these streets every year for the Printer's Row Lit Festival and someday she can be part of it. I tell her how in the late 1800s the buildings surrounding us housed printing presses and linotype manufacturers, the foremothers of the books we read today, a century of back-and-forth between reader and writer. I tell her that when they built the University Center super-dorm the year before, they had to reroute the entire Brown Line and I'd stand beneath the broken tracks scared the "El" would fall. I tell her about a bar called George's where I drank during grad school. I tell her about a diner called the Harrison, a waitress called Flo. I tell her I'll sit with her until her triage appointment and that if they can't give her one today, I will burn the building to the fucking ground.

"I know," she says, smiling. "That's why I asked you to come."

So much has changed. Gourmand is a bike shop. 76.4 percent of college professors are adjunct. The University Center sold to a developer for 200 mil.

But god. So much is still the same.

2010

I'm at Cafecito, a blink-and-you'll-miss-it Cuban place on Congress. I don't want to give this place away—the line is already too long, out the door and onto the street. It has ropa vieja. It has caldo gallego. It has the best café con leche I've had in my life. My coffee intake is forever on the rise. I have a full-time job at the college in faculty development ("Can we meet for coffee?"), a night class at a different college (student conferences in coffee shops), a two-year-old child (omg coffee), a bitch of a thyroid disorder, the primary symptom of which is fatigue (hence coffee), a two-hour daily commute (coffee to go!), little to no sleep (duh), and this, my friends, is the American Dream.

The truth?—I love it.

"Where have you been?" says the man ahead of me in line. I work with hundreds of teachers; it's not possible for me to remember everyone's name, but I remember that I like him à la Maya Angelou: *People will forget what you said, people will forget what you did, but people will never forget how you made them feel.* I know he teaches in the journalism department. This was back before journalism merged with, I think, marketing? There have been a lot of merges.

"Took some time off," I tell him, leaving out specifics: the postpartum depression, the mess in my head, the ongoing work of healing and how happy I am to be back in the world. My tiny son is healthy now, thriving. I'm writing again. Every day I talk to teachers trying to change things for the better and about how lucky we are to do work that means something in this beautiful mess of a life.

"Well," he says. "Welcome back!" and I feel like singing. I feel blood in my veins. I feel a little bonkers but who the hell cares? I get my café and head east up Congress, the long way around to my office. The sun climbs over the lake. People everywhere with their coffee and their stories, waiting for the bus, rushing to work, walking lazily through the park at 8:00 a.m. on Wednesday. A thousand cars zip by, speeding and furious to Lakeshore Drive North and 290 West and South on 94 and here I am in the middle of everything, alive, alive, alive.

2015

I'm at the Starbucks at Michigan and Balbo, just below the lobby of the Blackstone Hotel. You've been to this place, or one exactly like it: long line. Crowd waiting at the back counter. Separate station for cream and sugar; the chalky, grating sound of the steamer; little to no seating. This location doesn't let you sit with a laptop or a friend, no endless conversations about books, just get your caffeine and GTFO. It serves the whole South Loop, as well as tourists in Grant Park and the entire college community, literally thousands of students and faculty looking for a jumpstart after all-nighters writing papers or reading papers or grading papers—*writereadgrade writereadgrade* in a never-ending ouroboros loop.

"Hey, honey," says Kathy, and puts in my order. She knows what I like. She has a photographic memory for all our stupid, frothy adjectives: *nonfat no-whip double-shot with room.* I don't let anyone call me "Honey," but from her, it's lovely. Like she's looking out for me.

Lord knows.

I come here every day, sometimes twice. She makes my drink and we talk about our kids. It's nice to talk about something other than what's happening at the college: programs cut, scholarships gutted, faculty fired or jumping ship.

Think about the kind of person you want to be.

"Shit. You, too?" Kathy says, nodding at my backpack, an enormous outdoor sport model that you'd take up a mountain for a month, plus several paper-packed tote bags hanging at my sides. I'd just cleared out my cubicle. My file cabinet. My bookshelf. My back hurts. My head, my heart.

"I'm sorry," she says. I know she means it.

"It's okay," I say, and I mean that, too.

I walk out onto Michigan Avenue; the summer, the sauna. I turn the corner at Harrison; asphalt, sidewalk, brick. There are condos. Townhouses. Specialty grocery stores and commissioned murals and tourists. The neighborhood—the city—is so different from when I first arrived. I'm trying to remember myself back then. I had an apartment in Ukranian Village. Later, I moved to Wicker Park, then Logan Square, then four years in four apartments in Humboldt Park. Five years in Uptown. Six in Rogers Park. I waited tables in Little Italy, River North, and Bucktown; a decade at the Bongo Room on Milwaukee Avenue; teaching in Hyde Park, Oak Park, Ravenswood, Evanston, Cabrini Green, the Gold Coast, the Loop—I can't remember everywhere anymore. What I do know is this: in my twenty years of trying to get by and make things in this beautiful, complicated city, the only place that was ever constant was that corner of Michigan and Harrison.

It's not my place anymore.

Doesn't mean it was easy to leave.

On the way to my car, I pass the food counter where the Harrison used to be and watch the college students through the windows. Their desperate dreams, their tables stacked with books. Jesus, they put a lot of sugar in their coffee.

The Loop:
Life in Chicago's Front Yard

RACHEL CROMIDAS

If Millennium Park is Chicago's "front yard," then for three years it was also mine; I lived on Wabash Avenue, just one block away. My apartment overlooked a Madison Street Pizano's, and when I stuck my head out the window, seven stories up, I could hear the CTA trains and buses and I could see the park, the giant white, head-shaped sculpture *Awilda* by Jaume Plensa that was installed at the park's entrance from 2014 to 2016, and the lake beyond that.

Chicago is a city of neighborhoods, but one of the fastest-growing of them almost doesn't feel like one at all. I'm referring to the Loop; it's where the "city that works" literally goes to work, but it's also experienced a surprising population growth and development boom_over the past decade. More people are moving downtown—even as the populations of other iconic Chicago neighborhoods stagnate or decline—and more high-rise residential buildings are going up. Yet it still surprises many longtime Chicagoans to hear that people actually live around here, coun the Chicago Cultural Center and Block 37 among their neighbors, and consider Millennium Park a kind of shared front yard.

I moved to the Loop in 2014 and stayed there for three years. I was drawn to the neighborhood-that-isn't by a sleek condo with surprisingly affordable rent (my landlords bought the place as a short sale in 2011, around the time the real estate market bottomed out; they used Airbnb to pay the mortgage) and the promise of a short walk to my job at the Tribune Tower. When I told friends I was moving to the Loop, they almost always asked, "Do you mean the West Loop, or the South Loop?" And you couldn't blame them. Those neighborhoods have come to epitomize trendy city living, with their hip restaurants, dog parks, and glass and steel apartment towers. But no, I meant the corner of Madison and Wabash, Five North—right in the center of the action.

Our building was a former office building and jewelry store in the Loop's historic Jeweler's Row. According to a list of historical facts on the building's website, Mr. T used to buy diamonds there, before it was turned into condos in 2003. Our nearest CTA stop, the Washington/Wabash superstation, built to replace the Madison/Wabash station that was decommissioned in 2015, is the same CTA station that nearly 10,000 Chicago-area commuters use to get to and from work or school on a typical weekday.

Between all the students, office workers, civil servants, and tourists who make the Loop their home base from 9:00 to 5:00 and beyond, it can be hard to find a sense of community as a resident. Most shops and restaurants close by 8:00 or 9:00 (and even earlier on the weekends, if they're open at all), and you'd be hard-pressed to find familiar faces in the city's ever-changing crowds. In the early hours of the morning, even the Loop's busiest streets are virtually empty. After weekend nights spent out in other, more hip parts of the city, I could hear echoes between the buildings as I rushed home from the train in the early morning, slightly unsettled by the emptiness.

But I grasped for familiarity where I could, for example by becoming a regular in the lobby of the Chicago Athletic Association Hotel, a boutique Michigan Avenue hotel inside a renovated, century-old sports club, where I could get free wifi during the workday without hassle, and order coffee or a drink any time. My boyfriend and I befriended a single fellow "local" who lived around the corner from us in another century-old building, whom we met on a loosely organized downtown architecture tour. (We were always game to go on downtown architecture tours.)

I also embraced my role as a convenient stopover for friends in the liminal space between their homes and whatever it was that brought them downtown. Of course no one wanted to drive into the Loop to visit us, but it felt like everyone wanted to stop by my apartment after their trips to the DMV, to crash with me during conferences and big summer fests, or to get a home-cooked meal during their lunch breaks (just as often, I would have someone bring *me* Chipotle). On one occasion, a distraught friend hauled the entire contents of her office to my house in bags, minutes after being laid off. Losing your job is a hollowing, humiliating experience regardless of the reasons, and I was relieved my home was there for her to finally break down in before trekking home, as opposed to the sterile Panera around the block.

In the beginning, my boyfriend and I marveled at the conveniences of Loop life, bragging that we lived within walking distance of the Art Institute and the symphony. But eventually we longed for a return to the quiet, almost quaint-by-comparison pace of life on a tree-lined, purely residential block—especially once the CTA began construction on two major projects literally right outside our building, the LoopLink bus station and the new Washington/Wabash superstation. For the better part of two years, our corner thrummed with the sounds of construction at all hours, hurting nearby businesses and driving many of our neighbors to either move out or just complain loudly in the elevators about how the drilling and hammering kept them up at night (we were lucky—our landlords and the apartment's previous inhabitants had left us with double-paned, soundproof windows). The final straw came later, when we both began working from home and realized that living within walking distance of friends—or really, any friendly humans whom we could encounter regularly besides each other—was more important to us than being able to pop over to the Art Institute on a whim.

We also didn't quite fit in with the sleek, high-rise dwelling, suit-and-tie wearing vibe of many Loop denizens (our people are more likely to live in an intentional community, or some other multiple-roommates situation, in Avondale or Rogers Park, and spend their nights and weekends at a circus school or acro yoga jam), but we did learn a lot about how the city works while living there.

In the Loop, even the most mundane-sounding local news becomes the draw of dozens of reporters—for example, the time a hive of bees decided to make a bicycle parked on Madison Street their temporary home and every news outlet in town sent someone out to film it. It's also the neighborhood that City Hall arguably cares most about keeping pristine—between Millennium Park, Maggie Daley Park, the "cultural mile" on Michigan Avenue, and the newly-renovated Riverwalk, there's a whole team of people in charge of keeping the neighborhood pretty in a way that no other neighborhood has. When you live in the Loop, the news and events that define Chicago are inescapable—every time you head home you're bound to run into something, whether it's an emergency, a protest, a press conference, or the filming of another Dick Wolf show or *Transformers* movie. Plus, you're a part of every city-wide celebration, whether you want to be or not—from the hapless Chicago Fire Festival to the Blackhawks' and Cubs' victories, to the annual tradition of dyeing the river green for St. Patrick's Day. (You know city life is easy when you're biggest complaint is that you can't get across the street to go to the grocery store because you forgot about the special spring day when the city lifts the bridges over the Chicago River to allow boaters to return their boats from winter storage to Lake Michigan's harbors.)

Construction projects, like the record-setting Vista Tower in the Loop-adjacent New East Side, which promises to become the city's third-tallest building and bring 406 luxury condos to the area when it's completed in 2020, and several other "supertall" skyscraper projects yet to gain city approval that would bring new residential units to the Loop market, are poised to further shift the character of the Loop toward a place where people actually live. But most likely, the Loop's cost of living will remain out of reach for all but the wealthiest Chicagoans.

I moved out of the Loop on the morning of August 3, 2017—right in the middle of Lollapalooza Day One—and watched a literal wave of suburban teenagers decked out in crop tops and bodysuits beeline for Millennium Park as our movers loaded up their truck. I sighed in relief that I wouldn't have to push my way through another Lolla crowd, parade, or Stanley Cup celebration again if I didn't want to. And I promised myself that I would definitely still visit the Art Institute—which I have done exactly once.

Gold Coast:
The Alleys of the Gold Coast

LEOPOLD FROEHLICH

Chicago has plutocrats and paupers in the ratio of more than sixteen to one—boulevards for the exhibition of the rich and alleys for the convenience of the poor.
—Eugene V. Debs

This part of the city has two dimensions: streetfront—the ideal version of a community, the ruse that faces observer or visitor—and alley, which provides access for delivery and service and garage, but is not designed to be seen. In the Gold Coast, the false front is especially well developed. Streetward are presented garish ornaments, filigrees, amenities, Beaux Art follies, and half-hearted claims to Florentine grandeur. There are façades on Lake Shore Drive that aspire without irony to the rectitude of the Petit Trianon. Yet such grandiose efforts exist on only one side, the side that faces the street. As if weary with pretext, the other three sides don't bother with romance. The tree-lined aspect of the neighborhood, the side presented forward for the sake of appearance or propriety, stands for morality. The city always presents this veneer eastward, toward the lake, toward aspirations and legacies of the East Coast, while turning its baboon ass toward the backyard prairie. The city of god faces the lake and the city of man faces the alley.

The alley is the clever side: Chicago has 1,900 miles of public alleys. There is no Hellenic pretense to these walls. Instead, there is rude brick, untreated lumber, and the utilitarian reality of a city, distinct from the streetside's failed efforts at delicacy. The pure workings of urban life operate with neither adornment nor ambition. There is no need for the vanity of stonework or wrought iron on this side of the city, a side A. J. Liebling regarded—once he got past two or three blocks inland—as "a vast Canarsie."

Perhaps this dichotomy between formal front and pragmatic back is what inspired Louis Sullivan to announce that form ever follows function. The alley is the real thoroughfare. It speaks to the effortless brutality of place, and attests to man's tentative dominion over nature. Chicago's supposedly majestic order is belied by the city's inability to conquer and control what remains wild.

The Gold Coast alleys show the preposterousness of the city's claim to urbanity, to *urbs in horto*: there is mud, wild onion, slack water, decline. There is garbage and ice and salt, rats, and coyotes. The land reveals itself in primeval form, and we see how poorly the city asserts its control, how it struggles to keep alleys from reverting to their natural organicism, to prairie and sand dune. Concrete buckles, asphalt melts, and we return almost overnight to the marshland, with dragonflies and bent rims. Chicago's dominion over nature is tenuous, as the city has been around for only two hundred years. The imposed grid of the streets and avenues has always been more theoretical than practical, an order more ideal than actual.

This inversion of order—front for back, back for front—exemplifies Chicago's true hidden hierarchy: pragmatism trumps appearance, function prevails over form, praxis over theory. An alley in the Gold Coast, as elsewhere, represents the city as it really works, not as we wish it would work.

Everywhere in this Chicago is spoken the real lingua franca: bribery, kickback, payoff, quid pro quo, nod and wink, one hand washing the other. Inhabitants barely bother with the so-called *real world*, being for the most part unconcerned with the need to appear legitimate or honorable. These are words for children or the naive, indeed, sure to elicit guffaws and eye-rolls from any normal, ham-fisted Chicagoan. Small-timers also pursue their gains and abide by these crooked rules, so all transactions—major and minor, dime store and merchant bank, public and private—are ruled by low passions. Virtue, it can be said, does not thrive in fertile soils, but cunning flourishes.

The backsides of the Gold Coast buildings, with only the intermittent tar paper exception, are surprising for their muddy but pragmatic uniformity. The fronts of the post-fire edifices are a resplendent mix of styles and variegations, but the backs are nearly all brown brick, most of which sprung from claypits in West Ridge and Northbrook. During the building heyday of the 1920s the Illinois Brick Company and the National Brick Company turned out 300,000 bricks a day to build apartments and houses in the aspiring metropolis.

Chicago was sown in dishonor and born in sin. The very material on which it is founded is corrupt. The clay baked for these ubiquitous bricks—the most efficient material with which to build a city quickly—was subject to appropriation by the city's ruling class. Everything, even the primeval muck, the lacustrine clay and silt of ancient glacial lakes, is up for grabs. Chicago's materials companies have long made incredible money by charging the public for what was in the ground and belonged to the public. Arch-physiocrat Henry Crown made his fortune selling gravel and sand.

In 1933 Judge George E. Q. Johnson denounced a dozen concerns that controlled nine-tenths of Chicago's brick manufacture for engaging "in a conspiracy to violate the criminal laws of the United States as well as the state of Illinois." This criminal consortium, according to Judge Johnson, was able to maintain brick prices between 1921 and 1931—a period of significant growth for Chicago—at $12 a thousand, when the average price during competitive periods was $6 a thousand.

The president of the Illinois Brick Company, which at that time manufactured and distributed nearly two-thirds of the bricks in the Chicago area and was said to be the largest brickmaker in the world, was William Schlake. At the time of Judge Johnson's denunciation, Schlake was serving as commissioner of Lincoln Park. The other manufacturers alleged by the court to be "engaged in an enterprise outside the law" were Illinois Brick Company, National Brick Company, Chicago Brick Company, Carey Brick Company, Bach Brick Company, Tuthill Building Materials Company, Lake View Brick Company, Lutter Brick Company, Brisch Brick Company, Behnsack Brick Company, and the Builders Brick Company. Nothing seems to have come of Johnson's charges.

For all the vainglory of its failed grandeur, Chicago is and has always been a city of firemen, butchers, and teamsters. It will always be the alley that unifies this city, a passage of service from North to South, lake to prairie. Look at the city from the west and look again from the east: you see two different places.

Which is not to say the Gold Coast—which in the days of John Wellborn Root was the city's wealthiest and most cultured neighborhood—is a place without heart: after all the getting is out of the way (as if getting is ever out of the way) there is time for backslapping, awards, hospital visits, wakes, funeral cards, charity for widows and orphans, lace handkerchiefs, cash envelopes. It invariably assumes maudlin and sentimental forms, from Galway tenor to one-eyed tavern philosopher. But it is rarely inauthentic or without solicitude. Fall face down in the mud, and a resident of the Gold Coast will help you up.

It is not as if any of this is secret or hidden. It is always apparent to anyone who cares to see. Schoolchildren know who drives the black Escalades. Immigrants three days removed from Sarajevo or Katowice or

Quetta know enough to see that in Chicago reality is not durable, and truth is contingent. There has always been little use in Chicago for the chimerical world of civitas or law, which fools only Episcopalian priests and dimwitted residents of the Gold Coast.

NORTH
SIDE

Lakeview:
On Belmont and Clark

EMILY MACK

It was either a warm night during winter break or a chilly night during spring break of college. Too cold, we realized, to drink our bottle of five-dollar chardonnay at the harbor as planned, so we walked from the lake to Starbucks. I asked the barista for three grande cups of ice water, then poured the ice water out in the bathroom and poured the wine in. The three of us drank, all sitting in a row at the long table against the Starbucks window. The window looked out to the corner of Belmont and Clark which seemed nearly empty on a Sunday night. The two girls I sat with were old, old friends.

Facing the window I could see, kitty corner, an H and R Block that took up two storefronts bordering a cornball costume shop, Hollywood Mirror. And directly across: the new mini-Target built on a triangular axis (eight stories high, after the apartments) so that the beige building extended down both Belmont and Clark for a quarter-block each way, its red bullseye only visible from the corner by the Starbucks window. The Target had no other signage, just the still, red circle opened like a moralizing evil eye toward the intersection. I noticed no pedestrians until two drag queens tottered past in glittery platforms toward the sole club, Berlin. One of them momentarily leaned on an empty *RedEye* paper dispenser for support. I finished sipping my wine through the green straw, not quite buzzed but maybe just enough to feel nostalgic.

The first time I ever ditched class, I went to Belmont and Clark. A bunch of us girls all snuck out and took the "El" up from our middle school in Greektown. We couldn't have been older than twelve or thirteen. I had never even been to Lakeview before, but one of the more audacious girls who had her train lines memorized confidently strode from the Red Line to the vintage shops and we all followed. It felt like hours spent in Belmont Army, the five-floor behemoth of consignment and army surplus where we tried on pillbox hats and motorcycle helmets and bought polyester Chicago flags (two blue stripes, four red stars). We hung out on couches near the dressing rooms drinking root beers. We stopped across the street at the

Alley, an old goth head shop-superstore, and one of the girls got her ears double pierced. While everyone squealed as the gun neared her earlobe, I pocketed a fifteen-dollar locket of Al Capone. At home I ran upstairs to hang my flag before anyone could ask me how school was.

Throughout my adolescence, I identified Belmont and Clark as the reliable third place outside of school and home. If I didn't have plans after school, I hopped on the train and wandered through Lakeview with no exact routine. Next to the train stop was an American Apparel where some friends worked. I could hang out there for a while, flipping through the day-glo racks of skin-tight dresses and bullshitting with the cashier. Sometimes I bought a Stephen King paperback next door at Bookman's Corner to read in the Starbucks. If I didn't know what do for a date with a boy, I always said, "Let's just meet at Belmont," and with a bottle of vodka, we would sneak onto the roof of the army surplus or just walk around, slowly making our way east toward the lake to make out in a park. Sometimes we stopped for a donut. Our parents said that in the eighties, the Dunkin' Donuts there was called Punkin' Donuts and had a real parking lot nightlife full of leather-clad, rockabilly freaks leaving clubs that I will never know the names of. When I was in high school, the Dunkin' Donuts didn't even let us use the bathroom.

Belmont and Clark, as I knew it, was always half-sterile. Few remnants of Lakeview's eccentric roots remained, but I still found colorful spaces to socialize in the storefronts down Belmont. The Alley was overpriced, but I liked poking around. Starbucks was a chain, but I found comfort in its modest dependability and free plastic cups. When I was a senior in high school, I got a job at the Belmont Army selling women's clothes on the second floor. I took cigarette breaks with the girls from American Apparel, leaning against red brick facades. On bad days we ate stale long johns from Dunkin' Donuts. On payday we went to Chipotle. That was the same year Mark Thomas, the owner of the Alley, ran for alderman against incumbent Tom Tunney, who planned on opening a Walmart-Express down Clark street and allowing a mini-Target right here on Belmont and Clark. After forty years in business, Thomas could have just retired, but he clung to the hope of a funky Lakeview with the Alley at its heart. It was a nice commercialist sentiment, but even as a high school senior I sensed the deracination of this stucco utopia was totally inevitable.

That was the same year I visited LA and saw factory workers from American Apparel marching through the garment district chanting "Save Our Store!" Both the Alley and American Apparel closed down in 2016.

While the popular chain spot remains an empty storefront (between two other empty storefronts), the local landmark became one third of the mini-Target complex. So did the Punkin' Donuts. Belmont Army will likely close too; I recall several days that summer closing the floor register with only forty dollars' worth of sales. Sometimes the only shopper for hours was the old lady with wild white hair who smoked her cigarettes inside. There was no use asking her not to. She had fake eyelashes glued a centimeter too high and used to try on the most expensive pieces. She never bought them though. She always wore sequined berets and over-the-knee black stiletto boots. She had trembling, acrylic fingertips. I remember because once I saw her do cocaine in the Starbucks. For years that old lady shopped around Lakeview, high as hell and ashing all over the place with no money to spend. We all used to talk about her. She appears in my memory now like tan ghost, or harbinger, flitting out from behind paisley dressing curtains.

Certainly most Chicagoans would not consider the years in which I bummed around Lakeview any golden age for the neighborhood, which was already full of chains and new construction. I didn't really mind. Us kids had made do even when the mini-Target left Belmont and Clark unrecognizable, casting the avenue in looming eight-story shade. Last month though, I hurried past the Target toward the warmth of my Starbucks and discovered something much more dismal: they had remodeled, removing all the tables and chairs. The entire floor space is now reserved for the anticipation of a line. The bathroom is locked. When I asked the barista what happened, he told me Starbucks is trying out "a new look" at some of its more popular locations.

When I left, I drank my coffee on a bus stop bench facing the spot where the Alley once stood. And I remembered last spring break, or was it winter break, when I sat drinking chardonnay at the Starbucks with two girls from high school. That night we had noted the banal changes to our favorite block, but recognized that when we worked and shopped at those gimmicky stores, we were so young and without responsibility. Maybe that's why it was so fun. We could have had fun anywhere. And we sat talking and wondering where we might move after college, to what neighborhoods or even what cities. We sat talking until the Starbucks closed.

Lakeview: The Blue House

ELEANOR GLOCKNER

The blue house isn't blue anymore, and the cops don't come as often as they used to. We all knew that it would happen eventually—Andy's father Ed had a reverse mortgage, so whenever he died the bank would reclaim the property—but the neighbors were split between wanting things to finally quiet down and knowing that we would miss the excitement, the fuel for gossip and dramatic stories to impress out-of-town relatives. Vanessa Schneiderman told me that the guys who cleaned the place out couldn't believe that anyone had been living there: they were sure that it was abandoned and had been sitting for years. It took the two men three weeks and several full dumpsters, shouting warnings to each other in Spanish as they tossed rotten beams and old furniture out the front windows, before it was finally clear for renovation.

Luce Cowell was the only outsider we knew who had been inside, a transplant from Australia who naively accepted an invitation when she first rented the house next door with her husband Brett and daughter Maisie. There was a fresh deer head hanging from the blue house's second-story back window, but she figured it was just an American thing. The last occupants of the Cowells' house—Carol Higgs and her family—had moved to rural Wisconsin, and the neighbor they hired to rent out their house knew enough to pay Andy to stay away when he had showings. How was Luce supposed to know that Andy was someone we all generally avoided?

"Eleanor, you don't know how *creepy* that house is," she told me one summer night when we were sitting out on her front steps, all the grown-ups on the sidewalk talking about real estate and city politics while the kids played hide and seek, running through darkening gangways from backyard to backyard. "I went inside and it just reeked of smoke—like seriously, I started coughing and my nose got plugged up. Piles of junk everywhere, foam egg cartons stapled to the ceiling for insulation. . . . I don't know how they live like that. Andy wanted to bring me upstairs to show me his knife collection, but by then I was just like, 'No, thank you,' and we went back outside. I was so glad that Maisie wasn't with me."

We were never quite sure how many people lived there. There was Ed, with his floppy white hair, floppy tattooed arms, floppy belly under a white ribbed undershirt, and his floppy lower lip that always stuck out like he was pouting. I never heard him say a word or saw him do anything more than step onto the porch, look up and down the block, and then sit down on a faded plastic lawn chair to smoke. This was Ed, the patriarch, father of Joe and Andy; Ed whose second marriage was to a fare from his taxi-driving days who left him the blue house when she died; Ed of the late, one-armed ex-first-wife named Rose who moved in after the taxi wife's death and would sit on the front steps with a bottle in a paper bag, yelling at a small white dog whose name was, at least the way my dad tells it, Shutupshithead.

There was Mophead (we never knew his real name), who looked like a train-hopping hobo from the Great Depression chapter of my fifth-grade social studies textbook and who helped us break into our car when we locked the keys inside. Darlene was a young woman who wore purple shirts that rode up past her belly button and lived in the basement for a stretch; Joe explained that she was a friend of the family who had no relatives but received a monthly check for $1,000. In exchange for that they let her stay in their house to look after Ed, although she had a way of wandering off that made us think maybe she needed someone looking after her instead. For a few months there was Uncle Louie, who I could see from our front window as he stood in the blue house's doorway, looking like Mr. Clean but with no smile and more tattoos. My mom heard from Meg Sayeed that he had just been released from prison and needed somewhere to stay for a while.

But the real stars were Joe and Andy, Ed's grown sons, two men who loomed large in the block's mythology. Most adults had a soft spot for Joe, a quiet guy with a shaved head often covered by a baseball cap. He knew that his brother was a handful, and I think he felt like he had to make up for that: drawing a startlingly recognizable cartoon of all the neighbors for our block party T-shirts one year, joining the brigade of parents and kids chipping ice off vacant houses' sidewalks, advising neighbors of suspicious goings-on in the area. "Joe's a weird one, but his heart's in the right place," was one of Lisa Morgan's common refrains during the moms' wine-and-gossip parties on her front steps.

Lisa was, until she moved around the corner, the uncontested mayor of our block. Her biggest claim to fame was successfully auctioning off her eight-months-pregnant belly as advertising space in exchange for two tickets to the 2007 Super Bowl. The Bears lost, but her then unborn son made it through the experience to provide me with a high school career's worth of babysitting income.

She showed less affection for Andy, who had long brown hair, a large beer belly, and a tendency to sit shirtless on the blue house's front porch, calling out to passersby.

"You know what Andy told me the other day as I was getting out of the car?" Lisa would begin. "He told me he has some kind of cancer." This anecdote made its first appearance at the Schneidermans' glogg party one Thanksgiving, a tradition that seeped its way into the block social calendar along with soup night at the Sayeeds' and the big summer block party. Greg Schneiderman is a fireman—compact, intense, an old-school South Sider with the accent to prove it—who cooked for his firehouse before joining a special ops team, and he knows how to feed a crowd.

Lisa had the room's attention. Everyone liked a good Andy story. "'Yeah, Lisa, I don't know, I might not have that much time left...' Seriously." She scoffed and leaned across the short table in the Schneidermans' crowded kitchen. "There's no way he has cancer. I mean, he's got plenty of other problems but that's bullshit. I was just like 'Oh no Andy, hope it's not terminal,' and then he keeps following me, and trips over the sidewalk, and goes 'See look—it's already affecting my balance!'" Andy didn't have cancer, and the story lived on.

Andy drove a pickup truck that was a dark plum purple with a large green patch painted on the side and the duct-tape-lettered slogan, "METAL BY DAY, METAL BY NIGHT." Even without the lettering it would have stood out on our block, dented and rusting, hubcaps gone, amid the hulking minivans and sensible sedans and the Bukowskis' red Mustang convertible. "Metal by day" referred to the scrap he collected from alleys to sell at his friend's junk yard. "Metal by night" referred to the band he claimed would be big someday, but their most successful gigs so far seemed to be rehearsals at the blue house from 9:00 p.m. to midnight that always happened during the hottest parts of summer.

The room that my sister and I shared directly faced the blue house, and despite the screeching electric guitar we weren't about to close the window when it was ninety degrees with the fan on and we were tossing and turning in the lightest pajamas we owned, sheets tangled around our ankles.

"Eleanor," my sister would mumble from across the room, as if sounding groggier would better convince me that she was on the brink of slumber and Andy was the only thing stopping her. We both knew that it was too hot to sleep, and she was nowhere close to drifting off.

"What?"

"Make it stop."

"Mim, it's Andy. There's nothing we can do. Go bug Dad if it's bothering you so much. Or put your head under a pillow."

"Doinky poo."

"Just go to sleep."

"I *am* going to sleep, that's why I want you to go downstairs and tell Dad to make this idiot shut up."

I would sigh and sit up, scoot to the end of my wobbly loft bed, and step carefully down the squeaking ladder.

My sister didn't realize that pestering our parents often came with a bonus bowl of ice cream, but I had made the trip downstairs enough times to know what to expect: the kitchen lights still bright, fan whirring overhead, WFMT turned on so low that the announcer's voice was just a murmur in the background. Out the open back window, streetlights glowing over the alley and turning the faded red brick of the factory building a soft orange. My parents in conversation across a corner of our square wooden table, looking up in surprise from their blue bowls of mint chocolate chip. I would pout, play the unfortunate child, hope for some ice cream, and beg my dad to go tell Andy to quiet down. I was testing him, knowing that the last thing he wanted to do was go across the street and knock on that door, but curious what would happen if he did, pushing him to tell me exactly why he was unwilling to go, getting a different excuse each time: "It's only ten. He'll probably stop before too long." "Just wait a bit, they're usually done by eleven." "Are you sure you can't just close the window? I'll bring up another fan."

For a few years Andy or some other blue house resident could be counted on to stir something up at the annual August block party once it hit nine or ten at night, the street dark and strewn with tables and chairs as kids raced up and down the asphalt, wired at being up so late and running so free. Lisa Morgan would be presiding over her posse in a court of cushy outdoor furniture at one end of the block, a movie playing on a makeshift screen at the other, my mom and Meg Sayeed dancing to a Michael Jackson song in front of the pop-up tent in DJ Doug's greenway, my dad and I still sitting at our dinner table in the middle of the street, chatting with the Schneidermans about the flyover for the lakefront bike path that's taking forever to build.

Then Andy or one of his friends would start with boasts that escalated to threats that escalated to punches, Lisa or Greg would go try to calm things down, Vanessa or my dad would call the cops, and a few minutes later, spinning blue and white lights would appear. Sometimes someone would leave in handcuffs, sometimes they would just storm away. It was always fine by the next morning.

Luce Cowell divorced Brett years ago, little Maisie is now a high school senior with 200 likes on her latest Instagram post, and their old house—really the Higgs's old house—next to the blue house belongs to a lively Croatian criminal defense lawyer named Viktor, along with his wife and their son. In the summer, my mom walks with Viktor and his empty stroller to pick up Henry from preschool. If it's a Thursday, on the way back they stop by the farmer's market under the Southport "El" tracks for tamales and beer while Henry watches the trains rumble overhead.

When Carol Higgs was in town for business last September, my mom talked Viktor into hosting a party at his place. The past three residents were all back in the house next to the blue house. Carol was the guest of honor, Luce came over from her apartment two blocks away, and of course Viktor was there, along with the rest of the usual crew, but the neighbors I heard about most from that party were Zach and Javier, who had just moved in between the Schneidermans and another set of new neighbors who had caused quite a buzz. A Fox News contributor from the Trump campaign's Hispanic Advisory Council had bought a new construction house, painted his teenage daughter's bedroom candy pink, and hung a large painting of a rabbit over her bed, easily visible through the illuminated window as we walk home from the "El" at night. Zach and Javi were a much more welcome addition. While Javi headed in early to get some sleep before work the next day, Zach stayed up late telling wild stories, talking the rest of the group into a 2:00 a.m. run to the twenty-four-hour liquor store on Ashland for more wine.

They are the first real neighbors to be here since the blue house hasn't been the blue house. It happened gradually, all the harder to remember because we had been expecting it for so long. Even my parents' recollections were fuzzy, and I had to go searching through our messages to piece together the timeline. The best we could figure was that Ed died in the spring of 2015, just another instance of muted sirens and lights coming down the block, stopping in front of the blue house because that's where they always stopped, neighbors peering out from behind their curtains to see whether it was police or paramedics this time, my mom texting Viktor and Greg to ask if they could tell what was happening. And then one day Ed was carried out on a stretcher again, red lights rolling, and that time he didn't come back.

The rest of the family had a year to move out, slowly disappearing until it was just Joe, renting a basement room from a six-kid family three doors down, coming out the gangway to water their tomatoes. Public records show that the blue house sold in June 2016, but not until this past fall was it finally ready for new inhabitants.

At Christmas Eve dinner this year, Viktor's wife Lydia told us that there is a ghost haunting the former blue house. We were at their table with her and Viktor and his parents, silver tureens of fish stew glowing in the candlelight, wine glasses ringed with purple. Lydia is a no-nonsense contract lawyer, the reserved and sensible one of the family, but she's from Guyana, a country that takes its ghosts seriously. She knows more about these things than we do. "Don't you know? Meg Sayeed told me that a little girl died there long ago. Other people have seen her around." Henry sat on his dad's knee, hunched over a glowing iPad as the same video flickered again and again. "I can feel it," Lydia told us.

Later that night one of Viktor's candles caught on fire. My mom had sent me down to their basement fridge to get an extra jar of cherries for the cake, and on my way back up I noticed a small cauldron of flames under the television, on top of a stack of paperback books. A jar candle had burned so low that its wax ignited, and the fire had just jumped to the label outside the glass when I realized that this wasn't what was supposed to be happening. "I think there's a fire in the other room," I told the grown-ups. My dad and Viktor and I stood there looking at the soft orange flames, struck dumb by the potential for disaster and unsure how to stop it. My sister figured it out first: she smothered the jar with a frying pan, Viktor grabbed a baking sheet and oven mitts, and we carried the still-smoldering candle out the front door to set it on the porch, watching as the glass snapped and melted green wax solidified into a puddle in the snow. By the time Zach and Javi came over for drinks after their own Christmas Eve dinner with parents, it was just another funny story to share. "Where's Schneiderman when you need him?" we joked.

After we said our goodbyes and Merry Christmases, as we collected our empty Tupperware and stepped carefully over the ridge of gray slush from the snowplow—it doesn't feel right, to be leaving somewhere in Chicago in winter without a coat, but we were only going across the street—I turned back and looked at the blue house. It's a respectable gray now, square white columns holding up the porch roof and a red jingle bell wreath on the door. The only reason it wasn't torn down was because it's one of the tallest houses on the block, taller than the current zoning code allows; the only way to keep a building that big was to save its skeleton and gut everything else. The new owners are a couple in their forties with no kids. What are they going to do with all that house, we wonder.

North Center: Signs in Bloom

KIRSTEN LAMBERT

The lawn signs started sprouting up a few years ago. "We are #committed to Coonley," announces a yellow sign with blue-and-white letters staked in the grass outside a wood-frame two-flat. "We Are a St. Benedict Prep Bengal Family!" shouts a sign nestled between the bushes outside a brick bungalow. Each lawn sign proclaims the resident's allegiance to a local elementary school, signaling a friendly rivalry between the schools as well as a bit of swagger.

It's not clear who first thought of having people stick these signs in their lawns. But they're plentiful in North Center. Sometimes the sign in front of one home seems to do battle with the sign in front of the house next door, like a grown-up version of the childhood taunt, "My dad is tougher than your dad!"

Like the signs outside a polling place, the lawn signs also imply support for either public or private education in the North Center neighborhood: the area bounded by Montrose Avenue on the north, Diversey Avenue on the south, Ravenswood Avenue on the east and the Chicago River on the west. Spanning about two square miles, the neighborhood is home to five public and three private elementary schools, all of which compete for students. Kids from different schools often live next to each other or play on the same AYSO soccer team.

Three schools—Bell Elementary, Coonley Elementary, and St. Benedict Preparatory School—sit within a half-mile of each other, just east of Western Avenue off Irving Park Road. Students sometimes transfer between schools, and some families have siblings in two of the schools at once. The schools' fortunes are intertwined, and they've helped shape the entire neighborhood.

Alexander Graham Bell Elementary, named after the inventor, celebrated its one hundredth birthday with a balloon release in 2017. Bell's three-programs-in-one model is a rarity for a public elementary school. Bell doesn't just draw students from the neighborhood; students from other parts of the city also attend its regional gifted center and deaf/hard-of-hearing program. When the weather is nice, students linger after school on the grounds till dinnertime. On weekends, families might toss a football around on the artificial turf while first-graders swing from the monkey bars and teenagers skateboard. High-schoolers have been known to sneak a few beers outside Bell after the homecoming game at nearby Lane Tech until someone calls the cops.

With consistently high test scores and a reputation for sending graduates to top-tier high schools, Bell saw its enrollment shoot up from about 725 in 2000 to almost 1,050 in 2014. At one point, some teachers had to teach classes in the hall due to lack of classroom space. An addition in 2014 relieved the overcrowding, and then enrollment seemed to plateau.

Just half a mile northeast of Bell sprawls the brick and stone facade of another public school: John C. Coonley Elementary, named after a Chicago businessman who helped found the Union League Club of Chicago. As at Bell, its playground and a field of artificial turf make the school grounds a gathering place. The Coonley soccer team practices after school, teenagers shoot hoops, and a baseball backstop makes the field an ideal alternative when diamonds aren't available at nearby Welles or Revere Parks.

Coonley has seen its fortunes change over the past fifteen years. Not long ago the school educated a large population of lower-income neighborhood students, and the school's standardized test scores were mediocre. But parental involvement and fundraising, along with an influx of public money, allowed the school to renovate its building and grounds in 2009. This rejuvenation helped the school blossom, and its gifted program, added in 2010, also markedly boosted Coonley's test scores— and its appeal. Nowadays that gifted program, along with a program for special-needs students and the neighborhood program, echoes Bell's three-in-one concept.

Coonley's burgeoning popularity nabbed attention citywide after *Chicago Magazine* dubbed it one of the city's best fifteen public elementary schools in 2016. Top home prices in the Coonley boundaries rose past the $1.4 million mark that year as buyers wanted into the neighborhood. As with the lots in neighboring Bell School territory, developers have been razing aging houses and multi-unit buildings around Coonley to make way for large single-family homes. Census numbers suggest that Coonley's enrollment will continue its upward growth through at least 2022.

Facing south on the Coonley playground offers a clear view of a six-foot-tall clock, part of the St. Benedict Parish bell tower. At 150 feet, the tower is the tallest structure for miles around. In fact, people might not know where North Center is, but say "St. Ben's" and they'll nod in recognition. Although the church and school originally opened as a wooden structure in 1902, the building—with its stained-glass windows imported from Munich—put down roots in its current location in 1918. Residents can hear St. Ben's church bells, which toll each hour on the hour from 8:00 a.m. to 6:00 p.m., from several blocks away.

BenFest, the summer festival that St. Ben's hosts each July, has been going strong for almost forty years. But the parish school's hold on the neighborhood seems to be loosening. St. Benedict Catholic Preparatory, which began educating students in 1902 and opened its high school in 1950, quit accepting new high school students after the 2018–2019 school year. Although it will continue offering a preschool and elementary program, the lack of interest in St. Ben's high school forced it to phase out grades nine through twelve.

Searching for homes in North Center often brings up listings that mention proximity to St. Ben's or include phrases like "the award-winning Bell School," or "the coveted Coonley school district." Real-estate agents use the term "the ABCs" to refer to three of North Center's elementary schools: Bell, Coonley, and Audubon (which is just a few blocks south of Bell, in Roscoe Village).

In addition to seeking good schools, people who move to North Center view it as a better choice for families than other North Side neighborhoods such as Wrigleyville or Wicker Park/Bucktown. Kids can play basketball in the alley or ride their bikes down tree-lined side streets. Parents can squeeze in a night out by walking to restaurants along Lincoln Avenue, catching a music show at Martyrs', or watching a World Cup match on the big-screen TV at the Globe Pub. Those who work downtown can hop on a bus or ride the Brown Line into the Loop. Singles or couples without kids move to North Center for the convenience of the city, but with a community where neighbors shovel each other's sidewalks.

Official 2016 figures say that the face of North Center is 77 percent Caucasian and 12.5 percent Hispanic/Latino, with the remaining residents identifying as Asian, black, and other races and ethnicities. Almost 57 percent of residents are between twenty and forty-nine. The median household income is $97,703; 30.3 percent of households have an annual income of $150,000 or more. More than two-thirds of residents have completed at least a bachelor's degree. If you meet a new neighbor, asking what he or she does for a living might yield the vague reply, "Finance."

The neighborhood didn't always look the way it does now. The first North Center residents, European immigrants, settled here in the late nineteenth century. But by the 1990s, most of their descendants had left for the suburbs. The neighborhood was racially and socioeconomically diverse, with teachers and police officers making their homes in the area. Firefighters might grab a beer after work at the G and L Fire Escape, a corner bar that got its name from the cross streets of Grace and Leavitt. Residents in pockets such as Roscoe Village might shop at family-owned grocery stores such as the Cardeñas supermercado on the corner of Roscoe and Leavitt. Public schools like Audubon and Coonley were not seen as "good schools"; students scored below the state average on standardized tests, and parents who sent their kids there weren't bragging about it. Some North Center parents enrolled their kids in private schools or applied for public schools with gifted or magnet programs. But with the influx of double-income families, test scores at the public schools went up, diversity went down, and the neighborhood began to change.

While much of the demand for housing in Chicago shriveled up in 2007 and 2008, real-estate developers and rehabbers saw opportunity in North Center. As areas such as Lincoln Park and Lakeview were reaching maximum density, development started creeping north and west. Developers found aging housing stock and an appetite for luxury homes. So down came the two- and three-flats and up went the single-family homes. As longtime owners sold and renters moved, in came double-income couples who could afford 3,000-square-foot houses, each with a two-car garage, many of which had a deck on top—sometimes with a basketball court. House flippers came in and did gut rehabs, leaving the structures intact and ripping out everything except the studs. In contrast to many areas in the city and suburbs, housing prices in North Center more than doubled from 2000 to 2015.

The developers faced few barriers because Chicago zoning codes allow builders to construct single-family homes in any residential area. Many residents also welcomed the increase in their property values. However, at Bell, administrators and parents noticed that as single-family homes replaced multi-unit buildings, enrollment was leveling out.

Not all the schools in the neighborhood hold the same allure for affluent renters and buyers, however. The southwestern portion of North Center, near the intersection of Diversey and Clybourn, houses more low-income families than the tonier areas of North Center. In fact, more than 60 percent of students at Friedrich L. Jahn Elementary are considered low-income. As a result, even though CPS ranks Jahn as a desirable "Level 1" school, Jahn's students score below students at Audubon—less than a mile away—on standardized tests. So real-estate listings don't generally advertise the fact that a home is located in the Jahn boundaries, although families who send their kids to Jahn say the school offers a safe, supportive environment with strong instruction.

Some homeowners are hoping Jahn will follow in the footsteps of Audubon and Coonley. "Committed to Jahn," asserts one lawn sign near a "Hate Has No Home Here" poster. But over time it's become clear that the growth in the heart of North Center has yielded thorns: the deconversion of two- and three-flats to single-family homes means the population is dwindling. This results in a smaller tax base and fewer customers for retail stores and other businesses. Young adults often can't afford the rents in North Center, and—with prices starting around $250,000 for a two-bedroom condo—first-time buyers also may find themselves fenced out.

Aldermen are trying to regain the lost housing by pushing transit-oriented development (TOD): affordable high-density housing near transit stops such as the Brown Line that could help offset the loss of two-flats and three-flats. They aim to attract young adults with affordable rentals, hoping those renters will eventually mature into homebuyers who will stay in the neighborhood for years afterward while raising their families . But TOD projects have faced resistance from homeowners who fear increased traffic and lost parking spaces.

That NIMBYism could prove poisonous to North Center.

Many working-class residents can no longer afford to live in the neighborhood. So they either move elsewhere in the city or head to the suburbs. And despite the flourishing elementary schools, other families pack up and move out of Chicago if their children don't get into selective-enrollment high schools such as Payton, North Side, or Lane Tech.

Public officials say they want homeowners to stay in the neighborhood even after their kids have grown up and moved away, but the housing costs are also driving older residents out of their homes. If they're homeowners, they often sell the homes they've lived in for decades—even houses they inherited from parents—because fixed incomes don't allow them to reshingle roofs and replace water heaters.

These facts are not lost on elected officials in the area, who have banded together to create a program called GROWCommunity. The initiative spans four wards and involves educators, parents, neighbors, elected officials, philanthropic partners, and community leaders in an effort to keep families in the neighborhood with strong schools—not just elementary schools, but also high schools.

There is a downside to the GROWCommunity idea, though. If North Center's main draw is its schools, what will happen if those schools start to wither? It's hard to envision that now, when students at the "ABCs" are scoring in the ninetieth percentile on standardized tests. But the continual Chicago Public School budget cuts could eventually choke those schools like the ones in other neighborhoods.

Unlike St. Ben's, which collects tuition of about $7,000 for each elementary student, public schools like Bell and Coonley depend on parent-driven fundraising to supplement the per-student money they get from CPS (which rounds out to almost $4,400 in 2019). Through fundraising, the "ABCs" offer a variety of "specials": classes like art and music and drama, even libraries and librarians, a rare species in Chicago's public schools these days. If the private funds dry up, those schools will have to cut their "specials" and the bloom will be off the rose.

But for now, North Center is thriving. Construction fences surround properties on almost every side street. Longtime bars and restaurants such as O'Donovan's (which has been around for more than a century) and Laschet's Inn (established in 1971) are bustling, as are newcomers such as Japanese restaurant Kitsune. There's a Starbucks every half-mile or so. The strategy of nurturing the neighborhood schools to nurture the neighborhood seems to be working. It's as easy as ABC.

Ravenswood Gardens: Chicago River Life

ROB MILLER

Not so very long ago, you'd be branded a maniac or a fool for canoeing the river, the canal, the unremarkable ditch—whatever you thought of it, if you thought of it at all—that skulks through the North Side of Chicago. The easy-to-miss stretch near my apartment in Ravenswood Gardens, where the North Branch meets the North Shore Channel, just south of Foster, down to Irving Park Road, had been ignored, abused, neglected, defiled, dumped in, and dumped on for decades

Since the mid-1990s, I have been that maniac and that fool.

It would be a delusional romantic's errand to conjure adventure and Hiawatha-level serenity out of a river that one cannot read about without repeated references to "flushing," "run-off," "sewage," and "drainage." After a heavy storm, when the water turned from wan green to an end-of-shift dishwater gray, the septic tang and noisome, mucky high-water marks were stark reminders of the waterway's original purpose and the respect it was thus accorded.

The current doesn't flow so much as seep. It mysteriously and worryingly never, ever freezes. Tattered plastic detritus flaps from low branches. Drooling their way downtown are small flotsam rafts of bottles, cans, tennis balls, Flamin' Hot Cheetos bags, and, wait, is that a diaper? If you still feel the innate call to the waters our seafaring ancestors carried with them over unknown oceans, down Western cataracts or deep into the hearts of darkness, take note of the "Avoid all contact with skin; Seek medical attention if ingested" signs.

Yet.

The river was alluring, sublime, offering a strange and untrammelled vantage point of the city. In the years I've paddled it, I've cherished the peace in the early evenings; the angry knot of traffic on Lawrence Avenue muted as I drifted below, the fading light hitting water instead of streets, dancing on ripples instead of dying on asphalt. Hot summer days cooled when a wind blew over the water. Ducks plied the river, leaving a calm v-shaped wake. Remarkably large fish jumped out of the "nutrient-rich" effluent by the pumping station—a grand-era-gone-by building that, in a perfect world, would be a dreamy 1920s dance hall. The east bank was lined with modest bungalows. Their terraced backyards led down to piers of questionable sturdiness with lawn chairs and tiki torches stuck in five-gallon pails filled with sand. Decrepit, stained-at-the-waterline party barges bobbed lazily next to NO WAKE signs. A friend living along this bank once left a cooler on a flotation ring near the shore with a sign saying "For Rob." I paddled over and found a chilled bottle of Polish buffalo grass vodka, ice, soda water, and a couple of limes—a magnificently unique cocktail break. During the holidays, the piers and terraces were festooned with lights. Such was the river community to the few who paid attention.

The west bank has the more stately houses of Ravenswood Manor, with the river providing paddlers a voyeuristic backyard peek of hidden grandeur. Past Lawrence, there were the "parks" on both sides, with their tangles of dying ash, junk sumac, and scrub oaks spilling over the water's edge.

I'd paddle hard upstream to Foster or Peterson, beyond Chicago's only waterfall, with a drop of four feet and all the postcard charm of a concrete spillway. Then I'd drift back downriver, needing only the occasional steering stroke. An hour at dusk. An hour out of the city, in the city. A part of it, but apart from it. Far away, but just down here. So close to so much, but so off by myself.

And most of the time I was by myself. Other paddlers were rare. Water Reclamation District barges, piled high with tree limbs, rusted car doors, and sodden giant stuffed animals puttered past me on some days. I'd get bemused looks from people walking on the bridges and from teens in beat-up sneakers smoking weed under them. The pair of Hispanic men who always seemed to be sitting on the outlet pipe drinking Captain Morgan's, their fishing rods by their sides and not in the water, gave me the thumbs up. There was a homeless person who set up his summer box by the river, when the sumacs and locusts were in full bloom, hiding him from the prying eyes of the park or the police. He even set up a hammock one year. He always laughed and waved at me. Maniac and fool, he likely thought. And there was the corpulent couple I'd really rather not have seen naked laying on a blanket in a post-coital reverie. They waved at me dreamily. I paddled faster.

Most of my company, though, was the surprising amount of wildlife thriving in this unexpected, irregular refuge. The wholesale neglect of the river for years enabled a hidden ecosystem to swim, to paddle, and to stalk undisturbed right under our disinterested noses. To simply be.

There were the great blue herons, five feet tall with six to seven-foot wingspans. Awkward at takeoff, but majestic in flight. Green herons and night herons, hiding in the low branches with hunched, scowling demeanors, grouchily shaking their wings at me to stop scaring the fish as I drifted past. Belted kingfishers, darting out of the brush and diving into the water, then gone again before I could process what I'd seen. Wood ducks, black ducks, mallards, teals, canvasbacks, buffleheads, goldeneyes, and the odd merganser. Quacking and jabbering with curmudgeonly cheerfulness. Red-tailed and Cooper's hawks, eying the proceedings from the higher branches with a menacing stillness. Swallows at dusk—dozens and dozens of them—darting around me. I mean, I *think* they were swallows. They might have been bats.

Then there were the feral parrots. Neighborhood scuttlebutt had it that several years prior, a person with a questionable grasp of societal conventions owned a few South American parrots. When she moved away, she let them free. They hung around the river for a few years, their outrageous jungle plumage offering thoroughly incongruous and thrilling riots of color as they moved from tree to tree.

Less thrilling were the Canada geese. Their ubiquity in urban landscapes has numbed us to their presence—and, sure, when they have eight or ten fluffy goslings trailing them in an adorable little line, they seem congenial enough. But watch it! They are the leather-jacketed thugs of the bird world. They will come at your boat, hissing and flapping at the slightest provocation and I, for one, feel incredibly stupid paddling in a panic from them. One must maintain an aura of dignity in one's watercraft, after all.

The river is more than just a bird sanctuary, though. Often I'd see fifteen or twenty painted turtles at a time, basking on a single fallen tree limb. There was the mother beaver and her three kits. At first, all I saw was an indistinct brownish lump riding the current in front of me. Given the river's historical usage as a sewage outlet, this gave me disgusted pause until I realized what it was. The four of them swam serenely in front of me for a few dozen yards, then disappeared underneath shrubs overhanging the water. On a paddle one spring, I noticed movement to my left and thought, *hmm, what's that dog doing down here?* Then I saw the magnificent, unmistakable tail of a fox. It vanished into a den not thirty feet from where a Streets and Sanitation Department street cleaner noisily idled above.

During evening walks, my dog Gromit has the jauntiness of Gene Kelly in *On the Town*, all high stepping and high spirits. One night, on the west side of the Montrose bridge, his shore-leave giddiness gave way to manic trepidation. I swung my flashlight down the bank and two pairs of eyes reflected back at me. Coyotes were scavenging about with malicious intent. Gromit looked at me as if to admit, "I'm tough when that snotty Cockerdoodle mix gets all up in my face, but can we go home now? *Please?*"

And then there are the rats. Yeah, I know. But, seeing a functioning multilevel rat complex just above the waterline, like a busy condo rendered in mud, is much more fascinating than seeing a lone rat scurrying behind the dumpster with a scrap of Italian beef. I developed a grudging respect for the pestilential vermin in this environment.

Now the river is a much different place. It's safer, cleaner, and feels less remote, which is good and bad. Where there once was isolation are now rowing teams and kayaking pods. The quaint bungalows with quirky backyards are getting knocked down in favor of gaudy eyesores pulled from the dreary architectural playbook of a Hoffman Estates developer. The manor is more manorial. While gang tags and shamefully misspelled "Hail Satin" graffiti still mar the undersides of bridges, the wild overgrowth along the banks has been thinned and tamed, making access to the water easier. There are restored oak savannahs and prairie plantings. Floating bike trails will replace crumbling concrete slabs and even the waterfall has gotten a makeover, transformed into a friendly simulacrum of rapids. There are more teens, now sporting designer beat-up sneakers and smoking a higher grade of weed, haunting spots along the river—avoiding eye contact as if I'm some sort of River Narc. There are more dog walkers than AWOL shopping carts along the shoreline, and more fishing lines are actually getting wet. And the completion of the Deep Tunnel has (finally) lessened the frequency and severity of post-storm olfactory assaults.

But it is what we do in the wake (pun intended) of these developments that determines what the river becomes. An improvement in the water quality is objectively good, but will the river now be "better," or will it be the gateway to another sort of intrusion? With all the increased access to the riverbank, will I ever see a fox den or a family of beavers again? With logs and downed trees being removed more diligently, where will the mallard couple find quiet eddies to do their preening? With fewer dead limbs along the shore, what will the turtles sun on and stink-eye-giving herons stand on? For so long we had turned our backs on the river, and thus inadvertently created the opportunity for wildlife to find its way into our shared space. Therein lies the tension: What's good for us isn't always what's good for nature. And hasn't that often been the case? So, perhaps we could still benignly neglect the river a bit. Treat it with respect, not as a garbage can or a toilet, but still keep it a bit wild.

While I miss my spoiled but oddly unspoiled river, it is still easy to lose myself out on the water, to be transported out of the city yet still be deep within the city. My paddle strokes echo softly under a bridge. The mighty falls drown out the sound of the jets, so the flights seem to lazily and silently glide on their approach to O'Hare. The faraway feeling still slips over me like a warm coat on an autumn afternoon when the light is a little flatter and the leaves color the horizon. It's still a kick to see the L, especially in the summer when the trees are fully leafed out, burst from the treetops as it goes over the river. There's more human company on the water now, and with it the inherent value that comes from sharing an up-close and day-to-day appreciation of our river. It's a new community, of sorts. You would have to be a maniac and a fool *not* to see the city this way.

And I'm not likely to see that naked couple again. I'm definitely okay with that.

FAR NORTH SIDE

Uptown:
A Trip to the Argyle Museum of Memories

VITALIY VLADIMIROV

Imagine yourself holding a thick stack of oversize, lined sticky notes. You look down and see that someone has written in a delicate script an unsigned message that says:

"My departed friend Ted used to buy bulk basil on Argyle in the late '80s. The steeples of the L stop remind me of grocery shopping in my twenties."

You turn to the next one, which has a smudge from where a drop of water made the ink run, and it says:

"When my mom immigrated from the Philippines, Argyle was the first neighborhood she would come whenever she felt homesick. As an adult I still come here for food. I go to Hon Kee because that's where my parents took me when I was little. The owner still knows me."

You turn to yet another, printed in a neat, all-caps script and with a big lopsided heart drawn at the bottom. It states:

"Since '78 my family has been enjoying the Argyle area. Picking up roast duck and staring at the mini turtles for sale were great memories. Long live Argyle."

Each of these is a glimpse into a stranger's past, all tied to a place that sounds pretty incredible. These tiny letters share either a moment from childhood, note a favorite dish at a nearby restaurant, or speak of finding home right here in Chicago's Uptown. At once pedestrian and profound, as a whole they are little love letters to a very special corner of the city.

Argyle is just one piece of the larger puzzle that is the Uptown neighborhood, a lake-facing community six miles north of the Loop.

Conceived in the 1880s as the model suburb of Argyle Park, it was named to honor the developer's ties to the Scottish Dukes of Argyll. Annexed to Chicago in 1889 with Lake View Township so as to meet the one million population threshold required for cities to compete to host the 1893 World's Fair, the area grew quickly after railroad tracks were extended north from the Wilson Station, linking Argyle to downtown. These tracks were elevated by the 1920s, creating the city's famous L, and a boom in the construction of fanciful terra-cotta-clad hotel and apartment buildings followed. Uptown was also Chicago's proto-Hollywood, and it was on Argyle Street where Charlie Chaplin briefly worked at Essanay Studios in 1915 before the film industry moved to California. Uptown's zenith was in the Roaring Twenties, when its movie palaces drew huge crowds and when it was Chicago's busiest shopping area outside of the Loop. Argyle, too, had its own smaller movie theaters and emerged as an Orthodox Jewish community. But the Great Depression, World War II, and an era that glorified newly built suburbs as holding the cures for urban ills meant that Uptown became passé.

The neighborhood's decline coincided with deinstitutionalization—a push to close state-run psychiatric hospitals in favor of community-based clinics. People with disabilities and mental illness suddenly abandoned by the state could reliably afford apartments and rooms in Uptown's cut-up, once grand buildings. Migrant Appalachian whites, Puerto Ricans displaced from Lincoln Park, and the Black Panthers also made their home here and joined forces to fight police brutality. It became a neighborhood synonymous with poverty, crime, and arson. Business interests campaigned for federal dollars to clear "blight" and vintage blocks made way for glassy high rises, strip malls, and a new community college. Here, forces tugged at the threads of a densely woven urban fabric to remake it in their image. Today, Uptown is a place where you will see ornate century-old buildings next to brand-new luxury housing, panhandlers next to yuppies, and Nigerian headdresses next to women in hijabs. And then, of course, there is Argyle.

"Living and working in the Argyle area makes me remember the time when I was in my home town. The Asian community is amazing."

"My favorite memory was going to Furama to play Bau Cua Ca Cop for the Vietnamese New Year."

"Every time I come the food is amazing & the people have great stories. I find so much culture and history. I hope to be a part of it for many years to come!"

These memory fragments—several hundred in total—I gathered from strangers in a project that I dubbed the "Argyle Museum of Memories," a movable, pop-up that grew out of research for my master's degree in urban planning and public policy at UIC. I lived in Uptown then—on Argyle— and each day that I walked down the street, with every meal of pho or banh mi, and every time I bought lychees or Thai holy basil, I became more curious about the area's history and why, within just a few city blocks, there are over a dozen Chinese and Vietnamese restaurants next to pan-Asian grocers, herbalists, acupuncturists, salons and salon wholesalers, travel agencies, and nonprofits catering to a vast mix of people from Southeast Asia and elsewhere.

Turns out that in the 1970s a group of Chinese entrepreneurs selected Argyle as the site of a grand vision for a "New Chinatown"—a pedestrian mall replete with fanciful Orientalist architecture and dragon gates. Displaced by the construction of downtown's triangular prison, the Metropolitan Correctional Center, these businessmen saw value in Argyle's transit and cheap housing at a time when everyone wrote Uptown off as woebegone. A 1974 *Tribune* article called it "a shabby, beer-guzzling, bone-weary old slum," and yet a 1975 *Tribune* headline read, "2nd Chinatown planned for North Side," and touted that the development would serve a reported 7,000 Chinese living in the vicinity.

Since then, this pocket of Uptown around the Argyle Red Line station has been settled by waves of Chinese, Vietnamese, Cambodian, Hmong, Korean, Laotian, and other peoples, who transformed a corner of a disinvested slum into a vibrant, bustling place. Refugees and immigrants, many of them fleeing the 1975 Fall of Saigon, learned English, had children, opened businesses, held festivals, and in the process gave Chicago an invaluable cultural and economic asset that is diverse even for a neighborhood famous for its diversity.

"Great people! Walking down the street, sometimes you forget you're in Chicago."

"I recall Argyle in the early 1990s as a special place to come with friends. So happy to see it is even more vibrant!"

"Argyle was so magical as a kid. Many shops and restaurants today are a remnant of my childhood, which I hold dearly to this day."

There was real urgency to do this work because while Uptown is a rare exception to Chicago's calcified racial and economic segregation, its diversity is a precarious thing.

Today, the area is bustling but it is clear to everyone that change is afoot. Talk to people who grew up here and you'll hear that its current vibrancy is nothing like what it was like in the 1990s. They'll say there were more Buddhist monks in saffron robes, more street festivals, more active organizations, and more people. Census data supports this, as Uptown's population has declined by 11 percent just between 2000 and 2010, with notable decreases in its Asian and Latino populations and an increase in the proportion of white residents. And while neighborhoods are always in flux, this shift is troubling for a community where diversity has been taken for granted for so long. Thus, gathering local memories was necessary, before they were lost either to age or displacement.

"Argyle: my kind of neighborhood. I love it! I have been here 23 years and looking forward to another 30, 40, 50. . ."

"We moved to Uptown in 1977. One of my earliest memories were attending carnivals at Foster & Sheridan. Uptown instilled in me a love of food that remains today."

"Back in '84 we were evicted & moved to the Argyle area. I attended Stewart Elementary. I recall feeling like I was the odd one out yet made a couple of friends. My mom & I bonded more with little knowledge of the area. Now that she has passed I look at that time fondly as in that time we only had each other."

Most interesting was how the range in responses highlighted that, despite Uptown's diversity, Argyle is still embedded in Chicago's racial politics. Many were excited to see the historic materials and had detailed questions. I had people from every demographic come and tell lovely stories of the crucial role this urban space has had in their lives and how it instilled in them values of cities' potential for acceptance and inclusion. Some even seemed transported when they saw the photos and their faces lit up with wonder as they reminisced. Meanwhile, I noticed that responses among some of the white passersby were congenial, but less enthusiastic. I spoke to many long-time property owners who said they long avoided the area, but were excited for its recent shifts. Many wanted nothing to do with Argyle in the 1980s and 1990s but now adore it. Concerns over crime are of course common tactics for white folks to talk about minorities without broaching race. They avoided writing anything down, lest they seem insensitive. One woman did write:

"When I moved to Argyle in 2005 I would sometimes avoid getting off the L stop because of vagrancy. . . . I've come to appreciate the mix of ethnicities and income levels. I love this neighborhood."

She may love it now, but the fact is Uptown's network of social service agencies and varied housing stock made Uptown what it is and has helped support countless poor residents. Luckily she's come around but many remain steadfast in seeing diversity as a shortcoming rather than an asset. Still, this underscores that people can have highly varied experiences of the same urban space and that diversity alone is not cause for engendering tolerance and acceptance—both things also confirmed by numerous studies.

Changing demographics are making it harder for some of the minority-owned businesses to stay open; there just are less Asian customers to patronize their stores. Also, the CTA plans to rebuild the Argyle "El" station and viaducts that will entail several years of long closures, which will have oversized impacts on the nearby ecosystem. And business owners themselves are aging.

But why does Argyle Street matter? Research confirms that spaces where minorities cluster—Chinatowns, Little Indias, gayborhoods even—are valuable for many reasons. These places boost social capital, the invisible networks that tie communities together. It's borrowing a cup of sugar from your neighbor, or going to a restaurant so often the owners know you. For those who just arrived in America, places like Argyle offer resources that help them acclimate to life in a foreign country via nonprofits like the Chinese Mutual Aid Association, which can connect them to ESL classes, citizenship tests, and more. Social capital helps minority entrepreneurs not only open businesses, but also navigate forces such as city bureaucracies, rising commercial rents, and shifts in consumer behavior that force many businesses to close soon after opening. Plus, clusters like Argyle draw tourists eager to experience a city's unique culture. But Argyle's most important contribution is that it is living proof of America's plurality. This is a nation of immigrants after all, and places like Argyle are a testament to the contributions of those born abroad.

All this means that along Argyle there are many transformational stories of people overcoming great odds to become thriving members of our society. Take the owner of Tai Nam Market, Phieu Tran, who was one of the untold thousands of "Vietnamese Boat People" who survived incredible violence, came here knowing no English, and went on to a successful career at Motorola where he invented eleven telecommunications patents before co-founding the grocery store in 1993. Since then, Tai Nam has become a community anchor that supplies restaurants with fresh ingredients and is a destination for customers who will drive as far as one hundred miles just for a taste of home.

"My family used to drive in from Naperville to Argyle when I was a kid ('90s). My grandma would get her hair permed while we would go grocery shopping."

"Growing up, we would always take a day trip to Viet Hoa to get groceries. I have fond memories playing through the store aisles waiting for my grandma to get what she needed. Love coming back to see the new and old of Argyle."

"We used to come down to Argyle to shop, visit cousins, and have lunch at Pho 888. Food makes the culture & people keep it alive & thriving."

Still, all the immigrants' hard work in turning this area around has in ways helped hasten its gentrification. A 1985 *Tribune* headline reads: "Uptown: 'boat people' create comeback for realty on Argyle Street." It's as if now that the Asians have fixed up the area, some are eager to cash in on more than thirty years' worth of sweat equity that has made Argyle what it is. But there is hope still. New minority-owned businesses are still opening and some young people are stepping up to take over their parents' stores. And many of the memories I gathered are full of hope and optimism for Argyle's future.

"It's my hope that we can preserve Argyle for future generations to enjoy, to keep it vibrant and preserve our pan-Asian culture."

"I hope that we will continue to build upon the beautiful, diverse spirit of Argyle. I love coming here and seeing so many lovely people living, working, and celebrating together."

"Argyle. I love your energy. I feed off your vibe. I look forward to your future & am inspired by your past!"

So visit Argyle, eat at the restaurants, buy herbs, spices, and gifts, and donate time and money to local nonprofits. Attend the summer's Argyle Night Market or the winter's Lunar New Year parade and bring your friends. Recognize the street's uniqueness as a place of meaning and you will be rewarded with memories of your own and one day you might hear yourself say: *"I remember Argyle when. . ."*

Andersonville: The Precarious Equilibrium

SARAH STEIMER

Time ceases to exist in my apartment, or so I'm told. It's a phenomenon noticed most frequently around 3:00 or 4:00 a.m., table cluttered with drained glasses and cheese rinds. It doesn't help that our only clock is in the bedroom, but I would wager that it's because there's a sense of comfort that permeates the space that, when surrendering to it, keeps people from chronically checking their phones and realizing just how many hours have passed.

It's not just my apartment. The entire building strikes a certain close-quarters equilibrium. The building is purportedly about one hundred years old, celebrating its centennial with a few minor nips and tucks (updated cabinets, roof repairs), but remaining modest, creaky, and solid. Its U-shape hugs a vine-filled courtyard, embracing the residents within its red brick walls.

If neighborhoods are the microcosms of a city, then the apartment buildings within those neighborhoods focus the microscope ever closer. In the eight years I've lived in Chicago, I've watched friends jump ship from apartment to apartment, neighborhood to neighborhood in an effort to find their Goldilocks home: this apartment is too dark, that neighborhood overcrowded. But I've stayed put in Andersonville. Sure, I've occasionally entertained the dream of a second bedroom, or living closer to my job in the Loop or my friends in their uber-hip Logan Squares and West Towns. I've even toyed with the idea of outright ownership (a daydream quickly squashed by the thought of replacing my own appliances). But springtime rolls around each year and we re-sign our lease, just as resistant to leaving the apartment as we are the neighborhood.

The connection to this home feels most acute when you realize how delicate the balance of comfort really is. I lament the loss of businesses along Clark Street; I take it personally and I wonder what could have been done to keep them alive. The wine bar Ombra, with its outdoor seating—did I not visit you enough? The eighty-eight-year-old Swedish Bakery where I picked up a (supposed) traditional baked good that a Swedish friend insisted she'd never seen nor heard of before—should I have placed more orders? And Icosium Kafe, an Algerian restaurant whose savory crepes and sweet potato soup lured us to the neighborhood in the first place, only to close within the year we first moved a block and a half away—what more could I have done?

I most fear the future losses that could irrevocably tip everything off balance and wreck the precarious comfort of relationships created over the years, of affordable rent, and of neighborhood identity. I'm grateful for this community, but my gratitude is tempered by anxiety. How long it can possibly last—a neighborhood and a building that teeters on a pinhead of livability?

I thought about it after I was given permission to use my spare key to Jamie and Mike's apartment across the hall. I needed to borrow a cup of sugar, and they insisted via text that I let myself in. I lingered in the pantry, ever in awe of their well-organized dry goods, knowing the sounds and smells that float out of this kitchen when I'm one or two doors removed and hoping to catch a glimpse of whatever it may be. Sometimes I catch a picture of the baked good on Instagram, or—better yet—a knock on my door leads to a sourdough biscuit palmed over like a deck of cards. I don't mind a friendly baked good one bit, nor their cat, which may only be particularly friendly from previous weekends I've spent feeding it while its owners are away. I don't pretend to be a cat lover, but I can appreciate a kitty that spends its days listening to public radio while Jamie and Mike are at work or out of town, I assume so that Queso doesn't get lonely.

But what happens when they move? Who keeps the radio on for the rest of us? Will the next neighbors be so willing to lend me whatever item I failed to add to my grocery list? Will they care when it's 9:30 p.m. and we're all wearing our oldest sweatpants and I come knocking for a square of parchment paper? Can I barge over after work, balancing martini glasses and a full cocktail shaker?

The building reminds us of change in its own subtle ways. The intersection of past and present flickers when the sun hits our stairwell just right, highlighting the engravings on the since painted-over windowsill. These are purportedly from gangs that once lived in the neighborhood, as is some of the graffiti in the basement. Andersonville likes to look fondly at its deeper past as a Swedish enclave, even raising $165,000 to replace its damaged water tower painted with the Swedish flag—money that frankly could have better served the community in myriad other ways. A more recent read of Andersonville history is less about Swedish Chicagoans and more about a much wider swath of people.

My neighbor across the courtyard, for instance, came to the neighborhood as a child from Cuba. You can hear Gladis and her wife, Olga, shouting to one another over the vacuum on weekends or gearing up to head to the beach in summer, wagon of drinks and other amenities in tow; or you may catch a good chat in the laundry room, peppered with just a skosh of neighbor gossip. I asked them over one evening, expecting to proffer the refreshments. Instead, they came toting a bottle of chianti and Gladis's homemade empanadas. They're caretakers in every sense, keeping the building tidy and its residents safe with words of caution and offers to accept packages if you're away from home.

They also represent a piece of the LGBTQ community that's being tipped out of town. Andersonville was once a haven for Chicago's lesbian community—this "Girlstown" being the answer to Boystown further south—with affordable rents and since-shuttered lesbian bars like T's and Stargaze. As real estate prices have climbed, households with two female incomes are at an obvious disadvantage, especially to households with two male incomes. Cook County data from 2016 show that in ZIP code 60640, there are 173 married lesbian couples, compared to 405 married gay couples. I know Olga and Gladis would like to stop renting and buy their own place, but I also know they've been priced out of the Andersonville market.

How much longer do I have to cash in on their invitation to join them at Mary's Attic? Or to hear Olga's stories from her visits to see her sister in Florida? Even though LGBTQ staples like Women and Children First bookstore remain, how can we stop pricing out its patrons?

It's not as though Andersonville hasn't been gentrifying for some time, but it's held a precarious social balance that just the right real estate or restaurant boom could tremble and tip.

So I am precious about this neighborhood and this building. I know that I am the woman who complains about change while locals around me internally shriek, "She's not even from here!" I can't help but feel precious about a place that helped me tap into my own internal ease and balance.

So while my friends and coworkers shrug at the idea of really getting to know their neighbors, we have ours over for Easter brunch. I teach yoga in this neighborhood, the classes filled with tall, small, and full bodies, many of whom pair their brand-name bottoms with cheap tees. Clark Street wine walks are countered with zombie bar crawls, and men in leather harnesses share the dance floor with toddlers at Midsommarfest. It's where I can meet up with upstairs neighbors for an ice cream date at George's, or split a cab home from O'Hare with a downstairs neighbor I happen to run into at the airport in Paris. The speed of working in the Loop diminishes the moment I step onto my small balcony, partly screened in by two nearby trees. It is balance.

But it's a fairly tiny neighborhood and a small apartment building, easily changed by the loss of a retailer or an inhabitant. The shift isn't likely to happen overnight, but it can feel more palpable some days than others. When luxury apartments rose on our corner, one station on my digital antenna began to flicker and fade, until finally static gave way to a signal that vanished entirely.

Edgewater Glen: Trick or Treat

KIM Z. DALE

When people ask me where I live I usually say "Edgewater." If that doesn't spark recognition I may say "really far north" or "near Andersonville" or sometimes simply "Andersonville." I know that unless the person has lived in the area, they probably haven't heard of my sub-neighborhood, Edgewater Glen.

For most of the year Edgewater Glen looks like a lot of residential North Side neighborhoods in Chicago—single-family homes of various historical architectural styles with large porches or sunrooms jutting out toward tree-lined streets. A few three-flats and six-flats hug more closely to the busy thoroughfare of North Broadway, flanking the neighborhood on the east and mirrored by North Clark on the west. We are within walking distance of Edgewater's eclectic variety of restaurants and shops, several small theaters, and the lake. Edgewater Glen is charming and welcoming on any day, but my neighborhood is most alive on Halloween.

There are those neighborhoods that people drive through at Christmastime to see the decorated houses. Edgewater Glen is like that in late October, with ghosts instead of reindeer.

A night or two before Halloween my kids and I walk the neighborhood to look at the often spooky, sometimes silly decorations: a pirate ship steered by a skeleton, giant spiders, an alien invasion, monster eyes peering from upstairs windows, life-sized scarecrows in a makeshift cornfield, motion-activated animatronics that come alive as we pass, and yard after yard spiked with tombstones.

We look at the decorations a few nights early because on Halloween we are far too busy.

When we first moved to the neighborhood people told us to expect more than 1,000 trick-or-treaters. I assumed they were lying or exaggerating (just as you might assume I am lying or exaggerating now). The strange thing was the consistency of their stories: "More than 1,000 trick-or-treaters." Either my neighbors had conspired to play some strange joke on us or they were telling the truth. I bought eight extra-large bags of candy just in case, but kept the receipts so I could return the leftovers.

There would be no leftovers.

I'm trained as an analyst, so I wanted to know exactly how many trick-or-treaters we really got. (That is, I wanted to verify how much of an exaggeration the fabled "more than 1,000" count was.) I grabbed a notebook and pen and made tick marks for each costumed kid. At 5:00 we had less than ten. By 6:00 we were up to a few dozen, still far below the 1,000 we had been promised.

But then Halloween in Edgewater Glen truly began.

When trick-or-treating in our neighborhood starts, really starts, there are no pauses. There is no waiting inside for a child to ring the doorbell. You sit on your porch or front stairs or even pull a chair up to the sidewalk as a constant crush of costumed kids crowd the walkway pausing at each treat-filled bowl just long enough to say, "Trick-or-treat!" then, "Thank you!" before moving on to the next house.

It quickly became impossible for one person to both hand out candy and put the marks in the book. We divided duties and let the evening fly by in a blur of miniature replicas of creatures and characters. Some cute, some clever, some creepy.

The moving, morphing mass of sugar-fueled joy didn't begin to thin until two hours later. It had slowed but not stopped at 8:30 when we ran out of candy (despite having briefly resorted to repurposing some of the loot my children had collected on their own trick-or-treat excursion).

Defeated, we turned off our porch light, went inside, and counted the marks in the notebook. They went on for pages. The final total came to 1,198. Solidly more than 1,000 trick-or-treaters as the neighbors had warned.

Since that first year, my family has fully embraced living in our Halloween neighborhood. I plan my decorations months in advance. I sweep away real cobwebs to put up fake ones. I obsessively compare candy prices, ultimately buying enough to fill an eighteen-gallon storage bin. We upgraded to a mechanical counter for tallying kids instead of making tick marks. We invite friends over as helpers and witnesses. We wave to our neighbors on their own kid-crowded porches.

Last year the weather was particularly good. We ran out of candy after hosting 1,628 kids. There has only been one year when we didn't get at least 1,000 trick-or-treaters. That year the weather was cold. It was sleeting and sometimes hailing. We still got 845.

Halloween in Edgewater Glen is chaotic and amazing and joyful. We can never move because my children would be disappointed by

Halloween in a "normal" neighborhood. This over-the-top version is all they have known.

I've heard there are other Halloween neighborhoods in Chicago that get the same kinds of crowds as we do in Edgewater Glen, but I will probably never see them firsthand. I intend to spend Halloween on my own porch for the foreseeable future, enjoying the neighborhood asset I would have never thought to ask my realtor about.

West Ridge: Rebel Girl

SARA NASSER

I was ten when some punks stole my little brother's new Nikes, the ones that looked like moon boots on his tawny legs. The thieves approached us as were walking near Green Briar Park, a place full of drum circles in summer evenings, adult softball games, and like much of Chicago, intermittent gang activity. Our neighborhood of West Ridge stood at the edge of Skokie and Evanston—richer, safer suburbs—and a world away from the violence of the South and West Sides. Growing up, the only thing I really worried about was the occasional telephone pole adorned with a sneaker barely hanging by a lace.

The two thieves were part of a larger family, shepherded by an eldest brother who towered over them. I often noticed them out and about as if they didn't have parents to call them home for dinner or homework. These boys looked younger than me, and it seemed that they approached us more out of boredom than anything resembling material gain.

"Assalamu alaykum," said the short one.

"You got some nice new shoes brother," said the taller one.

He disarmed my brother by grabbing his arms from behind as the short one pried the shoes off my brother's kicking feet. I was head and shoulders above both of them, and yet I just stood there, crying like a girl.

My brother didn't cry. He looked pissed while we walked home silently.

"Why is your face all red?" my mother screamed in Urdu. "Where in Allah's name are your shoes?"

My brother answered in English, his eyes cast down: "They were stolen."

"How? And where were you?" she asked me.

"I was there," I said in Urd-ish. "I didn't leave him."

"There were these two black kids from the masjid," my brother explained. "There was nothing she could have done."

While the theft of my brother's sneakers hardly constituted a violent crime, we were actually quite lucky that nothing worse had happened to us over the years. Police cars patrolled Green Briar Park to stop drug deals, while us brown kids played with each other, sometimes befriending some black kids we'd seen at school or at masjid, altogether avoiding the Hasidic kids, who avoided us in turn. We lived near our respective parts of Devon Avenue, with the Orthodox Jewish community to the north and the desis to the south, California Avenue crossing in between. Shorter streets named for Muhammed Ali Jinnah, Mahatma Gandhi, and Golda Meir honored the founding fathers (and mother) of our homelands.

After my brother had his shoes stolen, we weren't allowed to wear nice shoes anywhere, not even to the mosque. My mother warned that our shoes would be stolen while we prayed, since we placed them near the entrance during prayers sessions held upstairs. My family's mosque was a derelict building, without a sign or symbol of our faith. We hid our religiosity in plain sight. We traded in our minarets and arches for the square boxes of the Midwest, lines of brick that faded into flat terrain. Here I was surrounded by women from all over the Muslim world—Iraq, Bosnia, India, Pakistan—praying in unison to Allah. I aped the rituals of these women because I liked the pretty rugs I buried my nose in while bowing before Mecca, and the pretty scarves covering the pretty hair of women who exchanged freshly prepared meals, who treated each other's children as their own, and answered my questions with a pretty smile.

"Why do you cover up?" I would ask.

"Because women are diamonds. Their beauty is rare and it has to be hidden. You don't want people to steal them," they would say.

After I failed to defend my little brother, I began to detest this sacred feminine space. I figured that they, like me, wouldn't have grabbed the taller thief's neck so that my brother could lunge forward and retrieve his new Nikes, all because these women willingly separated themselves from the male world. Even at parties held in my family's apartment, men and women segregated themselves. As a young girl I had been privy to the inner workings of both spaces, traveling from the world of diapers and wedding plans to one of politics and current events, of the kind that would now make my Che-clad friends blush. I had preferred this male space. I could hang out with my brother, play with boys our age, and act like the older brother I felt my younger brother had wanted. I also found that I didn't like pretty things anymore because my brother didn't, and I wanted to be just like him, like my best friend, who I wasn't able to defend.

Sneakers were the only thing we splurged on; they made up for our K-mart wardrobes. As public school students, we adhered to a strict dress code of plain white shirts and dark slacks or skirts, but our sneakers could be as colorful as we liked. Unlike our clothes, sneakers spoke to who you were—Chucks if you were "emo" and didn't care for sports, Adidas if you played soccer, New Balance if you ran track, and if you were like me and played basketball, you wore the shoes of the city's pride and joy: Jordans.

I had bleach-white ones with an electric blue swoosh marked with "AIR" on the sides. They were Air Force Ones, like the Nelly song blowing up the airwaves at the time, and I loved them. I love them still. I bought the Jordans when I made the basketball team in sixth grade, and I kept them long after my feet had outgrown them, though the hot pavement of Green Briar's concrete courts had burned through their soles. The gangly brown girl racing up and down the court could be heard from anywhere, for only Jordans could make those magical squeaks. Classmates and teammates and crosstown rivals told me, "Dayum, you have some nice shoes." My choice of sneaks was my claim to fame.

I whiled away my days at school by wandering through the hallways on my frequent and extended "bathroom breaks." I couldn't stand to be in the classroom—looking at the clock, sitting behind the desk, copying definition after definition out of an American history textbook so tattered and marked I had duct-taped its spine and corners. The classroom was a bit of a war zone: your mother insulted, your hair pulled, your homework often stolen from your own desk. Teachers weren't there to teach history or literature or really anything worth learning; as they put it, they were there to "babysit" and give explanations for current events:

"Why did the terrorists attack us?"

"It's because they're jealous. They're jealous of our freedom."

"Why did they kill themselves?"

"Well, their religion tells them they would be rewarded in heaven for killing themselves."

Much of what I knew about my religion, and learning in general, came from my thrice-weekly lessons learning to read the Quran. On days I didn't have basketball practice, I would sound out the words and read entire stories in Arabic, despite not knowing the meaning. I loved the order and structure set by ustad-be, a teacher from India, who brandished a long and wooden stick that struck fear in my heart. She wouldn't even spare a quadriplegic when he read so softly that "Allah couldn't hear him." I would sound out "Allah's words" in a language I didn't understand, and get whacked for my mispronunciations and thus, my disrespect for Allah.

When 9/11 happened and the FBI descended on Devon Avenue, my family and I often heard stories of shops being raided, people being deported, of possible informants who might or might not have been in last

Friday's prayer. My dad, after watching a news special about the internment of Japanese-Americans after the bombing of Pearl Harbor, became wary of our situation. "That could happen to us," he would say.

Ustad-be never talked about such things. She instead encouraged us to keep learning about everything there was to know about anything. She would often say that a "life spent learning is the closest to God," and because I believed in Muslims like ustad-be, it pained me when she told me to wear shalwar khameez—modest, sub-continental female garb—to class instead of my Rocawear tracksuit. I obliged, but she scolded me on my choice of shoes: "Wear some nice chappals next time."

Chappals sucked. They were discreet, thin, and flimsy, shaping my toes into flat, slender points. There was no difference between right and left. They made me walk slow and measured. They were my corset. My beloved Jordans, however, fit the curvature of my feet; they were loud and large, and made me fast and fluid so I could jump. I ended up wearing the chappals out of respect for ustad-be, out of reverence for her.

When I turned twelve I was no longer allowed to wear shorts. I wore track pants instead. They were loud, an annoying swoosh in contrast to the magical squeaks of my Jordans, and they made me stick out because I was the only one wearing them; the only Muslim girl on the court. I found myself explaining why I had to wear the pants and getting into more fights on and off the court.

"I think I'm going to kill myself!" I once said after a frustrating first half.

"Yeah, you would, you people tend to do that. . ." said my opponent behind me.

I shoved her. She tried to slap me, but I grabbed her arms and pushed her to the floor. Her teammate grabbed my hair from behind, and before I knew it, I had started a full-on fight. I was suspended from playing the following two games, and I could not have cared less. I had finally fought back.

On the first day of eighth grade, a kid who had moved from Oklahoma two years earlier chose to sit next to me. At first I felt sorry for him and his drawl, the taunts he incurred for it, his lack of athleticism. He always carried a book around. *Leviathan* comes to mind, which I wouldn't touch until I was eighteen, so I doubt he understood it all at thirteen. He was smart and upbeat, though I found his poindexter glasses and questioning of me annoying:

"Why do you look so mad all the time?"

"Why is your hair always in a ponytail?"

"Can I have that picture you just drew?"

The boy from Oklahoma introduced me to the song that'll "change your life": "Rebel Girl." My music tastes up to that point were filled with the braggadocios of hip-hop, but this, this was something different. Kathleen Hanna sang with that guttural angst I wallowed in: "When she taaalks / I hear the revolutions / In her hiiips / There's revoluuutiooons. . ."

Sometime after introducing me to Bikini Kill, after I swapped my Jordans for Chucks, the boy from Oklahoma gave me my first kiss, and Green Briar Park was no longer a place that made me feel sorry for being a girl—it actually made me glad that I was one. At the time I had felt guilty because had my parents known, they might have disowned me, or worse, threatened to ship me back to India. But the kiss and his constant presence had turned Green Briar into a place of empowerment and defiance. It flew in the face of what was expected of me, that I would confine myself to the female space, never to reach out, feel, and actually touch the other side. It made me a sinner. For the first time in my life, I chose what aspects of Islam would apply to me, and in a funny way, I became a Muslim. That it was impossible to be wholly Muslim, or Indian, or even a girl, would seem to be conventional wisdom, but as a preteen indoctrinated in the absoluteness of all these things, it was a revelation.

West Ridge: Paan Stains and Discount Vegetables

STUTI SHARMA

A neighborhood still holding the tension of partition, West Ridge is a mix of all of the people—from the Jewish bakeries with their boxed cookies tied up in string, to the Mexican street cart vendors selling elotes, to the Pakistani sweet shops who make falooda green and creamy like I prefer, to the Indian daal and poori platters and dosa I choose for lunch, to the Ethiopian restaurant a mile or so away where Kenyan functions organize.

Western Unions are as necessary as pharmacies, as people congregate to send money back home or receive gifts from family. They are filled with a chorus of different languages. Once my mom, who immigrated to Nairobi from India when she was a teenager, picked out Swahili and had a joyous reunion with another fellow Kenyan. They sat to the side, by neon, blinking "Currency Exchange" signs, trading stories of friends, streets, shops, and churches they knew in the old country.

Gentrification hasn't yet taken hold in West Ridge. On Rockwell Street, there's a multicolored building that was supposed to be a parking facility and fancy shops underneath a condominium complex. Construction started the year before we moved out, and eight years later, it stands incomplete and boarded up.

When taking street photographs on a lazy September afternoon on Devon, I tried to capture the beauty of us all forming a community by celebrating our cultures. I'm most familiar with the South Asian portion of Devon Street, but I wanted to weave in the others who hold just as much right to this space.

Assimilation is not the order of this community; it resembles integration, which I treasure. I hope my words and pictures have shown you the rhythm and pace of West Ridge. I don't know which country claims me as an immigrant, but, as someone who grew up in it and later returned to work in a nonprofit with direct service to youth, this pocket of West Ridge has.

Fresh Farms has rows of almonds, pistachios, dried fruits, dates, olive oils, jams, and breads. The center of the store is a plaza of colors: greens of peppers and chard, purple of beets and eggplants, orange of papaya and persimmon, and brown of coconuts and potatoes. In the summertime, vendors stand outside with bundles of stalks of sugarcane they crush into juice with ginger. The store also has a fresh pressed juice bar, entirely run by locals.

Devon stores are well-stocked. Their eclectic inventory is reminiscent of small foreign convenience stores, with towers of cooking pots and pans, rows of luggage, cell phone cases, plastic combs, foreign snacks, rice bags, and cheap but quaint crockery.

Albany Park:
Edge Zone Chicago

BENJAMIN VAN LOON

I once heard a man call Albany Park the United Nations. He meant it in a bad way, but he was from the suburbs, so as all Chicagoans know, his opinion couldn't be trusted.

Of course, he was partly right. Albany Park, a neighborhood of around 52,000 on Chicago's Far Northwest Side, is one of the most ethnically diverse ZIP codes in the US, home to thousands of foreign-born residents from Mexico, Guatemala, Ecuador, the Philippines, India, Cambodia, Somalia, the former Yugoslavia (Serbia, Croatia, Bosnia), Romania, Pakistan, Iraq, Iran, and Lebanon. More than forty languages are spoken at its more than twenty public and private schools, and the stretch of Bryn Mawr Avenue between Kedzie and Kimball is Chicago's officially unofficial Koreatown.

In other words, as shorthand for cultural diversity, Albany Park-as-UN works. But that's where the similarities stop. Life in working-class Albany Park is about making it in Chicago. That's certainly what brought me to the neighborhood. It's home to two universities—one private (well-intentioned, but functionally insular) and one public (one of the most diverse public colleges in the US) and more than a dozen parks. There are residential blocks lined with apartments, bungalows, a few aging mansions, and corridors lined with small- and medium-sized businesses. It is home to some of the best Middle Eastern and Mexican restaurants in the city, as well as Marie's Pizza—Albany Park's second-best-kept secret—a restaurant tucked behind a liquor store, with red vinyl booths, dim lighting, and jazz nights straight out of a David Lynch film.

Because Albany Park sits so far northwest, at the terminus of the Brown Line—one of the CTA's more underutilized vehicles—it's not a neighborhood many Chicagoans know. It's too spread out, too polylinguistic, and too unexciting to be gentrified, which is why it has worked so well for so long, and why you can experience a range of food, culture, and especially nature that you'd otherwise never see in the city.

Take Ronan Park, at 3000 W. Argyle. Not much happens there. There's a running track, a soccer field, and the occasional smell of marijuana.

Most people know it as the home of one of Chicago's only waterfalls. It's manmade, but it's the best word to describe the six-foot-high concrete spillway where the North Branch of the Chicago River, still following its natural curves, dumps into the unnaturally linear North Shore Channel. If you were in a boat and headed north on the channel, you'd paddle past a slow succession of increasingly large and expensive backyards before ending up in Lake Michigan in nearby Wilmette. If you went south, you'd eventually end up in the Loop.

But the North Branch itself is an atavism from an earlier Chicago. In planning lingo, it's an Edge Zone; one of the few places where the city and nature still meet and blend, and where you're able to see, up close, how the river shaped—and continues to shape—Chicago.

Perhaps it was along places like the North Branch where the city's "stinky onions," or what the native people called (and the original French settlers transliterated as) *shikako*, once grew. When you look at the river, humming and swelling behind restaurants and repair shops and single-family homes, you can imagine the original prairie, spotted with wildflowers and maple groves, watered and whetted at the marshy riverbanks.

It was this pastoral scene that first attracted non-native settlers to the area, then part of Jefferson Township, in 1855. Immigrant Germans and Swedes brought their old-land agriculture and community to the area, and despite the business, progress, and murder happening in nascent Chicago nine miles south, the township remained in a bucolic bubble until it was politically subsumed in 1889, as city politicians sought ways to inflate the city's population and force a successful bid for the 1893 World's Fair.

The fair and associated gerrymandering led to an exponential population boom in Chicago, which doubled from 1.1 million to 2.2 million people between 1890 and 1910. The city's infrastructure was still weak and ad hoc, and the river, which was then dumping into Lake Michigan and Chicago's water supply, was mostly used as a toilet, leading to sickness and shortened lifespans.

Chicago's solution, famously, was to reverse the river. Between 1892 and 1889, engineers dug the new Sanitary and Ship Canal (SSC) on Chicago's South Side, effectively redirecting the city's flotsam twenty-eight miles down the SSC to the Des Plaines River, which eventually connects to the Illinois River and, finally, the Mississippi—a bona fide American solution.

While the toilet was getting flushed down south, engineers dug the North Shore Channel between 1907 and 1910 to complement the river reversal and raise water levels. The North Branch remained unaffected, except for the spillway at Ronan Park. If you follow the North Branch northwest through Albany Park, against the natural current, you'll find only a few areas of exposed riverbank, most accessible only by trespassing. But even if you were to risk the $250 fine, you wouldn't find much aside from the debris of teenage debauchery and graffitied professions of everlasting love.

When the North Branch finally meets Pulaski Road at the intersection of Foster Avenue and Pulaski, it forms the centerpiece of Gompers Park, a thirty-nine-acre park with crushed gravel paths and rainwater lagoons. But the river soon goes under Foster, passing through the north side of Gompers before disappearing into the woods, ultimately falling out of sight and out of mind.

Beyond Gompers, you'll find the LaBagh Woods—Albany Park's first-best-kept secret. Sprawling 600 wild acres, the woods are officially part of the Forest Preserve District of Cook County. The FPD has cut a few small groves and shaded picnic areas in the woods, but due to their proximity to the highway and relative isolation from the rest of the city, the public areas are underutilized—which makes LaBagh a great place to get away while still being in the city, and a forgotten but important chapter in the history of conservation in Chicago.

At the turn of the twentieth century, as the Northwest Side of the city continued to grow, the woods (yet unnamed) were starting to shrink, but the State of Illinois had no official mechanisms for conservation, so the onus fell on the public conscience. In 1901, Ella LaBagh, a Chicago resident and active member of the Irving Park Women's Association (est. 1888), was riding her bike along the North Branch and grieved at the continued destruction of the forest. Through photography, public speeches, and grassroots campaigning, she led a coordinated effort that drove Illinois to form its Forest Preserve District in 1915, saving the woods along the North Branch in the process. In 1940, when LaBagh was ninety-five, the woods were finally named in her honor, and today a small monument at the edge of the woods preserves her legacy "as a pioneer in establishing forest preserves."

While LaBagh's name doesn't have Daley-level fame, she nonetheless left her mark on Chicago real estate. That's a win for conservationists, sticking it to the man in perpetuity. That the woods are there—rather than houses or highway—means something, if only as a glimpse into the world that would be. But they're an anomaly, too. Smattered with city scree, the woods aren't quite agrestal, and aren't quite urbane. They're their own thing.

The best way to enter the woods is from Bryn Mawr, on a bike. If you start at Ronan Park, you'll head north on Kedzie and go left down Bryn Mawr, through Koreatown, past Northeastern Illinois University, and past the sprawling Bohemian National Cemetery, the largest in the US.

The road ends a few blocks after you cross Pulaski, indicated by a Jersey barrier sheathed in yellow reflectors. In years past, this point would have marked the intersection of the Weber Spur, a former Union Pacific Railroad right-of-way and part of the Chicago and North Western lines. The spur was used from 1897 into the 1980s, but fell into abandonment, with the tracks finally getting pulled up around 2010. In their place, a twenty-foot-wide gravel scar cuts through the heart of the LaBagh woods. The shoulders of the spur, as they open up into oak and hickory forest, are lined with goldenrod, milkweed, and aster, with teasels and saxifrage intermingled amongst the stacks of moss-covered ties and sun-bleached city trash left to decompose or disappear into the oblivion of earth.

A few hundred yards down the spur, the woods surrounding you will darken and obscure the fact that you're in a city ZIP code. The forest diffuses the sounds of the highway, which lies just a few hundred yards to the west, and in place of this, there's a breeze ruffling through the treetops and the whistle of a passerine. But there are also moments of reminder, as when the spur bridges the North Branch. The railings of the bridge have been plucked and pilfered, and in the dry months of the year, you can look twenty-five feet down to the river below. The spans of the bridge are covered in years of graffiti. Broken bottles, condoms, and rusted cans of spray paint pepper the steep riverbanks.

Various paths spin off the spur and wander into the forest. Some of these are used by cyclists or hikers, others by pleasure seekers and midnight partiers. But a human sighting in LaBagh is rarer than an encounter with, say, a deer. These aren't the muscled deer of the north woods, but their more cunning, omnivorous cousins, who might snack just as well on a patch of clover as they would a soggy bag of Doritos.

The forest has the earthy smell of an older, pre-Chicago. One we'll never get to see, but you can sense it in the woods. Or maybe it's the woods that remember it; ancient viridian tissues still clinging to its polluted riverbanks, reflecting both the obstinacy of creation and the surety of change. If a white-tailed fawn dashes through one of the small bluejoint meadows in LaBagh, under the shade of a towering McDonald's billboard, is this a victory, a compromise, or just banal survival?

In many ways, the LaBagh Woods are a metaphor for what Albany

Park is to Chicago. The neighborhood sits on the grid which has historically so divided the city, but in spite of these engineered demarcations, it's one of the few places in Chicago—and America—that still paints a good picture of the melting pot that, in our current political reality, is increasingly and violently becoming relegated to a more historical, mystical American lore. In many ways, Albany Park is an anachronism, like a 600-acre wood in the city. It only makes sense if you can see it for yourself, though by being there, you change it. Is this a victory, a compromise, or just banal survival?

NORTHWEST SIDE

Portage Park:
Six Corners, Many Changes

JACKIE MANTEY

In 2013, Kanye West debuted his music video for "New Slaves" by screening it onto sixty-six buildings around the world.

One of those buildings was a Walgreen's in Wicker Park. Excited fans on Twitter started describing the projection, calling out its location on the "Six Corners" of Wicker Park.

That was a problem.

See, a Six Corners already existed in Chicago, and not in the sparkling Wicker area. With alarm, residents of sleepier, admittedly less hip Portage Park on the Northwest Side took to the internet to set things straight.

"Hey!" they practically shouted in unison. "Name's taken."

One visit to Portage Park's Six Corners and you can't really blame newcomers for not knowing about it.

The shopping district is so named because it's a six-point intersection of Milwaukee, Cicero, and Irving Park Roads. Headlining from this Six Corners today are the following: an abandoned-looking Six Corners Plaza, a Sprint outlet, a Vitamin Shoppe, a Mattress Firm, a shuttered Sears, and a pit of mud that's a development that's sputtered and stalled, sputtered and stalled again.

The same year as the music video brouhaha, a team developed a master plan to help breathe life back into the place. It included recommendations for improving the mixed-use shopping available, making more public spaces where people would want to hang out, building on the nearby historic Portage Theater as a mainstay for entertainment, and making it a more pedestrian- and bike-friendly environment.

Several years after the fact and it's difficult to spot any of that. In short, there's nothing seemingly worth the ride out here.

I do, though, ride out to Portage Park a lot.

It started when I had to head westward from our new apartment in neighboring Irving Park to get to the nearest Chicago Public Library branch. On one of my visits, a fellow book lover told me about City Newsstand and Café, located on Cicero Avenue's forearm of Six Corners.

City Newsstand and Café is a cozy shop, its original neon sign beckoning, with a coffee counter, homemade chocolate truffles for sale, small tables for typing out the next great American novel, a smaller space near the street-facing windows where visiting musicians often play, and—drumroll please—the largest selection of print magazines in Chicago.

Owner Joe Angelastri bought the place in 1978, when he was eighteen years old and when City Newsstand was just a traditional outdoor newsstand on the now-Sprint tip of Six Corners.

Calling it "just a newsstand" is a bit misleading. It was a destination for many, including some of Angelastri's high school friends who, he says, "would come to the newsstand to hang out to see the girls who were coming to shop."

That's because Portage Park's Six Corners was once a hot destination itself. Though the neighborhood struggles to define itself today among Chicago's seventy-six others (beyond being where the Smashing Pumpkins played their first show), it was once *the* place to go shopping outside of the Loop. People would come from all over to visit Portage Park, shop its Sears, and watch a movie at its theater.

Angelastri's newsstand on the corner was a popular place for area residents, too. A beat cop could often be found there, as well as a slim jim tool, which saw a lot of action jimmying open car doors when keys were accidentally locked behind them.

"I liked the people and the excitement of the newsstand," Angelastri says. "Back in those days, there were papers coming in all day long. Even then people were talking about the decline of newspapers."

As we all know too well, decline they did, but City Newsstand found ways to survive. In 2000, it moved into its current indoors Six Corners location and Angelastri's growing team took over another legacy newsstand in Evanston.

Some of the regulars still get their news here. With 200 feet of magazine racks hosting 5,200 titles, newbies make their way to Cicero Avenue, too. Visitors have come from as far away as Iowa and Wisconsin to shop its selection.

"We kept the newsstand open until 2000, but trends kept going away from newspapers, so we went real big into magazines," he says. "Then smartphones came out. Now the magazines are under a lot of pressure."

So the store kept reinventing itself, adding more books and café entertainment. The shop is a stop for local musicians to play, including blues legend Lurrie Bell, who lives nearby and became a regular after coming to the store to get a music magazine that had written about his work.

"We were really optimistic at one point, where we thought the neighborhood was going to explode. It's a little bit sad to see it didn't turn out as we first expected, but there's a lot of new energy and ideas," Angelastri says, adding that though the neighborhood could be overlooked as a place to launch a business, it shouldn't be. "It's a good neighborhood, and you're going to get very dedicated people. That's going to get you through the rough times."

Portage Park is remarkable for its accessible real estate in a city where affordable, safe, and spacious housing is scarce. It was one of four West Side neighborhoods in *Chicago Magazine*'s 2018 roundup of best places to live in the city and was applauded for its "terrific housing deals for first-time homebuyers."

I've lived in Chicago for three years now, and most of the people I meet weren't born here and didn't grow up here. That's a common story for this city. Many of Portage Park's settlers were immigrants from Poland. Then as now, Portage Park was a place where working-class homeownership might be possible. Sixty percent of all families in the Portage Park area owned their own home in 1920, compared to only 25 percent throughout the rest of Chicago. The immigrants headed here for the churches, to be near neighbors and family from the old country, and to leave the suffocating, densely populated downtown for more rural living.

But, rural no more, Portage Park has seen its Polish population plummet. Between 2000 and 2016, around 41 percent had left the neighborhood. Many moved to more suburban areas for varied reasons, schools being one of the more prominent.

New people like me are moving in and taking their place. I grew up on a dairy farm in a small town in Marion, Ohio. I moved to Chicago so my husband could further pursue his career in comedy, and we mostly hang out with writer, designer, artist, comedian types from the city's growing creative class. We came to big cities like Chicago looking for jobs, higher salaries, culture, each other, and, dear God, anything else to do on a Friday night than the high school football game and Applebee's half-price happy hour.

But my family is still back in Ohio. My grandmother has Alzheimer's, which means she's suffering, confused about where she is and where she's been on a near minute-to-minute basis.

In a cruel twist of fate, everything in our world seems to be moving forward at rapid speed—everything except a cure for Alzheimer's. The most recent memory loss prevention drug was approved by the FDA a long fifteen-plus years ago. To watch a loved one regress to a state of child-like dependency and cognition is awful, especially for the people who counted on this adult to guide them through their own childhood.

I think it's a similarly surreal (though less personally painful) experience to watch a beloved place decline. In 1938, two years after my grandma was born, the Sears at Portage Park's Six Corners opened with great fanfare. Nearly 100,000 people came to see this exciting new spin on shopping. It was the five-floor future of American retail! Aw heck, the future of America! It even had air conditioning! And sprinklers! Escalators! Parking!

The location's life story soon paralleled what was happening in the country at large. The $1 million building featured an art moderne edifice to showcase the merchandise and was made out of, not brick or limestone, but monolithic concrete. The *Tribune* wrote about an "invasion" of tens of thousands of shoppers clamoring for Sears's shipment of war-scarce supplies during World War II. Later, as suburban malls grew in size and offering, Sears at Six Corners started to lose its all-star attraction traction.

So what does it mean when something like that metaphorically crumbles? It's a tangible marker that we've moved on, I guess. A reminder that nothing—not a landmark or a reputation or a culture or a business or a mind—can thrive forever.

Have you ever witnessed a department store closing?

It's a lot like letting go of a memory. It starts so slowly that you don't feel like it's really ever going to slip away. But then the barking, increasingly desperate warning signs crop up: "Store Closing Sale!" "NOTHING HELD BACK!" "Was it Betty or Alice who fancied Fred in primary school?" Until suddenly the whole thing is just a husk of what once meant a great deal to a great many people. The process of retreat feels like a lucid dream. Did that really even happen at all?

In the case of the last Sears in Chicago, the Sears in Portage Park, the announcement of its closing and its final sale would be months apart.

During that time, I visited often, amused at the emptying racks and strewn clothes (no need to fix it all at this point) and frantic customers and price cuts that plunged deeper and deeper as the door-closing deadline approached. They still couldn't seem to sell all that *stuff*, no matter how deeply prices got the ax.

On my last trip, I tried on some clothes in the changing room, which looked like the scene of a fresh looting, and thought about my grandma. One of my last memories of her was at a Sears or a JCPenney. I can't remember which, but these were two of her favorite places to go when we visited her Florida vacation trailer home. She bought me a sweater I liked. As her memories slip away, I'm sad that I can't hold on to more of them for her. Because at a certain point, that's all we can really give back to those who came before us.

The people of Portage Park expected this store's closing for some time. Things hadn't looked good for a while; the Chicago-based company was $1 billion in debt and the Six Corners land that Sears sat on was part of a sale-leaseback transaction three years before it closed. That deal gave a growth properties company, according to a Sears spokesman's statement at the time, the right to "recapture" the land if they wanted to do something else with it. (Interesting choice of words, considering the silver aluminum sculpture "Portage"—crafted by artist Ted Sitting Crow Garner—is an abstract depiction of a figure carrying a canoe on his back, a tribute to the Native Americans who traveled through Portage Park long before "'Merica" America was even a twinkle in Johnny Appleseed's hungry eyes.)

What will happen to the building that once represented so much to so many—expats and immigrants, locals and tourists alike? Will Six Corners recover its history as a hot neighborhood destination or redefine what a successful residential Chicago neighborhood looks like? It's all as uncertain as I am. About what will happen to my grandma. About whether my husband and I will buy a home in Portage Park and plant deeper roots here. About where our country is going and what my place in it will be.

There are some things I do know, though, as I wait for the 80 to scoop me up from the gritty Six Corners bus stop and deposit me at Independence Park a neighborhood away. In the Sears bag I'm carrying are some chocolate truffles from City News Café and carnage of the Sears closing: an electric blue skirt I found for 70 percent off, dangling from a rack half-toppled by the confused weight of left-behinds. One side of my lip turns up into a smile thinking about how my grandma would have appreciated the discount and hated the skirt.

Hermosa: Holy Hermosa

SARA SALGADO

On maps, the shape is graced by way of Bermuda Triangle—everyone lost
in here
Fullerton Avenue; hyped-up wormhole when the streetlights go dead
thanks to the city's very own ComEd

Everything is combusted into neon,
it's all heated—keep it heavy, not healthy like *carne asada* stationary in your
stomach
over coke as you do bus-runs from Ashland west
the others think it's unexplored
but when you hit your stop, you better pull the cord
Kostner
praying grandma doesn't call you *callejera*—

Can't mistake the coordinates con confusion
yes you may have visions gone pretty lucid
but your home isn't illusion

The crosswords of corners became a kaleidoscope I couldn't conquer
So it throbs still, sickly orange
I carry everything twisted from here
I burry everyone unknown and mystic here. I crow in the garden every
time I'm
allowed out & bellow in the hollow of my room like a wingless bird when
I'm not

Walt Disney was born here
My mother was born here

Article in the *Chicago Curb* called it "the little hood west of Logan Square"
do not think we are a product of the young yuppies land wasted
I play the gentrification game, count hipsters past Pulaski
"why can't I come over" that's what everyone's been asking

Sun Times headlines
"Boy. 16. Shot in Hermosa Neighborhood"
"Boy. 16. Shot in Hermosa Neighborhood"
Adam, I am sorry you are only "boy" now, I'm sorry your name was buried and
unknown and mystic—twisted under a sick neon, orange. Maybe that's the color you
shoulda worn so people could distinct the difference between animal and "boy."
Between Hunt and Hood. Maybe you are buried under Walt Disney's childhood home
here, maybe you are under the house like the Wicked Witch of the West, of the West, of
the West, little hood West

But reminds me again to say
Walt Disney was born here
Just a shame he took his American Dream come true with him

I'll bend you a new future Hermosa
the stories to justify your very name graced by Spanish prophecy
Beautiful
To make you whole,
finally.

Logan Square:
The Best Burger on
the Square

NICHOLAS WARD

The winter before I left Chicago I took a job waiting tables at Johnny's Grill in Logan Square. I'd just returned from a writing residency and my then-partner had been accepted at her preferred grad school. We'd be moving in August. I needed money. Fast.

When I interviewed, the restaurant had closed for a few days to open a mezcal bar next door; the cooler was shoved into the middle of the diner and plastic tarps covered the surfaces. This wasn't the Johnny's I remembered from my first years out of college. But the stools and Formica countertops all looked the same.

Afterwards, I met my friend Molly for coffee at Reno across the square. Reno, with its exposed brick and band posters, had once been Abril, a Mexican restaurant that closed about a decade prior. Both restaurants— Reno and the restaurant Reno used to be—looked out onto the Centennial Monument, a tall column with an eagle affixed to the top, that connected Logan and Kedzie Boulevards and thus formed the square. From the bank of windows, I could see the red Norwegian church and the "El" station recently beautified with a community garden and a neighborhood-approved wall of street art.

"You interviewed at Johnny's?" Molly asked. "I work for that company."

We sat the wooden community table while the restaurant transitioned from bagel sandwiches and Stumptown coffee to wood-fired pizzas and wine.

"They took over the space last year," she said. "I'll put in a good word."

Molly and I have been friends for over a decade. She and her husband lived on Richmond near Palmer Square, in a two-flat that he'd bought with a friend. I'd moved into my girlfriend's apartment in Pilsen the previous summer.

"I'm not that excited to come up here," I said. "It's so different from even a year ago."

Molly made a loud guffaw. "I was drunk with Malachy last night, yelling about it on our walk home. 'These damn interlopers!' I said."

I nodded in agreement. I didn't remind Molly that we were interlopers, too.

Though her family's roots are old-school Irish Chicago and her husband was raised in Edgewater, Molly is from outside Minneapolis. I'm from suburban Detroit. After college, in 2004, my friends and I moved to Chicago, where we found cheap rent in a brownstone on tree-lined Spaulding Avenue in Logan Square. Our landlords, Miguel and Lenore, lived across the street.

I fell hard for my first neighborhood. I loved the way the boulevard exploded from under the Kennedy's viaduct, the stately graystones that lined the wide street. The live music on Saturdays at the Winds Cafe, the smell of fried plantains wafting across the bar. The cheap rundown movie theater on Milwaukee, where five bucks bought a ticket and a bag of popcorn. And Johnny's Grill, the quintessential greasy spoon, perfect for sopping up last night's booze. When the Art Institute of Chicago was promoting their Edward Hopper exhibit, they chose Johnny's as the iconic Chicago locale for a remix of "Nighthawks." Even though the diner was hopping on weekend mornings, the loneliness depicted in the picture felt prophetic.

I'm romanticizing my old Logan Square. My memory is filtered through the knowledge of what happened next. Most of the time I lived in Logan, I spent my free time elsewhere, in River North where I worked or Wicker Park, the hipster playground, or the bland Southport corridor where I auditioned for plays. After two years I moved to Roscoe Village. I'd given up my car and hadn't yet discovered biking. I was starting to audition for and act in plays, most of which were on the North Side. Years before technology allowed me to track the timing of buses, a trip to Sheil Park for an audition could take as little as twenty minutes or as long as an hour. Shortening that distance felt like a necessity.

In 2013, seven years after I left Logan Square, I moved back. According to census data, in the fourteen years between 2000 and 2014, the Latinx population in Logan had decreased by 35 percent while the white population had increased by 47 percent. The Winds Café, once owned by Black Caribbean neighborhood residents, had been transformed into Longman and Eagle, a Michelin-star pig and whiskey joint run by a "concept and project development studio" called Land and Sea Dept. The

Logan Theater now served craft beer. A developer named M. Fishman was buying up properties and leveraging old tenants to move at an alarming rate. Not all of the changes were being made at the hands of mustache-twirling developers and new middle-class residents who wanted to remake the neighborhood in their image. The Logan Square Preservation Society has existed since at least the mid-eighties and their effort to preserve the historic homes and aesthetics of the boulevards went a long way towards making Logan Square an attractive destination for artists priced out of Wicker Park, college graduates new to the city, restaurateurs looking for their next project, and the developers who followed.

My second era in Logan was marked by falling out of and then back in love. In the summer of 2013, I moved into one of those graystones along Logan Boulevard. My girlfriend and I took over a second-floor unit, still affordable on arts administrator salaries, where we strung lights across the back deck and hosted parties that lasted well into the night. That winter, after we broke up, I moved into a bungalow on a side street, with a dog and two housemates. Our landlord, a Polish lawyer originally from Pilsen, lived upstairs with his two cats. He never raised the rent. I fell in love again, with someone who lived in Pilsen. For almost a year, I was back and forth between Logan Square, the West Loop (where I worked), and Pilsen, stopping in Logan only to drink cheap beers from cold mugs at Helen's Two Way Lounge with my roommate, or watch my cat and her dog run around our apartment together.

Before, there were a handful of inexpensive food options, Mexican-run restaurants like Café con Leche, El Cid, and Puebla that had been in the neighborhood for years along with Lula Café, then a pioneer in its promotion of farm to table dining. Now there was L'Patron founded by alums of Rick Bayless's kitchens; Cellar Door Provisions, which sold the finest pastries in the neighborhood; and Bang Bang Pie, first run out of a home and now expanded to a brick and mortar shop. There were a bevy of craft cocktail bars (Billy Sunday, Scofflaw, Lost Lake) where once there had only been the Whistler. There were brewpubs and fine-dining restaurants and coffee roasters and it all just seemed too much. That I was complicit in the too-muchness was what I had to grapple with.

I thought I just happened to land in Logan Square when I moved to Chicago; that was where my roommates chose. I just happened to return at the height of gentrification; that was where my girlfriend lived. I didn't yet understand how easily I was able to bounce from one location to the next, the city my playground. As a middle-class, white newcomer, unwilling to live in the all-white neighborhoods at the city's perimeter and unable to afford the ones at its core, I had to ask myself: what kind of gentrifier do I want to be?

In 2014 Johnny's Grill closed. Nicholas Kalliantsis, the longtime owner, didn't want to leave, he said, but the owner of the building decided not to renew his lease. For longtime residents, it was one of the last remnants of the old days. The MegaMall had long closed, the Logan had been remodeled, the abandoned rail tracks that would become the 606 park were patrolled by cops. There is no one tipping point as a neighborhood changes. But the demise of Johnny's threatened to break the neighborhood open in the dreaded direction of Wicker Park and Bucktown, the lands of upscale retail and sports bars.

Element Collective, the restaurant/real estate group that Molly worked for, won a bidding war for the rights to the restaurant space on the corner of the square, the hottest real estate property in Chicago. The old Johnny's became the new Johnny's. They installed a female chef, a veteran of some of Chicago's best restaurants and an immigrant to boot, to take over, and they annexed Fleur, the flower shop next door, to open a mezcal bar that connected to the diner. And I got a job.

On my first morning, I followed one of the servers during a busy brunch while she explained the menu, flow, and layout. I met the head chef, who'd organized the menu around classic diner fare and favorites from her native Ireland. Over eighteen years in the industry, I'd never worked for a female chef before. I'd never worked in a restaurant where the kitchen was majority women. In an industry that did the same thing over and over again, it was refreshing to find something new.

At one point during that first service, a Saturday brunch, the chef asked me to get some potatoes from the downstairs prep area. "Go get 'em tiger," she said, whacking me on the ass with her towel. I stopped. I thought briefly about saying something. I thought about how it was my first day and I needed money. I got the potatoes.

When I came back up my trainer pulled me aside. "I just want to tell you that I saw what happened and that's not okay and we will deal with it," she said. Later, after the rush, the general manager came over and said, "I want you to know that I've spoken with [the chef] about it and that will not happen again. We want to make sure that you feel safe here."

Sarah and I are friends now and occasionally we'll joke about that moment. "Hey, remember when I smacked your ass on the first day you worked for me?"

"Yeah, that was really inappropriate," I always respond.

I wonder how many rounds of sexual harassment had she endured coming up. The way that the leadership of Johnny's handled that situation endeared me to them. So many other restaurants would let that slide.

From the moment Johnny's re-opened, there was attention. The media wrote about it in ways they never did when it was a greasy spoon. In February of 2016, the house burger started receiving outsize praise. Two thin patties finished with sea salt, gooey melted cheese, and mustard aioli, the *Chicago Tribune* compared it favorably to Au Cheval's burger, the most famous sandwich in the nation. *Chicago Magazine*, the *Chicago Reader*, and *Eater Chicago* all hyped the burger. The local host of an NBC show called "Hungry Hound" dropped by with a camera crew. That brought the suburban crowd, people driving in from an hour away to have a $9 burger at our neighborhood diner.

It was absurd, and also the best job I ever had. Perhaps it's because I knew that I was leaving. I can't deny the tension between what I liked about the new Johnny's and what it represented about this rapidly changing neighborhood. The prices were double what they'd once been. It wasn't uncommon for people to walk in, scoff, and head back out the door. It also wasn't uncommon for weekday mornings to see Latinx families, construction workers of all races, suburban whites, hipster theater kids, mothers with toddlers, and people who just needed a cup of coffee sitting side by side at the diner counter.

There was an easy rapport between the staff and guests and I liked that, after all my time waiting tables, I could break down the artifice that comes with restaurant work. None of that would save the neighborhood from gentrification. None of that would make it easier for the city's vulnerable communities to thrive. But in a hyper-segregated city, I cherished our small, integrated space.

I'd rise early, sometimes before dawn, my body aching, my mind blurry. Without showering, I'd hop on my bike. As the sun rose, I'd pedal from Pilsen, alongside streets and parking lots, through the medical district and on to the West Side, over the Eisenhower, past industrial warehouses and residential streets. The West Side was changing too, connecting the development of the West Loop to the early gentrifying stages of Garfield Park. I saw shiny condo buildings and white families with strollers in places I knew they'd not been for decades. I'd zip through Humboldt Park and remember when people—mostly middle-class white folks who'd moved to Chicago before me—had told me that it was dangerous, that I shouldn't go there. I'd scoffed at their casual racism but still rarely went. But now that neighborhood was transforming too, into something shinier but not greater, whiter but not safer. I wondered if the whole city was like this, everything changing, already changed, about to change, the whole city churning and shifting and dying and burning and building back up, and I loved it, sometimes more than I ever thought possible, more than I deserved, and certainly more than the city deserved itself. I couldn't actually believe that I was leaving, couldn't fathom what I'd do once I got to where I was going, and knowing somehow that I was doomed from the jump, that I'd always want to come back to the only place I ever really thought to call home.

I did return to Chicago, a year after I left. I didn't work at Johnny's or live in Logan Square. One visit told me all I needed to know: it had slowed down. The shine had worn off. The customers weren't clamoring to get in and no local magazines were running adulatory reviews of the food, which was still very good. The media had moved on.

Johnny's closed again, for good, in the fall of 2017. The space on the corner of the square is now home to a swanky cocktail bar with long windows called Young American. Inside I can see shadows of Johnny's and the mezcaleria. A big open space with neon lighting, the new bar sticks out in the neighborhood, incongruous for those of who knew what it once looked like. But in five years, will anyone remember? In five years, Young American may well look like it's been there forever.

Wicker Park:
milwaukee avenue

KEVIN COVAL

it's Algren's triangle
called the Polish square
at Milwaukee, Ashland and Division
where there's a fountain that calls pigeons
by the hundreds to swoop and circle
and shit. hear the *quips and players*° gather.
men with metal in carts replaced by fruits
from a farmer's market. we huddled
here after Ferguson to stomp on electric
boxes and circle, cipher and song. across
from the Chopin where the old Guild Complex
lived in the basement. where i learned at the side
of Luis Rodriguez and the books he published
on Tia Chucha, that i stole when i worked the door
of a reading, where i saw Li Young Lee stop a room
from breathing and Dennis Kim keep an audience
living. the blue line and the Ashland 9, the division
street 70. all sure ways of travel at the six way
where no business used to be unless it was illcit:
prostitutes and junkies and furniture stores
who let you lay away. there was a big Kmart
where i bought socks in a surprise winter rain.
the wig shop is still here. there are green condos
and premium sneaker stores. there is so much new
i don't remember all that used to be on The Avenue
i used to walk damn near daily *my heart will break
thru causalness and appear in windows.* here are californian
imports from the nonprofit industrial complex. a slew
of potbellies and pet supply chain stores. the ark thrift shop
is there and old ladies in all white shopping for new dresses.

you can still get hit by a car or a bicyclist or someone moving
furniture. there is always someone moving, quickly, without warning
the whole city moves forward as a flame. fire and fire and fire again.

the jewel is there but no blockbuster, no video store
no way to bring entertainment into your home
unless comcast, unless monthly fees again, ad infinitum
always a way to drain the working. but there is still a man
who steps slow with a cane on The Avenue
but now there are white women in spandex jogging
around him, almost spinning his hat off, knocking him over.
men with beer bellies and dogs on leashes
walking dogs on leashes at 419 in the afternoon
do nothing to help the man, who seems lost
and here forever. there are taco shops
and massage clinics. all the while
the Avenue traced by the shadow of the blue
line slinking behind furniture stores empty
waiting on some remodel. store fronts still
ghost 20 years later. and I still have no money
to buy something 20 years later. *i scintillate like a glass of ice*
nervous when the late run of August comes, when i count
pennies and cans in the cupboard. all that has not changed.
still the city of a story of suckers and those with a savings account.
the bright primary colored block letters of the central furniture mart
name brand appliance store has never been buffed. they still say
they take credit. Harold's Chicken Shack #36 is next to Columbus's Curry
whatever that means. some horrible joke that is a perfect commentary
on colonialism. something Fanon would site. there's a cheesy pub and grub
coming. other corporate interests. outsiders and outside money.

you will say i am supernatural
at Wood Street when i'd sit on a bucket
the ones boys turn upside down to drum
and watch crews battle for an entire weekend
on murals with letters on the viaduct at the Walgreens.
all sponsored by the CTA, like some dream we had.
Hebru Brantley's wall flying, despite the removal
of Black men. there are still black girls in African dresses

looking for a deal on fly jewelry. there are mixed couples
and Queer folk still, though the avenue is so straight
now. I know, it's right here; 1414, 1418, 1420 where the loft parties
raged and it was house music and hip-hop and the dawn
of drum and bass, a Danny the Wildchild aberration, mashed
up dub and Method Man snippets over beats so quick we needed
speed to keep up. Brother Mike had a loft here on the south
side of the Avenue. a house artists squatting, dry wall rooms
erected, mattresses on the floor, the floor the length
of a six flat. he threw parties and open mics with food
and innocence and incense and drink and song.

it wasn't so white, so few white people I knew
i was one, of a few, on the Avenue, at the time
at least, a few, of the ones, i could see, who would come
out into the day, the opposite of vampires, and stroll
and look for work or work on the Avenue
at one of the new bars or restaurants i waited
tables at. the ones, the whites inside were gutting
and flipping and selling out from the under
the people. whites more like moles who'd burrow
beneath. i didn't know all that at the time
i remember i felt at that moment i'd made it.
a clear and different trajectory to a life
and neighborhood, mixed and in the mix
my life, like the people, an art of the everyday grind
to make and stay making regardless of cost or cot
you might have to live on, a choice and commitment
to making and making it. and now whites run
down the Avenue free. we walk dogs and pick up
dry cleaning at The Hollywood Cleaners, always there
but the Silver Room is no longer the Silver Room.
Eric packed up, and took his storefront party south.
the nail in a coffin, the straw on a camel sinking in
a vanilla dump. the damn near, the tidal wave soon
and wealthy and homogenous and boring but in the back
Max Sansing's faces scar in war paint, hero ghosts of who
and what was once   here.

                                    Black men hustle

still, got buckets of water and elongated polls to clean
windows for a few dollars. the men are still all Black
collecting street tax in 7-11 cups and devising survival
strategies. for how long, i walked up and down the Avenue
witness to the need of Black men, always Black men.
there was once a woman who had a family
sleeping in an abandoned bus beneath the blue line
under the monster of iron. Trina open her shop, close
a women's massage beauty parlor, Itch DJ'ed.
the Avenue was dirty, seething. now everything's
manicured, even the vintage stores are conglomerates
the stores like the Avenue with less and less gems.

but ah, the park!   peeks out at Honore   like a toe
or promise. the park where *all beautiful things*
become real on wednesday. the many women i walked with
and the more many times and i entered lonely, with a bottle
a brown bag glass holder of 22 ounces. the park i will come to...
but Rodan is here for now and all the DJs: Jesse De La Pena,
Pickle, smoking bidis and cloves outside a new club
the day it opened we loved paying, playing the opening
dipping to Slick's after. all the many times i've been
to an opening and closing along the Avenue
a store, an idea, a life, a body
of work, some work, somewhere
some one once worked

all the weird art parties above Lubinski Furniture
run by SAIC students. *it seemed there was no one there*
but children. odd weird drug parties filled with bad art
and white students and maybe Korean international
exchange students. there is only so much mumble cut
video performance experiences one can stomach. oh white
people, what luxury, what false hope knowing what will be.
there is no courage in that, no experimentation. whiteness
is a retention of everything. everything and nothing
to worry, that is why the art is bad and predictably
abstract for an audience of friends who also paid
were able to pay for, to manufacture, manufactured
fine bad art.

the mail still comes even in the rain. the garbage
still gets picked up even in the rain. wicker park
a testament to the lack of taste and preference
for garbage and the dollar. the flat iron building
has studios artists are able to afford, the rent
paid for in art fairs where those who can afford
to decorate, to match a crate and barrel couch
or photograph a child or wedding or dog patron
and patronize the idea of art not the artists who make
the culture and city and Avenue a new. in the rain
an assault of capital, american apparel provatives, vice
magazines, high noon saloons and whiskey rivers.

i want myopic to stay open forever and all night
so i can find Maude Martha with an inscription
from Gwen or a hard copy of Cornelius Eady's Brutal
Imagination. where saul williams is jumping in the stacks
waiting for something to fall from the shelves, open to a page
and the possibility of the magic around you. upstairs
Paolo Javier is giving lessons on 21st century pidgins
which sound like a future tongue everyone talks.
i want to kiss you on the first floor, in the back
near Marquez, Melville and Morrison.

at the Blue Note, Idris will always be getting on
the mic, cuttin heads and chops. Shadow Master
hosts and Alo, is somewhere close in a basement
with a blunt, trying to produce a life for his daughter
10 years before his time. the city's DJ Premiere too
few heads ever heard, when no one was listening.

Square One gave us space to gather and juice
before it was a fad and too expense for the working
to eat fruit and vegetables. where Doc Lee got out
her car with a driver and into a cipher and city
and its class structure shook or at least created
a class kids could take at college that could look
and sound more like they do and did that night.
the double door might go all-ages. might be

a space again for something regular, anything
that is not a riot fest poster for white people
who go to riot fest, something that honors
the origin of the music that was stolen
like the land and the land again.

and i must express the science of legendary elegies
YO mama's cafe and its owner, a painter, in a jump suit
in rollerskates, with tiny twists in his hair, in a gas mask
preparing for the coming armageddon, a foretelling
of the incursion with its decadent brunches on the horizon
all the hollindaze soon poured over easy free range mimosas.

Sharkula is forever
passing out flyers and asking if you like hip-hop
slanging his *Martin Luther King Jr. Whopper with Cheese°* tape.
he's one of the last relics on the Avenue whose got any hustle
left, grinding in bones, backpack and boots. get up and go
get the cheddar, the dollar, the guap, the cream
cheese lite but he is there standing, somewhere
near the 6-way surviving.

the all-night corner store is now a smoke-
shop, a Ramen furious spoon fad, whim of the white
tongue. the people used to cut through on the North
Ave side and step back out on Milwaukee. a bypass
where the Muslim brothers inside would sell you liquor
and hold folks down if they were short a dollar.
they knew our names, would say *As Salamu Alaykum*
have their mother's baklava at the counter and allow
you   to   wait   on   the   bus   if   the   hawk   was   coming   down
or the heat or beef, if you had to hole up or hide.

i think of Crystal and her twin
that Lamon introduced me to at the parties
they'd throw over the bank when it was still a bank
a singular bank, for locals in the neighborhood.
it' have lollipops and small business loans
it'd have a Spanish speaker or four. above

in rooms and rooms the twins made into boudoirs
and parlors to mess with your senses and sense
of time. a scene with scenesters and tricksters
a milieu of characters playing their part perfect:
tweakers, dealers, pretty boys and their boys,
a melange of models stuck in the midwest, land
locked artists hoping for a coast, an industry
to feed them. the bank is an Italian restaurant
a Mia Francesca's offshoot sister brunch spot

                                        again

but the six way all i think of and where
i think of all the possibilities. i think of the carnival
the Elastic crew and Stefon organized
when they lived in the church on Cortland
off the boulevard in Humboldt. i think of Sam I Am
the impresario rapper, six-ring leader. we used to
run the new city intersection every Friday night.
a Shabbat in the crown of the work week, a way
to announce the weekend. we were oddities
a freak show inside the show at the circus. each friday
before 10pm we'd move into the streets, sometimes
off a train, sometimes out a car, a cab Paully drove.
dancers, pantomines, contact improvisers, bucket boys
hornplayers, polaroid portraitists, kissing booth hosts
a revolving army, Stefon led like a general, each week
rotating in and out of streets that were packed with mobs
bar hoppers, new comers and those who might come.
The Avenue was avant-garde and pedestrian, pedestrians
by the hundreds. we'd wait for the clock on the bank
that is now a walgreens on the northwest corner
of the Avenue and Damen to strike ten and then
for ten minutes we'd put on a guerrilla variety show
a gathering of all the artists and one-trick ponies, anybody
with a talent, novices and highly trained artists, musicians
in the top of their form and field. every week we'd meet
and perform and after gather back at the church or Anna's
on North above a Colombian restaurant that is Handle Bar
that used to move weight and white before patrons and tofu.

a ritual and community formed around these friday circuses.
regular for the months (maybe year? longer?). we just showed
up and kept making a show. something about Chicago art
will teach you that. to show up and make. at the small island
of concrete at Damon south of North on the east side i would
type on top of a Chicago Tribune box composing wildly off top
banging at the keys and at my mind. sometimes in a suit
my finest garments to greet the Sabbath bride and sometimes
in a ridiculous get up, a thrift store concoction, Gemma, Stefon's girl
designed. we committed for the moment, to the moment, to the idea

to the Avenue.
i used to hop on and hop off the train at 1558 N. Damen Ave. stalk the
alley
looking for graffiti, for a new DZINE mural. i'd meet the train and ride
looking for blue line kings, seeing who was out and up. and sometimes
most times, i'd just post on the corner's concrete stoop, the throne
of The Avenue at Damen and North right where the Starbucks came
you could sit there and watch for hours. i'd record and drink
and witness the comings and goings of a wednesday and how it was
more rambunctious than a sunday, the little subtleties of how a corner
altered weekly, daily. i'd listen and write and think and be lonely
when i was ok with being lonely, a lonely i must return to. then
i'd walk to the park, always to the park, to see if i could see anyone
i knew although I didn't know anyone but i thought if i did they might
be going to the park.

Wicker Park est. 1871

a Burnham plan, for real. each neighborhood had green, you didn't have to
Central Park. every hood could have a patch, a place poor people could
swing
and sit in grass, before the wood chips, fiberglass protective playground
when it was enough to just have trees and a few inches of land to lie in or sit
right. near where the night ministry bus comes in service and gives to those
who need a dose, a check up, a test, some food or some juice, late night
lemonade or methadone or clean needles. the Fieldhouse is here still, open
to some games inside. on the court outside, i used to run, but i didn't come
for sport. i'd come to sit. i walked here high, maybe drunk, maybe off
three pills. i'd look, the pigeons were my friends and the fountain was
empty.

there's no water there. Mario once hosted a reading, the summer Bonafide
lived with me, and Alicia moved back to Jersey and Amanda was coming
home
after she was assaulted on campus. and Roxy, beautiful Roxy, was there
the starlet of the micro-cosmos, the applebottom jean of every man's eye
a Puerto Rican Princess from the neighborhood, who still lived in the
neighborhood
and was being forced to move from the neighborhood, whose brother
negotiated
a conversation for my father when the Latin Kings came to kill him, who
was just
himself out of prison and used to do security work for one of the generals,
before
daley tried to wipe out the gangs, when crack houses were homes slumlords
let dealers move into and out of. there is still no water in the park. the
benches
are bare, ghost. chessboards homeless men used to drag all their wares to
gone.
they'd play the day away sharpening their minds for the night, the long
night
ahead. the park is cleaner now, i guess. there is still the great green space.
some
throw a frisbee, some lie down and sun, some sleep now and gather under
trees
for shelter, for meal. there is now a dog run in the acute angle of the
southeast side
of the park. it smells like shit. all the owners are white.

the park that ends at Schiller
is one block from Greenview
where Nelson Algren used to live
at 1958, around the same years
for almost two decades. the door
reads 97 in stained glass. he lived
on the third floor and recorded
the characters in the neighborhood
the denizens few seemed to see
or give a fuck about. he walked
and watched and wrote here

black ribbon on the typewriter
about the man with the golden arm.

Algren, who wrote the city constant
love letters but it never wrote him back.

there is a sign, the city, the history
museum or historical society made
a marker to this small monument
in the new city, in this new neighborhood
unrecognizable and ethnically cleansed.

Algren is buried elsewhere, in new york
of course. he died in exile and never wanted
to come back to the city/neighborhood/country
Avenue that broke his heart and all its promises.

august 2015

Humboldt Park: Along Pulaski Road, from Irving Park to Humboldt

ALEX V. HERNANDEZ

By the time I got there my father had already picked up a barstool. He had swung it out in front of him with the legs facing away, like a lion tamer. The barstool kept the drunk's knife slashes at a reasonable distance. The other barflies, once they noticed the argument had escalated into an attempted stabbing, cowered at the far side of the bar, near the bathrooms, to watch.

My sister had hit the panic button under the cash register so police were on the way. But because it was a summer weekend in Humboldt Park, they weren't going to be there right away. So I picked up another stool and, following my father's example, joined in trying to corral the knife-wielding drunk. As I moved closer my father accidentally clipped me on the temple as he swung his stool in the scuffle. Slightly dazed, I was still able to help my father force the drunk into a corner, where my father deftly slammed the barstool against him once, knocking the wind from him, and then used the legs to pin him against the wall. He then yelled at me, his seventeen-year-old son, to help him pin the man there with our combined body weight until the police arrived.

Once the drunk was taken into custody, he wouldn't stop ranting about how he was going to kill my father for not letting him into a *quinceañera* he wasn't invited to. In my dad's statement to the cops he clarified that the parents who had paid for the *quinceañera* at his banquet hall were explicit in their instructions to not allow this man in because he'd cause a scene if he started drinking. In the twenty-five or so years that I spent working in Humboldt Park, this is the one and only time I ever felt scared.

My father, Carlos Hernandez, entered into an agreement to purchase the property at 1536 N. Pulaski Road from Efrain Bedolla in the late 1990s. At the time he had been working as a manager at Armanetti Fine Wines and Liquors near the intersection of Grand and Western. But my father, an immigrant from Mexico, had always had big dreams and even bigger ambitions. So in 1992 he convinced my mother, Dolores Hernandez, to use their savings to purchase a commercial property at 4111 W. North Avenue. The way he pitched it to her was that my sister and I would be able to one day take over the property.

"Vieja, I don't want them to have to work for anyone. I want them to be their own bosses," he said. "¿Qué piensas?"

My mother is as ill-disposed to risk as my father is enticed by it. She's a nurse and didn't like the idea of using our family's hard earned savings on a property in Humboldt Park's struggling commercial district. However, the idea of my sister and I being financially independent landlords after she died was too attractive to pass up. And it would be my father's ambition and desire to leave something behind for my sister and I that led my father to quit his job at Armanetti and dive head first into Chicago's volatile hospitality industry.

One of the first things my dad did once he took over the restaurant from Bedolla was name it Don Carlos Bar and Banquet Hall. "Don" is a Spanish honorific—the equivalent English appellation would be "Sir"—but people who knew my dad from his business, but only spoke English, always called him "Don" because they assumed his first name was Donald. When I was born my parents were living in Chicago Lawn. But after my sister was born we moved to the Irving Park neighborhood on the North Side. As a ten-year-old, the three and a half mile drive south to the restaurant seemed like an eternity. I remember my sister and I looking out the window of my mother's red minivan as we drove down there.

"I thought we were all the way on the South Side because Pulaski has this tendency of having a lot of traffic," my sister Michelle says now.

As the neighborhood changed from Irving Park to Humboldt, we saw fewer white people and more black and Hispanic people. The streets had more refuse on them and we saw more graffiti. Buildings had bars on their windows and doors. Homes had wrought-iron fences around their yards. There were more police cars on patrol and the officers inside didn't look friendly. In Irving Park, my sister and I were accustomed to riding our bicycles around with our friends unsupervised. What we were watching unfold before us was the systemic segregation and income inequity of neighborhoods like Irving Park and Humboldt Park. But as a child I didn't have the vocabulary to fully grasp how race, gender, and the location where someone grows up can have a huge impact on the opportunities they're afforded in life as an adult.

My mother has always wanted the family to do things together and the restaurant wasn't going to change that. After we got out of school and she got home from work, she would drive us to the restaurant so we could all work alongside my father. Monday through Friday after school and all day on Saturday we would be at the restaurant. My sister was trained by the waitstaff, and once she could balance five plates on her arms, she wore her roller blades as she served our patrons' food. I was trained in the kitchen and by the time I was a sophomore in high school, I was cooking a four-course dinner every Saturday for banquet parties of 200 or 300 people.

"It was a nice, close knit group of people inside Don Carlos. Outside the restaurant's doors anything was game," says Michelle. "But even then I felt like something bad was less likely to happen. Especially because we had a father who was very outspoken and would just blatantly yell at you if you were being a jerk. But he also went out of his way to help out regulars and friends in the neighborhood. I think that carried a lot weight with the people who knew him from Humboldt Park."

My sister and I worked at the restaurant until we finished college. And over the years we also got our high school and college friends after-school jobs there. We grew up in Humboldt just as much as we did in Irving Park. I met, worked alongside, and made friends with people from Humboldt Park at a very early age and was fortunate to quickly understand how ignorant people from Chicago's more affluent, often white, areas can be when they demonize a neighborhood like Humboldt Park and its residents without once ever really setting foot there.

Long before my father purchased the restaurant, its interior had already gone through many changes. It initially opened its doors as the New Apollo Theater in 1914, and the New Apollo name can still be seen on the ornamentation that sits above the Don Carlos mural on the facade. William A. Bennett designed the building and it was built on top of the site of the Old Olympic Theater, which was originally built by Peter Nasiopulos, John Ahamnos, and A. K. Kalodimos. When the New Apollo first opened it had a seating capacity of 1,136.

On weekdays, when I would sit in a restaurant booth and do homework, I would often look out the window at the building across the street from Don Carlos. When I was a child it was called the Pioneer Bowl and had thirty-five billiards tables in its pool hall and bowling lanes on the second floor.

Initially known as the Pioneer Arcade, it was named after the large Pioneer Trust and Savings Bank building which opened in 1913 at the corner of North and Pulaski. Designed by Danish-born architect Jens J. Jensen in 1925, the Arcade building is a beautifully ornate example of the Spanish Colonial Revival style popular during the twenties. It's one of Chicago's largest surviving buildings from that era and for over eighty years was home to some of the largest neighborhood and citywide "beer league" bowling tournaments. Around the start of the new millennium it closed down and, like the bank it's named after, is currently boarded up and more or less abandoned by its current owners.

My father's restaurant would soon follow Pioneer into boarded-up abandonment after my family lost it in 2012 to Plaza Bank. The Great Recession took away the family business, and our dreams of self-sufficiency, and in 2015 cancer took away my father. But when he was still alive and we still had the business, my father allowed my sister, my two best friends (Ricky Velez and Nick Barnes), and myself a chance to book rock shows in the hall.

We were just about to finish college at the time and had the idea of taking the name of our old high school punk band, Crimzon Spider, and using it to rebrand the banquet hall on Thursday nights as a rock venue. We knew it'd be an uphill battle because, while Michelle and I had a lot of experience in the Hispanic bar and banquet hall market, we knew nothing about booking live music shows and attracting a millennial audience to Humboldt Park.

The last time we'd invited our high school peers, their parents, and alumni to a fundraiser for Luther High School North's drama club at Don Carlos, we had a lot of parents express concern over the choice of venue. Most of them were from Portage Park and adjacent neighborhoods, and the only thing they knew about Humboldt Park was that it was "dangerous."

"Some of the Luther North alumni that were now part of the Chicago Police Department, when they came to the restaurant, were shocked," Michelle remembers. "They said they needed to come into Don Carlos with their own eyes in order to make sure that it was actually run by the family of two of the kids that go to Luther North."

We started Crimzon Spider about five years after the Luther North fundraiser. Up to that point our regulars were mainly older Mexican and Puerto Rican men who loved watching soccer, playing dominoes, and gossiping about each other. But the new Thursday night shows started bringing in "young blood," as my father used to say.

Crimzon Spider's first customers were our friends, and then friends of friends, and eventually acquaintances of those friends. After a month of booking garage bands, we started getting decent crowds and began hosting theme nights like N64 and Guitar Hero tournaments. By the end of 2009 we had over 200 people at our New Year's Eve party, headlined by Domenica, a grunge metal band that had been on tour in Chicago when a gig had fallen through at another venue. They'd reached out to ask if they could play Crimzon Spider and sell merch to make up the lost date. I was flabbergasted. Here was a professional band, leagues above the open mic garage bands that were our regular bookings, asking to play our stage. The same stage that had hosted hundreds of Mexican weddings and *quinceañeras* every Saturday since before my father had bought the building.

"I remember when I would go to Crimzon Spider I would have to take the Orange Line into the city and then take the Red Line to North Avenue and then the North Avenue Bus west because that was the way my parents would allow me to go," says Julie, my fiancée. At the time she lived in Mount Greenwood and would trek out to Humboldt Park with her friends to hang out on Thursdays. On New Year's Eve, she remembers, "We had parked down the street and the cops pulled up and told us to get the hell out of Humboldt Park. But I grew up in Mount Greenwood, where all the cops live, and on New Year's they just shoot guns into the air. You can't go outside at all because I learned very quickly as a child that bullets come back down after you fire into the air."

Our friends were eventually able to leverage their experience working alongside my father at Don Carlos into hospitality careers in upscale neighborhoods like Lincoln Park and River North. In 2014 I was hired as managing editor at *Extra* bilingual newspaper. Before that newspaper also closed for good, I would pass by my family's old business on the way home from work and wonder what would have become of Don Carlos and Crimzon Spider had we not lost the property to the bank. Some of my friends whose first job was also at Don Carlos have stayed in hospitality while others, like me, have gone on to other careers. But it's nice to know we all started off washing dishes, mopping floors, and taking out the trash.

The weirdest memory I have of the neighborhood is from 2012, the first year Riot Fest took over Humboldt Park. That was the first time I saw so many people, who would have been afraid of the neighborhood otherwise, swarm its largest park without hesitation. Police, instead of telling people that they'd never seen before to get the hell out of the neighborhood, blocked traffic and patrolled the neighborhood on foot to make festival-goers feel safe while they waited in line to see Weezer and Social Distortion.

"Before Riot Fest a lot of my friends would tell me not to jog around Humboldt Park. They'd say that the park was so big that it'd be hard for me to get out of it if something bad happened, or full on racist shit like, 'Do you see those lagoons? They find dead white girls in them all the time,'" said Julie. "I was like, 'Wouldn't that make the fucking news? Wouldn't I have heard about that?' I see a lot more girls who look like me jogging around Humboldt now because they went to Riot Fest twice and played in the mud."

Epilogue:
The Last Days of Rezkoville

RYAN SMITH

Birds of prey are a rare sight in Chicago. But on a blustery February day, I watch as a hawk perches comfortably on a telephone wire here in this sixty-two-acre expanse of land that lies just south of the Loop like it owns the place. Who's around to tell it otherwise? Certainly no human being. In a city teeming with 2.7 million people, the population here is zero.

For fifty years, this open lot the size of forty-seven football fields has been defined by the things it is not: it's not a neighborhood, not a park, not a nature preserve, but a phantom version of all of those things—a twilight zone. Try to find it on Google Maps and all you see is a gray-colored rectangular blank spot. There are no buildings, no streets, no people, just crumbling remnants of its former life as a train yard. It doesn't even have a formal name, just nicknames. The only one that has stuck is Rezkoville, a sarcastic nod to Antoin "Tony" Rezko, the infamous developer and political fixer who owned it for several years.

Now the site is slated for a sprawling, multi-billion-dollar real estate project called "The 78"—a reference to the city's seventy-seven official community areas. The 78, the company's marketing copy says, aspires to be "Chicago's next great neighborhood."

One day, several years ago, I stumbled across the area by accident. I was trying to find a shortcut to Chinatown from the Loop on my bike. One minute, I was pedaling on a road past a Target; the next, I rode under a bridge and into an eclectic ecosystem of urban ruin and accidental wilderness—bloated bags of trash, broken glass, cracked concrete, and discarded furniture nearly swallowed up by tall green grasses and a patchy forest.

The place was quiet but not lifeless: at that time, fifty or so people planted their tents or lean-tos in the thickets of trees. Walking around, you could find flora and fauna rarely seen in the city—fireflies, wildflowers, coyotes. Urban explorers, myself included, snuck in occasionally to get a taste.

That laissez-faire era ended in late 2016, when real estate firm Related Midwest, the Chicago office of New York-based the Related Companies, ordered everything inside Rezkoville's borders—all the trees, grasses, and improvised dwellings—razed. They ejected the transient population and erected chain-link fencing to keep interlopers out. An elevated stage appeared with "78" written in numbers large enough to be seen from an airplane flying overhead.

For most of the last two centuries, this future neighborhood was literally underwater, part of a mile-long crook in the Chicago River. Then in December 1929, city leaders completed a $9 million project to straighten the river to better connect the booming South and West Sides to the Loop. Rail companies built infrastructure to better connect to Grand Central Station, a passenger railroad terminal on West Harrison Street.

But Americans fell deeply in love with the car during the post-World War II era, and by 1969, Grand Central Station served an average of only 210 passengers a day, prompting the city to close it down that year. Without any other kind of urban infrastructure—no roads, telephone lines, water pipes—Rezkoville fell into a fifty-year slumber.

Efforts to wake it up have been mired in different circles of bureaucratic hell over the last two decades. In 1997, the city unsuccessfully bundled the former rail yard into a 158-acre "Vacated Railway Area" as part of a "River South" Tax Increment Financing district to attract development. (Tax Increment Financing districts, also known as TIFs, are a complicated bit of policy through which the city doles out funds from property taxes to pay for infrastructure improvements, in order to attract private investment and redevelop "conservation" or "blighted" areas.)

Tony Rezko purchased the land in 2002 but his multiple attempts to build big box stores and luxury apartments with subsidies from TIF dollars failed. In 2005, Rezko sold the property to a company owned by British billionaire Nadhmi Auchi.

Mayor Rahm Emanuel threatened to seize Rezkoville in 2014, using the powers of eminent domain, but before he could, Related Midwest acquired part ownership and announced that they intended to make something of the vacant land. Those plans were solidified in 2017 when a group of well-dressed government officials and other big shots convened on the site to announce that the 78 would be coming soon.

Assuming all goes according to plan, the site will soon be connected to existing streets, public transit lines, and the downtown grid. Meanwhile, thirteen million square feet of glittering new luxury apartments, office space, storefronts, and a possible public-private research center connected to the University of Illinois will spring up from the dirt over the next two decades. Five acres will be set aside for a paved, one-hundred-foot wide portion of the Riverwalk and seven more acres for a crescent-shaped park that follows the path of the old Chicago River, pre-straightening.

There's an outside shot that the 78 could include Amazon HQ2 as a corporate anchor if governor J. B. Pritzker can convince fellow billionaire Jeff Bezos to reconsider the site. With or without Amazon, the project is expected to cost $7 billion.

Supersized real estate projects are popping up all over the world. Dubai, for example, is getting an eight-million-square-foot climate controlled domed city called the Mall of the World. Remarkably, the 78 isn't even the first collection of impossibly expensive towers, plazas, and shops birthed on top of the bones of a former rail yard by Related. That would be Hudson Yards—the skyscraper-filled mixed-use development in New York City that *New York Magazine* described as a "billionaire's fantasy city."

Chicago itself is brimming with outsized development deals: the Obama Center, a $85 million police academy, and most significantly, Lincoln Yards, a $6 billion real estate deal on Chicago's North Side. Lincoln Yards is also a brownfield site along a branch of the Chicago River getting an upscale makeover in the form of luxury apartments, offices, shops, entertainment venues, and novel new ways to consume the riverfront.

It's no coincidence that a handful of metropolises like Chicago, New York, London, and Hong Kong are being retrofitted with these mega-developments and cities-within-cities. As all the world comes to be ruled by the same global markets, capital is increasingly being concentrated by geography. This concentration of capital is part of a trend that urban scholar Richard Florida calls "winner-take-all urbanism." It means that some places are winners, some are losers, and everyone is desperate to win the next pageant of investment.

During his two terms as mayor, Rahm Emanuel intentionally positioned Chicago as such a "global city." To sweeten the pot for both the 78 and Lincoln Yards, Chicago has promised nearly $2.4 billion to the developers in the form of two TIF districts, including up to $700 million for the 78.

For firms like Related, the advantage of building on sites like Rezkoville is that they're essentially blank slates. There are fewer residents to upset about the loss of their favorite bar or bookstore; no property owners to displace; few preservationists or NIMBYs to assuage.

Up until the 2019 municipal election, which ushered in a new era under Mayor Lori Lightfoot, as Emanuel bowed out, there's been little political resistance to the 78. Candidates running to succeed Alderman Danny Solis, whose Twenty-Fifth Ward includes the 78, began to question approvals for the development after news broke that he was a target of an FBI corruption investigation. But few substantially questioned the idea of handing the keys of large swaths of land to big developers in the first place.

Nearly two years after Related bulldozed it clean, the Rezkoville land is stubbornly returning to wildness. It's a brownfield site where brownfield doubles as a literal description. Some shade of brown permeates nearly everything in sight, from the beige and tan-colored grasses on the banks of the Chicago River to the dusky dirt paths marred by scattered bits of litter.

At the field's southern border, patches of copper-colored prairie sway in the wind on a gentle ridge. When you stand at just the right vantage point, underneath the defunct bascule bridge on the southern border of the field, the view is startling: waist-high grasses are juxtaposed with the background of Chicago's iconic cityscape.

Squint hard enough and you can nearly trick yourself into thinking you've been thrust into the kind of dystopia portrayed in Veronica Roth's *Divergent*, the young-adult book and movie series in which Chicago's man-made built environment has been slowly reclaimed by nature because of a societal collapse.

At first glance, the 78's plans seem like the utopian opposite of this *Divergent* scene. The conceptual art depicts crowds of ever-smiling, ever-diverse people strolling on concrete paths or lounging on carefully manicured lawns amongst squat buildings topped with lush gardens. It looks like a futuristic and verdant blend of city and suburb—or "surban" as real estate developers have begun to call the trend. Surban development, the thinking goes, will attract wealthy white millenials who enjoy the amenities of the city and short commutes, but who also want the bucolic suburban calm that comes with lower-density zoning and private green space.

What the drawings don't illustrate is the high cost of living in a neighborhood created entirely by a luxury developer. At one of Related's Hudson Yards buildings, available apartments reportedly cost from $4.3 million for a one bedroom to $32 million for a duplex penthouse.

Related's description of the project claims that the 78 "is imbued with

Chicago's culture and history, blending seamlessly with the neighborhoods it borders," but what it seems more likely to do is expand the geographies of inequality of a city that urban planner Pete Saunders has described as, "one-third San Francisco, two-thirds Detroit."

Those chain-link fences now surrounding the boundaries of the 78 will be replaced by barriers of the invisible kind, the ones that increasingly segregate Chicagoans by race and class. Only 500 of the proposed 10,000 housing units are designated as affordable. Related will avoid building another 500 and pay a $91.3 million fee to the city's Affordable Housing Opportunity Fund.

The 78 is poised, then, to become another monument to today's "winner-take-all urbanism" and its inherent racism and inequality.

Given all that, when Related brags on their website that "city by city, property by property, experience by experience, we transform what it means to live, to connect, to belong," it sounds like a promise.

A promise and a threat.

I better warn the hawk.

Contributors

Gint Aras (Karolis Gintaras Zukauskas) has been trapped on planet Earth since 1973. He's the author of the novels *Finding the Moon in Sugar* and *The Fugue*, a 2016 finalist for the Chicago Writers' Association's Book of the Year Award. His memoir about a racist upbringing, *Relief by Execution*, is forthcoming in late 2019 from Homebound Publications. Check out his website gint-aras.com.

Zipporah Auta is a young photographer and audio storyteller. She has been part of Yollocalli Arts Reach since 2016, joining the audio, radio, and journalism program, "Your Story, Your Way!" and the experimental video and photography program, "Camera Flux."

Lily Be is arguably the best storyteller in Chicago, but she would never say so because boasting and bragging about one's achievements is *not* done in her family, her neighborhood, or her city. Lily's passion is giving voice to *everyone* that is never heard, anyone that is "othered," and anyone that feels like they don't matter. In addition to winning multiple Moth Slams and Grand Slams, Lily has performed at virtually *every* storytelling venue in Chicago and has been acclaimed as an actor, writer, director, and producer of her own one-woman shows. Over the last ten years, she has hosted hundreds of storytelling workshops at Northeastern University, Northwestern University, DePaul University, Loyola University, University of Illinois at Chicago, Harold Washington College, Malcom X College, Truman College. Second City, iO Chicago, and Hairpin. She has been invited to be an artist-in-residence several times, including at the prestigious Ragdale Foundation, has been sent to Paris to begin one of several memoirs, and has become a master sound editor for her own podcast series. She recently celebrated the six-year anniversary of her own storytelling show, *The Stoop*, which runs the last Thursday of every month. When you meet Lily Be, ask her about her greatest accomplishment, her son, the scientist and playwright.

Raymond Berry is a native Chicagoan and author of the poetry collection, *Diagnosis,* and the forthcoming book, *I Still Have The Name*, by Finishing Line Press. His other publication credits include *Reverie, To Be Left with the Body, Spaces Between Us, Warpland, City Brink, Cactus Heart, Assaracus*, and *Rust Belt Chicago: An Anthology*, by Belt Publishing. He is an English professor at the City Colleges of Chicago.

Josh Burbridge is a historian and writer currently living in St. Louis who has worked for the National Archives, the Landmarks Association of St. Louis, and the St. Louis Public Library. He studied Chicago firsthand as a buyer of rare soul and jazz LPs for the legendary record store Dusty Groove and he worked with oral history collections as a volunteer for the Southeast Chicago Historical Society. He currently writes about the history, culture, and peculiarities of midwestern urban neighborhoods for his website, *Pizza Hounds*.

John Lloyd Clayton is a writer and teacher in Chicago.

Kevin Coval is a poet and author of *A People's History of Chicago, Everything Must Go: The Life and Death of an American Neighborhood*, and more than ten other full length collections, anthologies, and chapbooks. He is the founder and editor of The BreakBeat Poets series on Haymarket Books, Artistic Director of Young Chicago Authors, which won a MacArthur Award in 2016, and founder of Louder Than a Bomb: The Chicago Youth Poetry Festival, the world's largest youth poetry festival, now in more than nineteen cities around North America. He's got a lot of hustles. He also is the recipient of the 2019 Gwendolyn Brooks Youth Advocacy Award, the 2018 Studs Terkel Award, and the 2017 John Peter Altgeld Freedom of Speech Award. He co-hosts the podcast *The Cornerstore* on WGN Radio cuz he is in love with listening and can be found on the interconnected networks @kevincoval.

Rachel Cromidas is a writer and editor living in Chicago's Logan Square. She has written for the *New York Times*, the *Wall Street Journal*, and the *Chicago Tribune*, and she served as the editor in chief of the news site *Chicagoist*. She recommends grabbing falafel in the back of a jewelry store on Wabash Avenue the next time you're in the Loop.

Kim Z. Dale writes plays, essays, and short fiction. She was a longtime contributor on *ChicagoNow.com* and is a Listen to Your Mother Show alumna. Her work has been published in several anthologies, including a Norwegian English textbook. Kim is an information security specialist, wife, and mother. She has lived in many places, but Chicago definitely feels like home. She tweets as @observacious.

Sheila Elliott was born and raised in the Chicago area and has written for or contributed to area publications like *Lerner Newspapers*, the Illinois edition of the *Hammond Times* (now the *Times of Northwest Indiana*), *Near West Gazette*, and *Southwest Community Newspapers*, where some assignments brought her into the Garfield Ridge neighborhood. She was also a contributor to Lake Claremont publication's *Native Guide to Chicago* (Fourth Edition). Elliott now focuses most of her writing energies on essays, poetry, and fiction.

Leopold Froehlich is a senior editor at *Lapham's Quarterly* in New York City.

Jonathan Foiles is a social worker and the author of *This City is Killing Me: Community Trauma and Toxic Stress in Urban America* (Belt Publishing, 2019). His writing has also appeared in *Slate*, *Belt Magazine*, *Chicago Review of Books*, and *Psychology Today*, where he blogs regularly.

Kirsten Ginzky is an Illinois native from a family of downstate farmers, steelworkers, and public school teachers. Ginzky is an AM/PhD student at the University of Chicago School of Social Service Administration, where her research focuses on diversity and creativity in the community provision of social resources. In her spare time, she enjoys studying architectural and art history, walking along the lakeshore trail, knitting, and browsing bookstores in Hyde Park, where she lives with her partner, Ben.

Eleanor Glockner is a Chicago native and a K-12 CPS alum. She lived on the block described in her essay until leaving Chicago to study Chinese in Beijing after high school. She is an undergraduate majoring in bioengineering at Stanford University, and is currently taking time off from school to work on design and outreach at Foldscope Instruments, a startup producing low-cost paper microscopes.

Miranda Goosby (she/her) is a twenty-four-year-old writer, organizer, and creative from the DMV. She collaborates and contributes to the work of nonprofit and social justice organizations through journalism, research, and data collection. Miranda has used her skills to advocate for reproductive justice and children's rights, and most recently, she has studied the impact of the criminal justice system within local Chicago communities. She believes in authenticity and expressing one's truth because you can't allow someone else to tell your story. In the words of one of her favorite writers, Audre Lorde, "your silence will not save you." She has been writer in residence at the Breathing Room and is involved in community organizing with organizations like BYP100, and she also enjoys creating moments through dinner gatherings and think tanks between other writers like herself. Miranda believes in the community coming together, creating change through using their collective voice. She always hopes to bring a warm energy, an open mind, and a strong work ethic to the space she shares with others.

Alex V. Hernandez is a reporter with Block Club Chicago. The Chicago native has previously written for the *Chicago Tribune, Chicago Reader, Chicago Magazine, City Bureau, In These Times,* and he is one of the founders of 90 Days, 90 Voices. Alex was a 2016 Peter Lisagor Watchdog Award finalist for his work on an interactive Chicago Reporter database that shows where, how, and when police misconduct happens in the city of Chicago, and a 2017 Peter Lisagor Award winner for Best Start-Up for his work with 90 Days, 90 Voices. When not reporting, he's either riding his Vespa or camping.

Sebastián Hidalgo is a Mexican American freelance visual journalist and digital producer whose work focuses on many social and systemic issues such as gun violence and displacement in many of Chicago's black and Latino communities. He believes in a community-oriented and civic journalism praxis and devotes himself to considering, giving back, and growing in conjunction with the lives he finds in front of the camera. At the age of twenty-three, he is among the *New York Times* "Twelve Emerging Photographers You Should Know." His work is frequently featured in hyper-local, regional, and national publications.

Jean Iversen is a Chicago-based writer and editor. She is the author of *Local Flavor: Restaurants That Shaped Chicago's Neighborhoods* (Northwestern University Press 2018) and *BYOB Chicago*. To find out more, go to jeaniversen.com.

Rasaan Khalil is a rapper, poet, and actor who grew up between Maywood and Chicago's Austin neighborhood. He is a 2016 Poetry Incubator alum with a bachelor's in history from the University of Illinois at Chicago. Influenced by artists such as the Roots, Lupe Fiasco, and Saul Williams, much of Khalil's work explores faith, race, and coming of age in Chicago. He plays the role of Haki in Manual Cinema's *No Blue Memories*, a production about the life of Gwendolyn Brooks written by Dr. Eve Ewing and Nate Marshall. Rasaan's debut EP is set to release in in 2019. His work has been featured in *Fake Shore Drive* and elsewhere.

Kirsten (Schnoor) Lambert is a freelance writer who tackles topics such as health, education, and parenting. Her work has appeared in publications including the *Chicago Reader* and *Chicago Parent*. Find her on Twitter at @ KirstenSLambert.

Ann Logue is an adjunct professor at the University of Illinois at Chicago. She is the author of *Options Trading: Idiot's Guide* (Alpha Books, 2016), among other things.

Emily Mack is from Chicago, where in high school she competed in the Louder Than a Bomb poetry slam. She currently studies at Columbia University and her writing had appeared in *Quarto Magazine, Tabula Rasa*, and the *Best Teen Writing* series. She is the recipient of the 2017 Maggie Nelson Nonfiction Prize.

Jackie Mantey is a creative writer, multimedia artist, award-winning copywriter and journalist, and forever Midwest fangirl. The Press Club of Cleveland's Excellence in Journalism Awards honored her with the title Best in Ohio: Freelance Writer in 2014. She moved to Chicago two years later. See more of her work at jackiemantey.com.

Ed Marszewski is the Director of the Public Media Institute (PMI), which publishes *Lumpen Magazine* and *Mash Tun Journal* and runs the low power community radio station, Lumpen Radio (WLPN-LP) on 105.5 FM. PMI also programs and facilitates the long-running experimental cultural center the Co-Prosperity Sphere, based in Bridgeport. Ed is also the co-founder of Version Festival, Select Media Festival, the MDW Fair, and other projects. He is the co-founder of Maria's Packaged Goods and Community Bar, Kimski, and Marz Community Brewing Company. He is also the senior vice president of Public Affiliates, Level G, for Infochammel.

Tim Mazurek is an educator, writer, feminist, and uncle who lives and eats in Chicago. He runs the award-winning food blog *Lottie + Doof*.

Gabriel X. Michael is a freelance photographer, artist, and writer living on the West Side of Chicago in East Garfield Park, also the subject and location for much of his photographic and artistic endeavors concerning Chicago's overlooked and neglected built environment. He has also produced architecture and history pieces for the Chicago neighborhoods website *Chicago Patterns* since 2014, and in 2017 he contributed to Theater Oobleck's immersive *A Memory Palace of Fear* production in West Humboldt Park. Along with his daily photographic exercises and obscure explorations chronicled as @_GXM on Twitter, Gabriel is currently working on an extended photo-essay/book concerning the past, present, and possible future of a formerly significant and largely unknown thoroughfare called Fifth Avenue on Chicago's West Side.

Alex Miller is a Navy veteran from Chicago, currently living in Harlem. He has been published in the *New York Times*, the *Washington Post*, *New York Daily News*, *Forbes*, *QZ*, and the *Guardian*, among other places.

Rob Miller is the co-founder of Chicago's Bloodshot Records and a contributor to Belt's *Rust Belt Chicago: An Anthology* (2017). If his story inspires you to get on the river, bring a plastic bag and fish out all the trash you come across. Every little bit helps. The strangest thing he's seen floating in the river was a six-foot stuffed panda.

Sara Nasser is currently a freelance journalist based in Istanbul. She was raised in the West Ridge neighborhood of Chicago and is writing a novel about the city.

Audrey Petty's first home neighborhood was Chatham. Her poems have been published in *Cimarron Review* and *Crab Orchard Review*, and her essays have been featured in such publications as *Callaloo*, *Columbia Journal*, the *Southern Review*, *ColorLines*, *Saveur*, the *Oxford American*, and *Gravy*. She also is the editor of *High Rise Stories: Voices from Chicago Public Housing* (Voice of Witness/McSweeney's) and co-editor of *The Long Term: Resisting Life Sentences, Working Toward Freedom* (Haymarket Books). She directs the Odyssey Project at Illinois Humanities.

Emmanuel Ramirez is a young creator that uses storytelling, audio production, and photography as his medium of expression. He has been part of Yollocalli Arts Reach since 2015, and in 2017, he joined the audio, radio, and journalism program "Your Story, Your Way!"

Sara Salgado is a Chicana poet from Chicago's neighborhood of Hermosa. She has appeared in several publications of *Rookie Magazine* and you can find her in *The End of Chiraq: A Literary Mixtape*. You can see more of her poetic work translated into film on her Youtube Channel "Sarita." She is a Kenwood Academy alum, but really graduated from her grandmother's house and now attends Harold Washington College. Her poetry delves into the scary truths and beautiful lessons from Latinidad, her neighborhood, feminity, family, her achy breaky heart, and more.

Dmitry Samarov was born in Moscow, USSR in 1970. He immigrated to the US with his family in 1978. He got in trouble in first grade for doodling on his Lenin Red Star pin and hasn't stopped doodling since. After a false start at Parsons School of Design in New York, he graduated with a BFA in painting and printmaking from the School of the Art Institute of Chicago in 1993. He has exhibited his work in all manner of bars, coffee shops, libraries, and even the odd gallery (when he's really hard up). He writes dog portraits and paints book reviews in Chicago, Illinois.

Stuti Sharma is an immigrant artist, poet, educator, and stand-up comic based in Chicago and the south suburbs. She's a poet in residence at the Chicago Poetry Center and is working on a chapbook. While juggling different projects, she performs comedy all around the Chicago area. Find her at @cyborgstuti on Twitter. She also loves food and only trusts restaurants where the cooks are simultaneously Facetiming their families.

Ryan Smith is a journalist and essayist in Chicago covering politics, history, transportation, and media. He is a native of Springfield, Illinois.

Scott Smith is a media strategist and Chicago fundamentalist. A child of the city's southeast suburbs, he's lived in Chicago proper since 1998. In his spare time, Scott enjoys comic books, scotch, and the oeuvre of the Faces. He lives on the South Side in Morgan Park with his wife and daughter where he hosts and produces the live lit show *The Frunchroom*, featuring stories of, by, and about the South Side. Follow his further musings on Twitter at @ourmaninchicago.

Sarah Steimer is a Pittsburgh native currently residing in Chicago with her husband and an ever-expanding jungle of houseplants. She's a journalist, podcast host, and essayist.

Megan Stielstra is the author of three collections: *The Wrong Way To Save Your Life, Once I Was Cool,* and *Everyone Remain Calm.* Her work appears in the *Best American Essays,* the *New York Times, Poets and Writers,* the *Believer, Longreads, Tin House, Guernica,* and elsewhere. A longtime company member with Second Story, she has told stories for National Public Radio, the Museum of Contemporary Art, Goodman Theatre, and regularly with the Paper Machete live news magazine at the Green Mill. She teaches creative nonfiction at Northwestern University.

Mare Swallow is a writer, storyteller, and public speaking coach in Chicago. She is the author of *Twenty-One Ways to Engage Your Audience.* The former director of the Chicago Writers Conference, she was named to New City's Lit 50 List three times. She hosts the occasional Bad Poetry Night, and she is one-half of the all-female ukulele duo the Ukeladies. She holds an MFA in creative nonfiction from Goucher College. You can find her on Instagram @swallowspeaking.

Claire Tighe is a journalist and multimedia producer whose work has appeared in the *Village Voice, Ms., Bitch, Belt Magazine,* the *New Territory,* and elsewhere. She has a master's degree in journalism from New York University and prefers to see the world by bike.

F. Amanda Tugade is a community journalist based in the Chicagoland area. When not on assignment, catch F. Amanda reading poems at an open mic, making rounds at her favorite record stores, avoiding mosh pits at a show, or eating ramen. For more of her published work, visit writefelissa.com.

Benjamin van Loon is a Chicagoland native, currently living in Edgewater on Chicago's North Side. He is a writer and communications consultant for economic development organizations, urban design firms, and nonprofits, and his writing work has been featured in *MONU, PopMatters,* the *Guardian, Curbed Chicago, Green Building and Design,* and others. He holds a master's degree in communications and media from Northeastern Illinois University, in Albany Park, where he also serves as an adjunct professor of public relations. View more of his work online at benvanloon.com.

Gloria "Nine" Valle is a young creator that uses radio, journalism, and painting as her medium of expression. She is originally from Little Village and has been part of Yollocalli's art apprenticeship since 2016, and in 2017, she joined the audio, radio, and journalism program, "Your Story, Your Way!"

Vitaliy Vladimirov is an urban planner, artist, and activist who designs zines, walking tours, and pop-up experiences to educate and empower urbanites to envision cities that are healthy, vibrant, and just. His interest lies in exploring how space, place, memory, and justice intersect in the built environment. He employs design as a means of critical pedagogy and is eager to bring his work to new audiences and welcomes collaborations with individuals and institutions! Learn more: www.vitaliyv.com.

Joe Ward is a Chicago-based reporter living in the Bridgeport neighborhood. Joe worked as a breaking news reporter for neighborhood news website *DNAinfo Chicago*, and covered the Joshua Beal story for the publication. His work appears in *Block Club Chicago*, the *Real Deal Chicago* and the *Chicago Sun-Times*. Joe only travels to the North Side to take his dog, Scout, to the Montrose Park dog beach.

Nicholas Ward's writing has appeared in *Catapult, Midwestern Gothic, Bird's Thumb*, the *Billfold, Hobart, Vol. 1 Brooklyn*, and others. He is a company member with the Chicago-based storytelling collective Second Story and the Booking Manager at Young Chicago Authors. He lives in Chicago.

Shaina Warfield is a twenty-year-old Chicagoland native studying English at Dominican University. She has been published in Dominican's literary magazine *Stella Veritatis*. Her work is a product of navigating many forms of hybridity through the day to day chronicles of being a queer, black woman working very hard to only speak on purpose.

CPSIA information can be obtained
at www.ICGtesting.com
Printed in the USA
JSHW040030051222
34264JS00002B/3